Younger-Generation Korean Experiences in the United States

Younger-Generation Korean Experiences in the United States

Personal Narratives on Ethnic and Racial Identities

Edited by Pyong Gap Min and Thomas Chung

LEXINGTON BOOKS
Lanham • Boulder • New York • Toronto • Plymouth, UK

Published by Lexington Books
A wholly owned subsidiary of Rowman & Littlefield
4501 Forbes Boulevard, Suite 200, Lanham, Maryland 20706
www.rowman.com

10 Thornbury Road, Plymouth PL6 7PP, United Kingdom

Copyright © 2014 by Lexington Books

All rights reserved. No part of this book may be reproduced in any form or by any electronic or mechanical means, including information storage and retrieval systems, without written permission from the publisher, except by a reviewer who may quote passages in a review.

British Library Cataloguing in Publication Information Available

Library of Congress Cataloging-in-Publication Data

Younger-generation Korean experiences in the United States : personal narratives on ethnic and racial identities / [compiled by] Pyong Gap Min and Thomas Chung.
p. cm.
Includes bibliographical references and index.
ISBN 978-0-7391-9141-5 (cloth : alk. paper) — ISBN 978-0-7391-9142-2 (electronic)
1. Korean Americans—History—20th century—Sources. 2. Korean Americans—Biography. 3. National characteristics, Korean. I. Min, Pyong Gap, 1942- II. Chung, Thomas
E184.K6Y76 2014
111'.85—dc22
2014010429

∞™ The paper used in this publication meets the minimum requirements of American National Standard for Information Sciences Permanence of Paper for Printed Library Materials, ANSI/NISO Z39.48-1992.

Printed in the United States of America

Contents

Foreword	vii
Acknowledgments	ix
I: Introduction	**1**
1 Theorizing Ethnic Identity through Comparison *Pyong Gap Min and Thomas Chung*	3
II: Personal Interviews with Sixteen Members of an Earlier Cohort	**19**
2 Authenticity Dilemma among Pre-1965 Native-Born Koreans *Linda S. Park*	21
III: Three Essays by Members of the Earlier Cohort	**41**
3 My Trek *Rose Kim*	43
4 A Handicapped Korean in America *Alex Jeong*	55
5 Reflections on a Korean-American Journey *Ruth Chung*	63
IV: Four Essays by Members of the Later Cohort	**75**
6 Growing up Korean American: Navigating a Complex Search for Belonging *Brenda Chung*	77
7 How to be a Korean *Sun Park*	89

8	Too American to be Korean, Too Korean to be American: A Second-Generation Outsider's Account *Thomas Chung*	101
9	The Way I See: Post-Ethnic Formation of Identity *Bora Lee*	117

V: Three Essays by Members of the Later Cohort — 131

10	*Miyeok guk* for the Korean Soul *Helene K. Lee*	133
11	Anyone Ever Tell You That You Look Like . . . ? *Dave Hahn*	145
12	Family Matters: Emerging Adulthood and the Evolution of My Ethno-Racial Identity *Sung S. Park*	157

VI: Three Essays by Members of the Later Cohort — 171

13	The Outlier *Katherine Yungmee Kim*	173
14	할머니 안녕? (*Halmuhnee Ahn-Nyung?*) *Alexandra Noh*	185
15	What it Means to be Korean *Hyein Lee*	197

VII: The Editors' Comments on the Essays — 209

16	Major Findings about the Cohort Differences *Pyong Gap Min and Thomas Chung*	211

References Cited and Additional References on Ethnic Identity	229
Index	237
About the Contributors	239

Foreword

Professor Min established the Research Center for Korean Community in 2009 to distribute social science data and information about the Korean-American population to Korean community leaders, teachers, social workers, researchers, and government and academic organizations in the United States and Korea. We established a community nonprofit organization, Research Foundation for Korean Community, to financially support the Center's various activities. One of the central activities of the Research Center is to publish books, research reports, and journal articles that are practically useful to the Korean community. Professor Min already published his edited book, *Koreans in North America: Their Twentieth-Century Experiences*, in 2013. That book, which provides a wide range of statistical data on Korean Americans, has been widely distributed to the Korean community and Korean government agencies. This book, the second book project of the Research Center for Korean Community, compares two younger-generation Korean-American cohorts in their ethnic identity formation. It is partly based on ten personal narratives presented at the annual conference organized by the Center in 2011. Ethnic identity among 1.5- and second-generation Korean Americans is one of the topics which Korean immigrant parents, Korean community leaders, and Korean government agencies have taken a great interest in at a time when many younger-generation Korean adults are emerging to the forefront of the Korean-American community. I have known Professor Min for over ten years. He has worked tirelessly in conducting research on Korean Americans. He has already published several books and numerous articles focusing on Korean experiences in the United States. I, along with the other Board members, would like to congratulate him on the publication of this important book for the Korean community. I am confident that this book will provide many insights for members of the Korean and

Korean-American communities, as well as for researchers in the field of immigration and ethnicity.

November 2013,
Hae Min Chung, President
Research Foundation for Korean Community (RFKC)

Acknowledgments

First of all, we would like to express thanks to the thirteen younger-generation Korean Americans who wrote personal narratives about their experiences related to their ethnic and racial identities. Three of them—Rose Kim, Ruth Chung, and Alex Jeong—wrote their essays in the late 1990s, which Pyong Gap Min and Rose Kim included in their 1999 edited book, *Struggle for Ethnic Identity: Narratives by Asian American Professionals.* We also would like to thank Rowman and Littlefield Publishers for giving permission to reprint these three essays in this book. The other ten essays were written in 2011 and presented by the authors at a conference organized by the Research Center for Korean Community at Queens College. The conference was held in Flushing, New York, in November 2011. Without these thirteen writers' willingness to share their personal stories and to take time from their hectic schedules to write and revise their essays, the publication of this book would have been impossible. This ethnic identity book project is of great importance for the Korean community and thus, its publication has been a high priority for our Research Center for Korean Community. Its publication has been made possible by financial support from Research Foundation for Korean Community, a non profit Korean community organization that supports our Research Center for Korean Community. We would like to thank all the members of the Board of Directors of Research Foundation for Korean Community. In particular, we owe special thanks to the following four leaders of the Foundation: Hae Min Chung, President of the Foundation; Yung Duk Kim, Chair of the Board; Peter Park, Vice Chair of the Board; and Henry Jung, the Personnel Committee Chair. They have worked for our Center tirelessly with their time, energy, and monetary contributions. We also owe a great deal of thanks to Jana Hodges-Kluck, Associate Editor of Lexington Books, for enthusiastically accepting our manuscript from the beginning. We would like to thank Natalie Mandzuik, and assistant editor at Lexington Books, and Catherine Mudge, our production editor at Lexington for this project, for walking us through the arduous publication process and for processing the manuscript as efficiently as possible.

I would like to acknowledge Thomas Chung, the co-editor of this book and the editor and webmaster for our Research Center for Korean Community. He spent numerous hours in communicating with the essay contributors and editing the essays over the last two years. Without his efficient communications and superb editing, we would never have been able to complete this book project. This is also a good opportunity to express my sincere thanks to Thomas for his hard work for and dedication to our Center in managing our Korean American Data Bank and editing numerous manuscripts and documents over the last two and a half years. He is a person of great academic talents, and I have tried to influence him to get into the academic world so he can utilize his talents fully for his professional career. I feel happy about his decision to start a Ph.D. program in sociology or English literature next fall. I also would like to thank Se Jung Yim, the best research associate our Center has ever had, for helping me very efficiently with a number of different tasks, including administrative work, proposal writing, data analyses, field work, and online research. I cannot imagine how I could run the Center without her varied skill set, disciplined work ethic, and good attitude. I am also delighted with her decision to pursue her Ph.D. in sociology in New York City, which means that she will continue to work for me and our Center. Finally, as always, I owe my wife, Young Oak Kim, special thanks for helping me with many of my own research projects, as well as administrative work for the Center, both at home and at my office. In particular, she has saved me from many potential disasters at nights and on weekends when I encountered computer-related technical problems. I would also like to thank my three sons (Jay, Michael, and Tony) and my daughter-in-law (Julia) for supporting me. For many years, I have always felt sorry that my extended graduate education prevented me from spending enough time with my sons during their formative years. I would also like to acknowledge the newest member of my family, Jake (Sunwoo), my one-year-old grandson, who has made my life more fun.

Pyong Gap Min

Working on this book has been an extremely satisfying, challenging, and enlightening experience. For much of my life, I have struggled with and rejected my own ethnic identity in many ways. This project has not only helped me to come to terms with my own Koreanness, it has also taught me about other Korean Americans' struggles. Although it doesn't necessarily make me feel happy that so many others have endured hardships, identity crises, and racial discrimination, it definitely made me feel less alone and also made me feel solidarity with others who understand. First and foremost, I would like to thank my co-editor, Professor Pyong Gap Min, for being my mentor, teaching me some of the nuances of academia and the world of writing and editing books, and supporting me and motivating me with his seemingly endless knowledge and superhuman work ethic. Without him, I would not have been part of this book project, and in all likelihood, I would not have stayed in New York City or be involved in academia. I would also like to thank Se Jung Yim, a good friend and one of my coworkers at the Research Center for Korean Community, for helping me embrace my Koreanness in myriad ways (including teaching me more about the Korean language and culture, and patiently correcting me when I say something incorrectly in Korean). I would also like to acknowledge all of the contributors, who took time out of their busy schedules to write essays for this book. Not only did these gracious and patient individuals take time to write thoughtful essays, they also put up with what seems like hundreds of email correspondences with me, and in many cases, several rounds of painstaking revisions. In particular, I would like to thank two contributors: my sister, Brenda Chung, and my best friend, Dave Hahn. Last but not least, I would like to thank my family for their constant love and support. In particular, I would like to thank my father, Kwan Sung Chung, for passing on his love of reading and writing to me and my siblings, for being a gentle-but-firm disciplinarian during my childhood, and for working so hard with my mother, Seong Ran Chung, so my siblings and I could enjoy better lives. I know that this dynamic is prevalent among all immigrant families, but it seems particularly salient among Korean Americans. On behalf of children of immigrants everywhere, I just want to say thanks to our immigrant parents.

Thomas Chung

I

Introduction

Chapter One

Theorizing Ethnic Identity through Comparison

Pyong Gap Min and Thomas Chung

THE NEED FOR THIS BOOK

It has been over forty-five years since the passing of the Immigration Act of 1965, which sparked a wave of immigration from South Korea, among many other nations. During this period, the Korean community in the United States has made remarkable positive changes, not only in population growth, but also in terms of economic adjustments and community organizations. Korean immigrants with severe language barriers have made successful economic adaptations to American society by developing labor-intensive small retail businesses, such as grocery and greengrocery stores, and labor-intensive service businesses, such as dry cleaners and nail salons. Many Korean-owned retail and service businesses are prominently visible in large metropolitan areas, as well as in medium-sized cities. Additionally, hundreds of Korean ethnic organizations have been established in each of the major Korean communities in the United States. Korean ethnic organizations include Korean churches, social service and empowerment organizations, Korean schools, cultural organizations, professional/business associations, alumni associations, and many friendship associations.

In recent years, many 1.5- (those who immigrated to the United States at the age of twelve or younger) and second-generation (the U.S.-born children of the immigrant [first generation]) Korean Americans have come of age in the United States, and they have gradually involved themselves more and more in community activities. The participation of younger-generation Koreans in the labor force and their emergence in the community is one of the most significant changes that have occurred in the Korean-American community. Min's own research on Korean social service agencies, business associations, and professional associations in the New York-New Jersey area also reveals that many 1.5- and second-generation young adults are involved in Korean ethnic organizations, either as staff or board members. Not surprisingly, younger-generation Korean adults compose much larger proportions of the Korean-American populations in Korean communities on the West Coast, such as Los Angeles, San Francisco, and Hawaii, because these areas have much longer Korean immigration histories than Korean communities in other areas of the United States. These West Coast Korean Americans are more actively involved in ethnic organizations in Korean communities than their East Coast counterparts in the New York-New Jersey area.

The extent to which 1.5- and second-generation Korean-American adults participate in Korean community organizations as staff or board members is partly determined by the strength of their Korean or Korean-American ethnic identity. Ethnicity has its expressive and instrumental functions, and their participation in ethnic organizations can be said to be the instrumental function of ethnic identity. Those who have strong Korean identity are more likely to work for Korean ethnic organizations than those who have weak Korean identity. Also, how often younger-generation Korean adults visit their mother country (South Korea) partly depends upon the strength of their Korean ethnic identity. Most importantly, the level of ethnic identity greatly influences how successfully Korean Americans will be able to preserve their cultural traditions and ethnic institutions over generations. Accordingly, research on the formation of ethnic identity among younger-generation Korean Americans is of practical significance as well as of theoretical significance.

Since ethnic identity is fluid and not fixed, situational, and multiple (Song 2003; Wallman 1978), we cannot fully understand the formation of 1.5- and second-generation Koreans' ethnic identity using survey data. We need qualitative studies to capture the complexities and changing nature of their ethnic identity. Thus, researchers usually utilize audio-taped personal interviews to study younger-generation Korean and other Americans' ethnic and racial identities (Danico 2006; Garcia 2004; Kibria 2002; Min 2002; Min and Kim 1999; Song 2003; Tuan 1999). Yet, even audio-taped interviews may not be ideal for studying identity formation, because informants need ample time (perhaps two to three hours or even longer) to answer complex questions about how their ethnic identity has changed during different stages of life. As opposed to in personal interviews, informants are more likely to answer these questions more effectively by writing personal identity essays. This book examines the ethnic identity of younger-generation Korean Americans, largely based on personal narratives written by 1.5- and second-generation Korean young adults. However, only Min and Kim (1999) previously used personal narratives to examine younger-generation Asian Americans' ethnic and racial identities. As will be discussed shortly, this book is also based on the ideas of its co-editor, Pyong Gap Min, acquired from his communications with younger-generation Korean high school students during his 2012 and 2013 lectures on younger-generation Koreans' formation of ethnic identity.

As will be shown in the following section, the nature and strength of younger-generation Koreans' ethnic identity are largely determined by the following four factors: (1) their retention of Korean culture, (2) their participation in Korean ethnic networks vs. non-Korean ethnic networks, (3) their linkages to their mother country (South Korea) and their perception of the mother country's global power and influence, and (4) their experiences with racial prejudice and discrimination in the United States. The earlier cohort of younger-generation Korean Americans who grew up in the 1960s and early 1970s had far more difficulty in forming their ethnic identity than the later cohort who grew up twenty years later, in the 1980s and early 1990s, for the following two major reasons.

First, the earlier cohort experienced far more difficulty and unfavorable circumstances regarding the aforementioned first three factors related to the Korean community and South Korea than the later cohort, especially in terms of positive ethnic identity formation. Second, racial prejudice and discrimination in the United States in the first historical period were more severe and overt than they were in the later period. In the first period (1960s-1970s), the Korean ethnic or Asian racial label was more or less imposed on Korean and other Asian Americans, because the dominant society did not accept them as Americans. However, there was far less racial rejection of Korean and other Asian Americans in the second period (1980s-1990s). Thus, younger-generation Korean Americans from the later cohort are more likely to have had positive Korean identities throughout their lives. Moreover, they are more likely to have voluntarily chosen their Korean ethnic identity, as opposed to having it imposed on them by the dominant society.

The above summary suggests that comparing the earlier cohort of younger-generation Korean-American adults with the later cohort will help us to understand more clearly the effects of the aforementioned four factors on their ethnic identity formation. This book intends to compare two cohorts of 1.5- and second-generation Korean Americans in their identity formation. Researchers use cohort analyses to examine the effects of particular time periods. Immigration scholars have often compared different waves of the same immigrant groups (Glenn 1983; Grenier and Perez 2003; Kitano and Daniels 1995; Yang 2011). But few scholars have compared different nativeborn cohorts of the same ethnic group (Eckstein and Barberia 2002). Since internal and external factors contributing to ethnic and racial identities have gone through major changes since 1965, it is important to make a cohort analysis to highlight the effect of the time period on identity formation. However, though many researchers have examined the formation of ethnic and racial identities among children of post-1965 immigrants (Danico 2006;

Kibria 2002; Min 2002; Min and Kim 1999; Song 2003; Tuan 1998), no study has used a cohort analysis. Thus, this book makes a significant contribution to studies of ethnic and racial identities by using the method of a cohort analysis.

It may be useful to tell the readers how Min came up with the idea for a book comparing two cohorts of younger-generation Koreans to explain the importance of the three internal factors and the external racial discrimination factor for the formation of their ethnic identity. Korean community leaders and Korean immigrant parents have shown keen interest in the topic of second-generation Koreans' ethnic identity. Many Korean organizations have invited him to give talks about second-generation Koreans' ethnic identity. The demand from the Korean community for information about second-generation ethnic identity issues has led him to conduct research on this topic for many years. In particular, the Korean American Youth Foundation asked him to give a talk about younger-generation Koreans' ethnic identity for its members, which consisted of junior and senior high-school students, in 2012 and 2013, respectively. In Min's 2012 talk, he emphasized to my audience of Korean-American teenagers that they had huge advantages in developing their ethnic identity smoothly, especially in comparison to younger-generation Koreans who grew up in the 1960s and early 1970s. He explained that they had advantages over their predecessors in virtually every possible way: their level of retention of Korean culture was much greater, they were far more involved in Korean social networks, and, due to technology, they were able to maintain much stronger transnational ties with their homeland, which, in and of itself, was much more powerful than it had been in the 1960s and 1970s. However, he also pointed out that they now have the luxury of developing their ethnic identity voluntarily rather than having it imposed upon them and being forced to accept it, compared to the earlier period, because they are also more accepted as Americans by members of the dominant group than their predecessors were.

Many Korean-American high-school students who attended Min's talk indicated that they were lucky and that they felt sorry for those who grew up in the 1960s. He realized that an ethnic identity book comparing two cohorts of younger-generation Koreans based on personal narratives would help both Korean immigrant parents and their younger-generation children to understand what factors are important for the development of the latter's Korean ethnic identity. Min knew he could not use data based on contemporary high-school students, because they have not fully developed their ethnic identity. However, he actually had two sets of personal narratives focusing on ethnic identity written by two different cohorts of younger-generation Koreans, one group who grew up in the 1960s and early 1970s, and the other who grew up in the 1980s and early 1990s. Although he initially did not collect personal narratives by the later cohort of younger-generation Korean Americans for the purpose of comparing them with the earlier cohort, he decided to publish a book comparing the two cohorts for the advantage of conveniently explaining the formation of younger-generation Koreans' ethnic identity. This is the background in which he started this book project.

FOUR MAJOR FACTORS AFFECTING ETHNIC IDENTITY FORMATION

Generally speaking, the following four major factors affect the formation of ethnic identity among younger-generation Americans' ethnic and racial identities: (1) their retention of ethnic culture, (2) their social networks with ethnic friends and involvement in ethnic organizations, (3) their linkages to the mother country and perception of the mother country's global power and influence, and (4) their experiences with racial prejudice and discrimination. The first three factors are closely related to the size and influence of the ethnic group in the United States and the mother country. Members of a very small ethnic group with few ethnic institutions have difficulties in preserving their cultural traditions and in maintaining ethnic social networks. Thus they have disadvantages in holding strong ethnic identity. Additionally, when the home country or mother country has low visibility or a negative image, members of those particular immigrant/ethnic groups will most likely feel ashamed of their ethnic background and try to hide it. While the first three factors have more to do with the home/mother country of immigrant groups, the last factor is closely related to the host society (in this case, the United States) and its level of racial discrimination and rejection against minority groups. We review the literature on the effect of each factor on ethnic identity in more detail in the following paragraphs.

Retention of Ethnic Culture

Ethnic culture and ethnic social networks, along with ethnic identity, are three major components of ethnicity (Gordon 1964; Yinger 1994: 304). As such, they influence each other. However, the influence of ethnic culture on ethnic identity seems to be more salient than the reverse. Ethnicity differs from race, class, and gender, in that it is characterized mainly by cultural distinctions—language, dress, food, holidays, customs, values, and beliefs. As Alba (1990: 76) points out, "ethnic groups generally define their uniqueness to other ethnic groups largely through the medium of culture."

Language is the central component of culture, and as such, it has the strongest effect on integrating members into a particular ethnic group. Yet language is also the first element of the immigrant culture to disappear over generations (Alba 1990: 4; Waters 1990: 116). In Alba's survey study conducted in the late 1980s, only 16% of his native-born white respondents said that "they actively use a mother tongue, either as a language for conversation or an ethnic garnish when speaking English" (Alba 1990: 94). By virtue of immigrants' strong transnational ties to their home countries and the U.S. government's active multicultural policy, children of post-1965 immigrants have more advantages in retaining their mother tongue than earlier white immigrant groups. According to the 2005-2007 American Community Surveys, 34% of native-born Asian Americans were found to use another language (most likely their mother tongue) at home (Kim and Min 2010: 240).

Research shows that ethnic food and ethnic holidays are much easier to maintain over generations than language. Studies show that even intermarriage does not do much to hinder the preservation of ethnic cuisines (Alba 1990: 91). Gans (1979) coined the term *symbolic ethnicity* to indicate the tendency of third- and fourth-generation white ethnic groups to maintain ethnicity without practicing much ethnic culture or participating in ethnic networks. According to him, by the 1970s, most third- and fourth-generation Jewish and Catholic white ethnics had achieved high levels of acculturation and social assimilation, losing much of their ancestral cultures and moving into non-ethnic primary groups. However, they continued to perceive themselves as ethnics and maintained their ethnic identity mainly through ethnic food and festivals—symbols that required little effort, and rarely interfered with other aspects of their lives.

Religion usually has stronger effects on ethnicity than the home-country culture. But it can have a positive or a negative effect on ethnicity depending upon the level of the association between ethnic culture/identity and religious rituals. When a religion is inseparably linked to the ethnic culture and history, as it is in the case of Judaism for Jews, it can help an ethnic group to sustain their ethnic culture and ethnic identity over many generations (Hammond and Warner 1993; Huntington 1998). Among contemporary immigrant groups, Indian Hindus become another salient example in which religious rituals are inseparably linked to ethnic cultural elements, such as language, food, festivals, and music/dance. Thus, Indian Hindu immigrants in the United States have advantages in preserving their ethnicity through religion (Min 2010). By sharp contrast, Korean Protestantism has not incorporated many Korean cultural elements, such as food, festivals, and other elements of Korean folk culture. Accordingly, Korean Protestant immigrants have difficulty in transmitting their cultural traditions and ethnic identity to the younger generations, though they themselves can enjoy practicing Korean culture in Korean immigrant churches (Min 2010).

Ethnic Social Networks and Participation in Ethnic Organizations

As already pointed out, ethnic social ties and ethnic identity mutually influence each other. Those who maintain close social ties with many co-ethnic members are likely to hold stronger ethnic identity than those who maintain weak social ties. Alternatively, those who preserve strong ethnic identity are more likely to choose co-ethnic members as close friends or dating partners than those who preserve weak ethnic identity. But the effect of ethnic social ties on ethnic identity is likely to be more common and stronger than the effect of ethnic identity on ethnic social ties. For example, second-generation Koreans who live in Flushing, Queens, a Korean enclave in New York City, are likely to have many close Korean friends. Their strong Korean friendship networks, in turn, are likely to strengthen their ethnic identity. We can consider an opposite situation. A second-generation Korean student attending a predominantly white high school in the South with few Koreans may develop strong Korean ethnic identity partly because of his/her parents' emphasis on his/her Korean background and active practices of Korean culture at home. Additionally, in this hypothetical example of a second-generation Korean living in the southern United States, racial rejection by white students can also contribute to a strong Korean ethnic identity. Nevertheless, the strong Korean ethnic identity is not likely to enhance his/her ethnic friendship networks.

As is clear from the above examples, both group size and the ethnic composition of the neighborhood of one's residence have significant effects on one's ethnic social ties. second-generation Koreans today have huge advantages over their counterparts in the 1960s and early 1970s for ethnic social networks by virtue of the presence of many potential younger-generation Korean friends in their neighborhoods, churches, schools, and workplaces. Those second-generation Koreans who live in large Korean population centers, like the New York-New Jersey area or parts of southern California, also have advantages for ethnic social networks over those who live in an area with a small number of Korean Americans. Moreover, younger-generation Koreans can maintain ethnic networks through participation in ethnic organizations. Large Korean communities in the United States, such as Los Angeles and New York, have many ethnic organizations in which younger-generation Koreans can participate as staff members, board members, volunteers, or simply as members of social and religious organizations. The mere participation of younger-generation Koreans in Korean ethnic organizations is likely to strengthen their ethnic identity. But their participation will also have a positive effect on their ethnic identity because it helps them to maintain social networks with other co-ethnic members of particular organizations.

Linkages to the Homeland and the Latter's Global Power and Influence

The linkage of immigrants and their children to their homeland or "mother country," and the latter's global influence, closely related to their ethnic culture, also strongly affects the formation of their ethnic identity. The dispersed peoples who live in diasporas against their will always have yearnings to return to their homelands (Tweed 1997). But even the voluntary migrants who left their home countries as adults are usually nostalgic about them. European immigrants in the United States in the early 1900s had difficulty in visiting their homes across the Atlantic Ocean. However, contemporary immigrants in the United States have strong transnational ties to their home countries by virtue of advanced technologies (Glick Schiller et al. 1992; Itzigsohn et al. 1999; Levitt 2001). In terms of the physical proximity to their homelands, Korean and other Asian immigrants have disadvantages for transnational ties to their homelands compared to Latino and Caribbean immigrants. However, Korean and other Asian immigrants have advantages for transnational ties over Latino and Caribbean immigrants by virtue of having greater class-based resources for using high-tech equipment for communication, such as smart phones, computers, e-mail, and online chatting.

The children of immigrants who were born or grew up in the United States maintain much weaker transnational ties to their motherland than their immigrant parents (Levitt and Waters 2002). However, younger-generation Koreans also maintain ties to Korea through different channels. First of all, the vast majority of 1.5- and second-generation Koreans have visited their mother country (South Korea) once or more, with a significant proportion of them having visited three times or more (Min 2012). During their childhood or adolescence, they may have visited Korea accompanied by their parents or through various roots education programs in the Korean community. Also, a significant proportion of them communicate with their relatives and/or friends in Korea frequently without physically visiting Korea, using advanced technologies. Moreover, most younger-generation Korean Americans maintain strong emotional and cultural ties to Korea through watching transnational Korean media. These ties to Korea undoubtedly have positive effects on their Korean ethnic identity.

The power and influence of the home country, separate from their linkages to it, also have a strong effect on the ethnic identity formation of younger-generation Americans. However, researchers who have studied ethnic and racial identities seem to have neglected to pay attention to its importance. When the mother country is perceived as weak and/or invisible, younger-generation children of contemporary immigrants are unlikely to feel proud of it and thus have weak ethnic identity. Alternatively, when their mother country exercises a powerful economic, political, and cultural influence globally, younger-generation children are likely to feel very proud of it and hold stronger ethnic identity.

The effect of the global power and influence of the mother country on younger-generation ethnic members is an important issue, especially for younger-generation Koreans, because there has been a remarkable change in the global influence of South Korea over the past three decades. South Korea has emerged as a major economic power in the twenty-first century since the middle of the 1980s. Korean-brand products, such as Hyundai cars and Samsung smart phones and TV sets, are very popular in the U.S. market. The occupation of the two top positions of the United Nations by Koreans (U.N. Secretary-General Ban Ki-Moon and World Bank Group President Jim Yong Kim) reflects the global political and diplomatic influence of Korea. Finally, the global influence of Korean culture all over the world, represented by Korean TV dramas, movies and K-pop, has significantly changed the perception of South Korea in the positive direction. No doubt, these global Korean economic, political, and cultural influences are likely to lead younger-generation Koreans to feel proud of their ethnic background.

Racial Prejudice and Discrimination in the Host Society

If retention of ethnic culture and linkages to the homeland are the only sources of ethnic identity, it is likely that most people's ethnic identity will wither away with their inevitable progressive acculturation to American society over generations. Yet African Americans still have strong racial and ethnic identities, although they have lived in the United States for several generations and have lost most of their African cultural repertoire. Patterns of post-migrant adjustment to the host society—especially levels of residential and occupational segregation and experience with prejudice and discrimination—have effects on the development of a particular group's ethnicity as well (Despres 1975; Olzak and Nagel 1986; Yancy et al. 1976). For highly acculturated multigenerational white ethnics who are accepted as authentic Americans, ethnic identity is a matter of personal choice to meet their psychological need to belong to a community (Waters 1990). However, for members of racial minority groups in the United States, no matter how acculturated they are, ethnic and racial identities are imposed on them by societal expectations or social perceptions.

African Americans, in particular, have endured more severe forms of prejudice and discrimination than other minority groups in the United States. Their ethnic and racial identities have been generated almost entirely by structural factors—their settlement in inner-city slums, their concentration in low-paying occupations, and their experiences with racial prejudice and discrimination. As a result, although they have lived in the United States for many generations, African Americans have strong ethnic and racial identities. Ronald Taylor uses the term *ethnogenesis* to refer to African-American ethnicity generated by the structural conditions under which most African Americans have struggled for survival in American cities in the twentieth century.

Asian immigrants in the nineteenth and early twentieth centuries encountered many legal barriers and racial violence (Chan 1991; Hing 1993; Takaki 1989). Although Asian Americans are now treated far more favorably than they were fifty years ago, as people of color, they still encounter moderate levels of prejudice and discrimination. Despite the prevalence of the positive image of Asian Americans (Hurh and Kim 1989), many Americans still tend to view them, regardless of their level of acculturation to American society and generation, as "foreigners" or "aliens" who cannot be fully assimilated (Espiritu 1994; Tuan 1998). Third- and fourth-generation Asian Americans, like multigenerational white Americans, are thoroughly acculturated to American society, far removed from their Asian cultural heritage. Yet, these multigenerational Asian ethnics were forced to accept their ethnic and racial identities because they were not accepted as full American citizens by the dominant society (Tuan 1998).

Typology of Ethnic and Racial Identities

The first three factors reviewed above—retention of ethnic culture, involvement in ethnic social networks, and linkages to the homeland—are contributing factors to ethnic identity that have much to do with particular immigrant and ethnic minority groups, although they are also affected by the policies of the host society and the level of technological advances. By contrast, racial prejudice and discrimination are mainly dependent upon race relations and minority policies in the host society. Accordingly, for the convenience of discussion in this introductory chapter, we will refer to the first three contributing factors to ethnic identity as internal factors; we will refer to racial prejudice and discrimination as external factors. Depending upon a combination of high or low internal and external factors, we can consider four types of ethnic identity among children of immigrants in the United States. We provide a typology summarizing four types of ethnic/racial identities with examples in Table 1.1.

One hypothetical situation for identity formation is when descendants of immigrants maintain very low levels of ethnic retention and ethnic social networks, but they are well accepted by members of the dominant group. This means that they are likely to have a very low level of attachment to their ancestors' homeland and a high rate of intermarriage to white Americans. Most likely, these individuals hold a low level of ethnic identity in the form of symbolic ethnicity (Gans 1979; Waters 1990). They are not forced to accept their ethnic identity, but choose it simply to belong to their ethnic

Table 1.1. Typology of Ethnic Identity Depending upon Combination of Low or High Internal and External Factors to Ethnic Identity

Internal	External	Type of Identity	Example
Very Low	Very Low/None	High Assimilation Symbolic Ethnicity	Multigenerational White Americans
Low	High	Acting White Ashamed of Ethnic Background	Pre-1970 Asian groups
High	Very Low/None	Hyphenated Americans	Jews
High	High	Separated National Identity	Black Nationalists

community psychologically, without holding ethnic content. Multigenerational white Americans hold this type of ethnic identity.

Another contrasting situation is when descendants of immigrants have low levels of cultural and social ethnic attachments and linkages to the homeland, but are racially rejected by white Americans. When small numbers of Asian immigrants settled in the United States on the West Coast in the first half of the twentieth century, they had difficulties in retaining their ethnic cultural traditions, partly because of their small population and community sizes and partly because of the U.S. government's strong assimilation policy. They did not have strong linkages with their Asian home countries, nor did they feel particularly proud of them. Thus, the internal factors pushed them toward assimilation to American society. However, they were not accepted as Americans by members of the dominant groups. Most second- and even third-generation Asian Americans pretended to be white, but they realized they could not hide their physical differences because they were rejected by white Americans based on their physical characteristics. Consequently, most of them went through serious psychological problems in the process of their identity formation. They initially had to accept the Chinese, Japanese, Filipino, and/or Asian label more as racial categories or assignments rather than ethnic option, and gradually restored their ethnic identity as they learned their ethnic language and culture. The experiences of the earlier cohort of younger-generation Korean Americans who grew up in the 1960s and early 1970s is a good example of this type of struggle for ethnic identity.

We can consider two opposite situations: (1) a case in which high levels of internal factors (ethnic retention, ethnic social networks, and linkages to the homeland) are combined with very low levels of the external factor (racial discrimination/prejudice), and (2) a case in which high levels of internal factors are combined with high levels of the external factor. When members of an ethnic group maintain high levels of ethnic cultural traditions and ethnic social networks, but are well accepted as American, they are most likely to maintain a hyphenated American (e.g., Korean- American, Japanese-American, or Polish-American) identity. Since they are fully accepted as American, they are likely to hold an American identity, but since they also have close cultural and social ethnic ties to their ancestral homeland, they are likely to voluntarily add an ethnic component to their identity label. When they have strong linkages to their homeland and feel proud of it, the ethnic component of their identity is even more important. This type of hyphenated American identity is different from symbolic ethnicity held by multigenerational white Americans, who use ethnic identity to symbolically belong to the ethnic community without the ethnic content, as discussed by Herbert Gans (1979). As pointed out above, most of today's multigenerational white Americans have not preserved many (if any) ethnic traditions and do not belong to ethnic networks. Thus, they are thoroughly assimilated to American society.

If we single out one white ethnic group whose experiences are closest to the hyphenated American ethnic identity type, it is the Jewish group. The inseparable connection between their religion and ethnic history/culture, their heavy residential concentration in several major metropolitan areas, and their rich community organizations have helped even multigenerational Jewish Americans to preserve their ethnic culture and social networks. Moreover, Jewish Americans maintain stronger ties to their homeland than any other white ethnic group in the United States. On the one hand, these high internal factors are likely to lead most Jewish Americans to hold strong or at least moderate ethnic identity. On the other hand, prejudice and discrimination against Jews in the United States, which were strong in the 1920s and 1930s, have been gradually reduced in the post-war period. Jews, like members of other white ethnic groups, are now accepted as full American citizens. This change, along with their strong ethnic attachment, seems to have led most Jews in the United States to hold Jewish-American identity, with equal weight on the ethnic and American sides of their identity.

As already pointed out above, younger-generation children of contemporary Asian immigrants, including younger-generation Koreans, have advantages over their counterparts in the pre-1970 period in retaining their ethnic cultural traditions and maintaining ethnic social networks. They seem to be both culturally and socially more ethnic than contemporary multigenerational Jewish Americans. Anti-Asian prejudice and discrimination, the external factor that affects the formation of ethnic and racial identities, has also been significantly reduced. No doubt, lower-class Asian immigrant workers with strong Asian accents still encounter racial discrimination (Lan 2012). However, 1.5-generation and U.S.-born Asian-American children growing up in large metropolitan areas like the New York-New Jersey area seem to experience far less uncomfortable incidents deriving from racial prejudice and discrimination. As a result, they are likely to voluntarily develop a positive and concrete form of ethnic identity, similar to the one held by multigenerational Jewish Americans. In terms of both the internal and external factors, the cohort of younger-generation Korean Americans who grew up in the 1980s and early 1990s had disadvantages for smoothly developing a hyphenated American ethnic identity compared to contemporary younger-generation Korean Americans. However, we expect to find that they had advantages compared to the earlier cohort.

Going back to the typology, the fourth type of ethnic or racial identity can be developed when children of immigrants or minority members have strong internal forces affecting their ethnic identity but continue to encounter racial rejection from the dominant society. In this situation, they are likely to develop a separatist national identity with little to no American identity component. There is no minority group in the United States that fits well with this type of identity formation. But we can consider Black Nationalists, such as Marcus Garvey and Malcom X, who were most influential between the 1920s and 1960s, as the closest example to this type of racial identity. Black Nationalists did not believe they could achieve racial equality by changing laws because anti-black racism was so deeply embedded into American social institutions. Thus, they argued that blacks should maintain separate institutions in education, economy, politics, and other fields (Jacques-Garvey 1986). African Americans lost their African cultural repertoires during the slavery period, but Black Nationalists tried to restore some of the African cultural traditions and emphasized black racial and cultural pride.

DATA SOURCES

We use mainly personal narratives written by 1.5-generation and native-born Korean Americans as a source of data. For the earlier cohort, we have used two data sources: (1) three personal-narrative essays written by 1.5- and second-generation Korean Americans who spent their childhood and adolescence in the late 1960s and early 1970s, and (2) Linda Park's recently published book chapter (Park 2013) based on sixteen audio-taped personal interviews with second-generation Koreans who grew up during the same period. For the later cohort, I have used ten personal-identity essays written by 1.5- and second-generation Korean Americans who grew up in the 1980s and/or early 1990s.

The three identity essays from the earlier cohort were included in a 1999 book I co-edited with Rose Kim (Min and Kim 1999). The book includes fifteen personal identity essays by first-, 1.5-, and second-generation Asian-American young professionals. I asked them to write personal narratives on their ethnic and racial identities by discussing (1) their parents' immigration and settlement experiences, (2) their retention of Asian culture, (3) their friendship and dating patterns, with special attention to co-ethnic vs. non-ethnic members, (4) their experiences with racial prejudice and discrimination, and (5) their struggles with ethnic identity. Three of the fifteen essays were written by 1.5- and second-generation Korean Americans who grew up in the 1960s and 1970s. Since these three essays do not provide enough data for the purposes of analyzing the earlier cohort of 1.5- or second-generation Korean Americans, I have also used Linda Park's book chapter focusing on U.S.-born Korean Americans' ethnic identity in the pre-1965 period (Park 2013). As previously mentioned, the book chapter is based on her personal interviews with sixteen second-generation Korean Americans who grew up in the late 1960s and early 1970s.

I started a similar edited book project in 2011, this time focusing specifically on younger-generation Korean Americans. I arranged for fourteen 1.5- and second-generation young Korean Americans to write personal essays focusing on their ethnic and racial identities. In writing their essays, I asked them discuss (1) their retention of Korean culture, (2) their friendship and dating networks (Koreans vs. non-Koreans), (3) their experiences with racial prejudice and discrimination, (4) their linkages to South Korea and the increased global influence of South Korea, and (5) their struggle for ethnic identity. They presented their essays at a conference organized by the Research Center for Korean Community in November 2011. Ten of the fourteen Korean Americans revised their essays for this edited volume. The ten authors of the essays spent their childhoods and adolescent years in the late 1980s and early 1990s. There was twenty-year average difference in age between this cohort and the group from the earlier period. I asked the recent cohort to address how the increasing power and influence of South Korea has affected their ethnic identity in a positive direction. However, I had not asked this question to the earlier cohort.

We expect to find that the later cohort preserved Korean cultural traditions more successfully, maintained stronger transnational ties with their mother country, and felt more proud of it than the earlier cohort. We also expect the later cohort to have encountered a lower level of racism than the earlier cohort. As a result of all these differences in their life experiences, we expect to find that the later cohort of younger-generation Korean Americans experienced fewer psychological struggles in forming their ethnic and racial identities and a higher level of ethnic pride. In comparing the two cohorts, we will start by examining their levels of retention of ethnic culture, and then move on to their transnational ties with and perceptions of the mother country, their ethnic vs. non-ethnic close friends and dating networks, and their experiences with racial prejudice and discrimination. Finally, we will compare the two groups in their level of inner struggle for the formation of ethnic identity. Although this is a qualitative study based primarily on personal narratives, it is analytical in that it compares the two cohorts of younger-generation Korean Americans systematically with regard to five major points of comparison.

We concede that using only three personal narratives for the 1960s and the early 1970s cohort, supplemented by a secondary source based on sixteen tape-recorded interviews, somewhat weakens our claim that this is a personal narrative book. However, a huge methodological advantage of our book is to compare two cohorts of younger-generation Korean Americans using personal narratives. As already pointed out in the beginning of this introductory chapter, there was only one previous book that examined ethnic and racial identities of younger-generation Asian Americans based on personal narratives by younger-generation Asian Americans (Min and Kim 1999). The book was largely based on the ideas of Min, a co-author of this edited book. Using only ten personal essays by members of the second cohort of younger-generation Korean Americans, we could have published a book. The advantage of a cohort analysis outweighs the disadvantage of insufficient data for the 1960s-early 1970s cohort.

ORGANIZATION OF THE BOOK

This book consists of seven parts. Part I is the introduction to the book. The introduction includes the need for the book, a review of the literature regarding four major factors to the formation of ethnic and racial identity, data sources, and organization of the book. Part II includes Linda Park's long chapter on pre-1965 native-born Korean Americans' struggle for ethnic identity based on her personal interviews with sixteen younger-generation Korean Americans who grew up in the 1960s and early 1970s. Part III includes three separate essays written by members of the earlier cohort of younger-generation Korean Americans.

The ten essays by members of the later cohort of younger-generation Korean Americans who grew up in the 1980s and early 1990s are divided into three parts. Part IV includes four essays written respectively by Sun Park, Brenda Chung, Thomas Chung, and Bora Lee. We put them together because they went through conflicts over Korean-American ethnic identity during their childhood and adolescence due to their experiences with rejection by both the Korean community and the larger American society. Yet, they had a fairly high level of Korean ethnic identity at the time of writing their essays. We put another three essays together written respectively by Helene Lee, Sung Shim Park, and Dave Hahn in Part V because they retained a low level of ethnic culture and only a moderate level of ethnic identity even at the time of the interview. Part VI includes the remaining three essays, by Alexandra Noh, Katherine Yungme Kim, and Hyein Lee. We put them together because they share strong Korean identity. Alexandra has strong Korean identity through her thorough learning of the Korean language and culture without visiting Korea much while the other two do it mainly by virtue of their extended residence in Korea.

Part VII includes the editors' comments on the essays, summarizing major findings and pointing out their theoretical and practical implications. The instructors who use this book for their courses relating to Asian/Korean American experiences, race relations, and immigration/ethnicity could use this part effectively to connect theories of ethnic identity with the stories included in the essays. The final reference section includes not only references cited in this book, but also other references important for research on ethnicity. We hope scholars and graduate students who conduct research on ethnic identity will benefit from this extended reference list.

II

Personal Interviews with Sixteen Members of an Earlier Cohort

Chapter Two

Authenticity Dilemma among Pre-1965 Native-Born Koreans

Linda S. Park

INTRODUCTION

The American-born second generation of immigrant families often struggle with questions of authenticity and fitting into their own ethnic communities within the U.S. This struggle is part of a larger question on who defines an individual's inclusion in a group. American-born Asians, in particular, struggle with authenticity in a unique way as they are often seen as "foreigners" in America because of their race (Tuan 1998) and as "cultural foreigners" in the home country of their parents because of their unfamiliarity with cultural markers defining that society (N. Kim 2009). Questions of authenticity arise when there is a conflict between your self-identification and how others identify you. Ethnic identity, an important element of self-identity, is established internally by the individual and is externally imposed by others.

Nadia Kim (2009) used the term "authenticity dilemma" for Korean Americans who experienced "cultural foreignness" in Korea. However, her focus was on the Korean-American experience in Korea. This chapter explores how participants in this study struggled with issues of "authenticity" as a Korean, and how being a "cultural foreigner" within the Korean community created difficulty in connecting with and being accepted by the immigrant Korean communities that have emerged since the 1970s. One possible explanation for this authenticity dilemma faced by the pre-1965 native-born Korean Americans arises from a conflict between a strong assimilation ideology, which led participants in this study to have heritage, language, and cultural barriers, and the deep-rooted sense of ethnic nationalism (known as *danil minjok*) of Korean people which create strong in-group/out-group boundaries. This conflict stems from how differences in the social construction of race in two different countries have created different definitions of "who" or "what" is Korean.

Immigration scholars tend to focus on adaptation and incorporation into the dominant host society in the form of acculturation and assimilation (Alba and Nee 1997, 2003; Berry 2003), while ethnic identity scholars tend to focus on ethnicity and heritage retention (Chong 1998; Min and Kim 2002). However, not much attention has been given to the issue of how assimilated individuals fit into their own ethnic communities. The data in this chapter call attention to how the consequences of assimilation influence ethnic identity and this issue of authenticity with one's own ethnic community rather than the dominant society. I shift emphasis to how individuals found meaning in or defined being Korean in a Korean community and not as assimilated Americans in the dominant society at large. Having spent most of their critical developmental years of childhood and adolescence in predominantly white communities created challenges when trying to associate with co-ethnic peers and the immigrant Korean community.

Data for this chapter come from my dissertation which focused on how a particular cohort of Korean Americans negotiated and defined the meaning of their ethnicity as adults in midlife. This cohort is made up of descendants of Korean international students who emigrated to the U.S. between 1950 and 1965, a very small group for which very little information is known (Hurh 1980, Kitano and Daniels 1995; Yu and Choe 2003-2004). Although there are a few studies that examined ethnic identity among children of the pre-1965 Asian immigrants (Min and Kim 1999; Tuan 1999), most studies of second-generation ethnic identity focus on children of the post-1965 immigrants. This study specifically focuses on children of the pre-1965 Korean immigrants—during a time when there were not many Korean and other Asian Americans, and when the U.S. government enforced a strong assimilation policy.

BACKGROUND

The complexity of Korean-American experience warrants some background information to situate the participants in this study. This section situates their parents' immigration experience and the ideology of assimilation within a social and historical context. The last part briefly describes differences in the social construction of race between two countries.

Korean immigrants to the U.S. arrived in three distinct waves. The first wave of 8,000 arrived in Hawaii between 1903 and 1924 (Hurh 1980; Min 1998; Takaki 1998). Although Asian immigration was banned between 1924 and 1965, certain circumstances allowed for their entry into the U.S. (Okihiro

2001; Takaki 1998). The second wave of about 14,000 arrived between 1950 and 1965 under three categories: Korean adoptee children (5,300), Korean War brides (6,400), and Korean international students (2,300) seeking postbaccalaureate degrees (Hurh 1980). The third and current wave of Korean immigrants arrived after the passage of a landmark immigration act in 1965, which ended discriminatory quotas and lifted the Asian Exclusion Act (Suarez-Orozco and Suarez-Orozco 2001). For fifteen years (1976–1990), a mass emigration of Koreans, approximately 30,000 per year, entered the United States. By the year 2000, the Korean population in the U.S. had reached over a million (Yu and Choe 2003-2004). Much of the research has focused on Korean immigrant families arriving after 1965. However, this study focuses on the families of a small group of students who were first scattered across the U.S. at different universities during the 1950s and 1960s, and later scattered in the suburbs of predominantly white homogeneous neighborhoods as the lone Korean (or Asian) family.

For over a century and a half prior to 1965, many immigrants had to establish their own communities while also feeling that assimilation for their children was a necessary process and outcome to survive in the U.S. (Eckstein and Barberia 2002). For decades, assimilation in the U.S. meant relinquishing one's cultural heritage and moving towards the dominant American culture, most commonly associated with middle-class white Anglo-Saxon Protestants (WASPs). Until the civil rights and affirmative action movements of the late 1960s, America's national identity had been rooted in this ideology. As long as the U.S. remained predominantly white, it was not problematic to expect immigrants to assimilate to white society. A strong command of the English language was prerequisite for assimilation and establishing American identity (Portes and Rumbaut 1996). Participants in this study were born during this time when laws severely restricted Asian immigration to the U.S. and when an assimilation policy required immigrants' strong command of the English language. This was the context immigrant families faced, and it influenced how immigrant parents socialized their children.

The crux of the authenticity dilemma that second-generation Korean Americans face in the Korean community seems to stem from differences in how race is socially constructed in the U.S. and Korea. Recognizing these differences enlightens us on how South Koreans view Korean Americans and vice versa. Although there is no biological basis of race in the U.S., race continues to be based on phenotypical (or physical) features and is frequently used to categorize people and establish identity (Yanow 2003). Race is also one element of ethnicity—referring to one's culture and ancestry (Omi and Winant 1994). American citizenship does not lend itself to a national identity as it does in many other countries. As a nation, the U.S. is not defined "by blood or ancestry, but by a set of shared ideas [e.g., freedom, democracy, and the Constitution]" (Jacoby 2004). For Korean Americans, their race, ethnicity, and citizenship are fairly independent (e.g., race is Asian, ethnicity is Korean, and citizenship is American).

However, this is not the case in a country like South Korea, where nationality is conflated with race, ethnicity and national identity (N. Kim 2008; Shin 2006b). South Korea is considered to be one of the few ethnically homogeneous nation-states in the world (H. Kim 2009; Min 1991). According to Shin (2006a), "Koreans believe that they belong to *danil minjok* (a unitary nation), one that is ethnically homogeneous and racially distinctive." This point is reiterated in H. Kim's (2009) observation of Korea as "a country notorious for its strong ethno-cultural definition of nationhood and its obsession with purity of blood . . . the unspoken and unquestioned yardstick for membership in the Korean national community." The ideology of modern *danil minjok* emerged during the Japanese colonial rule of Korea as a strategy to resist Japanese nationalism (Shin 2006a). To counteract Japanese assimilation policies, Korean intellectuals and historians used the legend of Tan'gun as the foundation to their ethnic homogeneity to create a strong blood-based ethnic national identity. Since its independence from Japan in 1945, Korea promoted this version of Korean nationalism for the next thirty-five years (H. Kim 2009; Shin 2006b). This deep-rooted sense of ethnic nationalism remains in Koreans' consciousness even when emigrating. Knowing this part of Korean culture and history helps to frame the experiences of Korean immigrants and Korean Americans.

METHODS

Participants in this study were born in the U.S. between 1953 and 1965. Due to difficulties in locating this particular cohort, convenience and snowball sampling techniques were used (the internet, books on Asian Americans, newspaper articles, and conversations with other people). Of the thirty-eight people found, sixteen people consented to an interview. Informants' demographic characteristics are presented in Table 2.1.

One-time face-to-face interviews, averaging one to two hours, were conducted in seven metropolitan areas with large Korean-American populations (Boston, New York, Washington, D.C., Los Angeles, San Francisco, Seattle, and Chicago). The interviews were completed between June and November, 2008. Names have been changed to protect the participants' identities.

Participants' stories were mostly retrospective. They recounted past events, but reported through present reactions, meaning their reflections represented their understanding of past events now as adults rather than when they were young (Scott and Alwin 1998). All the participants' stories together present valuable "oral sources" historically documenting a comprehensive portrayal of that social and historical time period (Portelli 1991: 26).

Table 2.1: Demographic Data (N=16)

Gender	Male= 6	Female= 10	
Education Level	College = 7	Post-College = 9	
Dominant Language	English = 16	Korean = 0	
Age at time of interview	40-45 yrs = 7	46-50 yrs = 5	51-55 yrs = 3
Marital Status	Single = 6	Married = 9	Divorced = 1
Ethnicity of Partner (n =9)	Korean = 1	White = 5	Other Asian = 3
Current Regional Residence	East Coast = 9	West Coast = 6	Midwest = 1

RACIAL FOREIGNER: ATTEMPTS TO "BLEND IN" WITH WHITE COMMUNITIES

The findings are reported here in two broad sections. This section illustrates how participants experienced being a "racial foreigner" as they attempted to blend in with their white peers. However, as participants struggled to blend in, they simultaneously understood how different they were. It is because of these experiences that participants sought out co-ethnic peers as the Korean immigrant communities grew around them. The next section focuses on participants' experience with "othering" and exclusion from their co-ethnic community and peers.

The 1940 U.S. Census listed less than two thousand Koreans in the mainland U.S. outside of Hawaii, signifying the virtually non-existent Korean communities outside of Los Angeles and Hawaii (Patterson 2000; Segal 2002). Also, because that small number of Koreans came to the U.S. to study, their points of entry were scattered across the U.S. at different universities during the 1950s and 1960s. Upon graduation, these families continued to be scattered mostly at different universities for employment (e.g., Massachusetts, Louisiana, Kansas, Virginia, Minnesota, and Ohio). Consequently, most participants in this study spent much of their developmental years growing up in predominantly white communities where oftentimes participants recalled that they were the only "Asian kid" around in their schools or neighborhoods. Growing up in this type of environment left the children no choice in who their peers were. Jessica aptly summed up many participants' experiences during their early school years: "I think part of it was growing up in such an overwhelmingly white suburban neighborhood as I did in Ohio, I had no choice but to hang out with white people." Time and time again, almost all participants stated similar scenarios about growing up in predominantly white neighborhoods and learning to "blend in" with the communities around them. "Blending in" was a term used by many participants to describe how they attempted to fit into their surroundings with their white friends. As Kathy reflected:

> Between the time I was born and middle school, we grew up I guess like a typical "American" suburban family with a house. We went to the local elementary school, got involved in some sports and played with our friends, hung out and did the usual, I guess, *Leave it to Beaver* type of thing. I think it seems like we were very blended in with every other "American" type family.

Mina made a similar comment:

> Did I think much about being Korean? When I was young, I think I really didn't. You know, actually it probably wasn't until college when I was really actively sort of thinking about my identity because I think that whole time until I went to college, I probably just tried to blend in.

During the 1970s, as Korean communities began to flourish in certain regions of the U.S. with the mass influx of Korean immigrants, participants continued blending in with the white community around them. In fact, blending in was so important that several participants told stories of how they distanced themselves from new Korean immigrant youth for fear that they would be mistaken as "one of them." Kathy remembered:

> But then I could always tell them [new Korean immigrants] that just came because they couldn't mingle in with me or my other friends. We still hung out but you could tell that they were the weird ones and I guess there was that term called FOB, "fresh off the boat." I didn't want to look like that. I wanted to look like my blond-headed American friends and do what they do.

Michelle recalled how blending in with the majority group (white peers) was more important than connecting with the newer Korean students that entered her school:

> Yeah, I mean growing up through high school, it was mostly white friends because again, there were very few Koreans and Asians where I lived. And I think that the few that were around tended to be, you know, more recent Korean immigrants. And, you know, again, you're just trying to fit in. And I think there was one woman in my high school that came from Korea. I didn't reach out to her and I felt that I had very little in common with her.

While participants were aware that being Korean was different, they continued to make efforts to blend in, as Jessica's following comments reflected her efforts:

> I just became like everybody else even though I wasn't. For the most part I behaved like they did. You know, I dated the same kids that everyone else dated. I did the same, you know, [. . .] went to the football game every Friday night. I didn't stand out in that many ways.

The consequence of growing up in predominantly white neighborhoods was that this was what they became the most familiar with. Unfortunately, this had consequences for many participants later in life as they tried to enter Korean communities during their college years and beyond. As participants grew older and the Korean immigrant communities grew around them, they soon felt the exclusion and realized they were outsiders in the Korean communities. This left them little choice but to continue surviving within the white communities around them, or for some, finding an Asian-American community to associate with.

However, this does not mean that participants were not conscious that they were Korean. When participants were young, their ethnic identity was ascribed to them by outside forces such as their parents and the dominant white society at large. They remembered being told by their parents that they were Korean. Although they wanted their children to assimilate, immigrant parents were proud of their Korean heritage (*danil minjok*) and so they taught their children that they were different from the majority community around them. Participants recalled these memories: "Haha, because we were told [that we are Korean] as we were growing up" (Wilson). "They [his parents] would talk about it when I was at a very early age 'We're Korean'"(Derek). "I think when I was really young my parents told me I was Korean and so that had a big influence" (Mina).

A common theme for many was the feeling of being different from everyone else around them. They were conscious of being racially different and yet wanting to fit in with their white peers. Patrick remembered when he started kindergarten in Kansas: "I noticed that none of my friends looked like me." And his awareness of being Korean became a negative reaction "because I didn't look like my friends so I didn't like being different from my friends." Elena had already graduated from high school and was in college by the time the Korean immigrant communities began to grow. As such, she hardly had any contact with Korean communities and has always been quite comfortable within the dominant white society. And yet, she remembered feeling different from her peers when she was young and going to school: "I wasn't in a place where there were a lot of minority students and so it was clear that I was different." Wilson's comment below illustrates the complicated nature native-born Koreans lived in:

> Oh early on, I think, I've always felt like I was the minority. We grew up in mostly white neighborhoods and the only Korean access was at church and it seemed like I was always surrounded by non-Koreans from early times. I thought ok, I'm different. I don't know why exactly but I have differences in everything—what we eat and what we talked about and the language [. . .] very early [. . .] as early as I can remember.

Some comments were based clearly on their phenotypic features. Kathy recounts, "I would consider myself Korean American because I still have the Korean look." Elena recalls, "I consider it's more accurate because obviously I don't look Euro-American so I guess I always kind of knew, even as a child that 'oh we're Korean.'" It could be argued that any racism participants faced was based on the fact that Asians are not phenotypically white. This could explain the constant need of wanting to blend in because, for many, there was lack of "full" acceptance into the dominant society.

Nativist attitudes have endured in the U.S. for over two centuries. The racial divide between whites and the African-American communities has remained long after the Civil Rights movement. Many scholars (e.g., Takaki, Tuan, and Kim) have noted the challenges that Asian/Asian Americans pose in the racial constructions in America. There are two common ways this occurs: constantly being mistaken for another Asian group (because all Asians look alike) or constantly being perceived as a foreigner in the U.S. As the data reflected in the previous section, this cohort of second-generation Korean Americans did culturally assimilate to the dominant white society around them because that is all they could do. Interestingly, participants were somewhat divided in their responses regarding their experiences with racism. Some participants recalled their experiences with racism vividly as racial slurs. Yoona painstakingly remembered and bitterly related this account, "It was very blatant. First of all, I can't date the white people. This is a small city in Texas. I was always considered 'Oriental' so it wasn't considered that I could date the white people. It's hard to explain. It's just, that's just the way it was." In this instance, the geographical location of where participants grew up had an impact on how much racism they experienced. Growing up in the South or the Midwest was different compared to growing up on either the West or East coasts. Some participants realized that they posed no threat to their white peers since they were the only Asian in their schools. However, for others, being the only Asian brought on more opportunities for racism. Yoona recognized how this experience can be exponential as she said:

> I mean, you know, because there's not that many of us [second generation] [...] so the amount of racism when there's only one or maybe two is a lot! Because you're the only one and so they pick one; you're like a circus show to them. If they've never seen an Asian before and you're the only one that's like not a good situation, you know.

Jessica grew up in the Midwest and was able to blend in with her white peers but that was also during a time before Korean and other Asian communities began to grow. Her younger sister, on the other hand, had some different experiences. Jessica recalled this particular incident:

I remember when my sister ran for student council in Ohio and she was like class president and all that, but someone scrawled on her campaign posters "Remember Pearl Harbor." I don't think the community viewed itself as racist even though I think it probably was extremely so.

Jessica continued to speculate as to whether an incident such as this would be tolerated today. It seemed like nobody was punished for this reference to Pearl Harbor back then. Abby, a Los Angeles native, described her childhood neighborhood as being more diverse with Latino- and African-American communities. And she remembered this:

All through your life you encounter these incidents where people make fun of how you're looking, make fun of your speech [. . .] [references to] the "ching chong, China man" as a child [. . .] and then as you get older, it's different because it becomes more subtle [. . .] Just realizing that in a place like LA, where it's diverse, the diversity still causes more tension and sometimes there's a clash because people have biases.

Both the reference to Pearl Harbor and the reflection from the Los Angeles native represent lingering negative attitudes associated with Asians. In this case, the first negative association is with the Japanese during WWII. The second negative association revolves around the tumultuous race relations between the African American and Korean communities during the Los Angeles riots on April 29, 1992.

It seemed that for many participants, subtle examples of racism were more common than incidents of blatant racism. It was difficult for Dylan to remember any incidents of racism in his life, but he did recall this incident when he was young and living in the suburbs of Maryland:

I think that most of the time, it's subtle. It's more, if it's related to being Korean but just being Asian probably. I don't have any recollections of anything blatant. But I do feel their subtle ways that are always there. I mean when I was in fourth grade, there were clearly very few Asians and I can remember kids, you know, name calling. I honestly don't remember what the terms were but I do remember that it existed and that it was always, you know, there was always some reference to what your race was.

Others felt racism was fairly minimal and attributed ignorance to the name calling. Since the U.S. is a country that has been predominantly white (until more recent years), there is a strong tendency and connection that "American" means white. Often the term "American" is a loose reference to a white person, just as Josie stated: "Because when I think American, I think of, you know, sort of Caucasian, sort of classic, although that's not really." So while European immigrants and their children are able to blend into the dominant white society over time, Koreans have a tougher time because they are not white. These participants were asked constantly "what they were," implying the lack of recognition as Americans, even though they were U.S. citizens by birth.

By 1924, when the Asian Exclusion laws took effect, it was estimated that there were already 225,000 Chinese and 72,000 Japanese living in the U.S. compared to 8,000 Koreans (Segal 2002). And because the Chinese and Japanese communities in the U.S. have longer histories and exist in greater numbers, participants were often mistaken for being Chinese or Japanese. As such, many people in the U.S. did not know where Korea was or who Korean people were. Many participants were mistaken to be Chinese, as reflected in the racial slurs they encountered. Several participants shared memories of being called "chink," but not many remembered being attacked physically, except Wilson, who remembered as a child, "being called 'chink' or something and maybe it would get physical, there would be a fight [. . .] there would be one or two."

Devin recalled a very familiar incident that resonates with many Asian Americans: "I get that all the time too, haha [. . .] 'What are you?' 'American.' 'What?! No, no I mean what ARE you?' Yeah yeah, I get that [. . .] hahaha." Participants in this study also experienced the perception from others that they were foreigners in the U.S. even though they were born with U.S. citizenship. For instance, participants were constantly asked what they were, where they were from, told that they spoke "really good English" and inquiries as to when they were going back to their homelands. For instance, Elena, who spent parts of her childhood between the East Coast and the Midwest said:

> Oh clearly there were a lot of questions like 'what are you?' I'm not sure if that was being discriminated against [. . .] I've been told I speak English very well and asked 'when are you going to go back?' [. . .] More people were just ignorant and I came to appreciate that later. Obviously it was becoming burdensome to have to continually explain who you were.

Many felt these remarks were often subtle and stemmed from ignorance. Wilson had friends who accepted him, but at the same time there were others around him who did not:

> Some were cruel [. . .] they reminded me all the time [. . .] new people, new situations. That first time, if they didn't know me but the first time they'd see me, I think it was pretty obvious I was different. Oh Chinese, Japanese, what are you? Then I felt that I was Korean. But most of the time I didn't.

For some participants, it was during these types of experiences of feeling like a racial foreigner that participants had no confusion that they were Korean. They were sent clear messages from their white peers that they were not white or even American. Min and Kim (1999) state that even later-generation Asian Americans cannot help but accept their ethnic identity because they are not accepted by "real Americans." Thus, while Asian Americans may want to assimilate (and have succeeded culturally) and identify with the dominant group (American), they are never completely accepted as American as the European Americans are. In this way, by the time many participants reached college age in the late 1970s and into the 1980s, they welcomed the opportunity to meet co-ethnic peers. However, their place as a cultural foreigner soon became evident.

CULTURAL FOREIGNER: "OTHERING" AND EXCLUSION FROM CO-ETHNIC COMMUNITY AND PEERS

The previous section explained how the efforts of native-born Korean Americans to assimilate and blend in to the dominant white community around them still left them knowing that they were different but affirmed that they were Korean. This section describes how, as opportunities arose, participants tried to engage with the Korean immigrant communities only to experience cultural foreignness. This section is divided into three parts. The first subsection illustrates how the deep-rooted consciousness of *danil minjok* affected the interactions between this small cohort of native-born Korean Americans with a significantly much larger cohort of 1.5-generation Korean immigrants. The second subsection explains how the influences of assimilation put participants at a disadvantage within a community that strongly values language and culture. The third subsection summarizes the end result of both the attempted assimilation efforts and the exclusion from the Korean community.

Danil Minjok and Strong In-group/Out-group Boundaries

Nadia Kim (2009) defines the idea of being a cultural foreigner in one's home country to individuals who have a Korean face but lack knowledge around Confucian norms, style of dress, sense of history, and most important, Korean language skills. She goes further to say, "They [Korean Americans] are especially foreign in a nationalistic society that conflates race and culture (e.g., Korean blood explains our diligence; Koreans naturally love kimchi). In this way, children of immigrants completely disrupt South Koreans' sense of identity (N. Kim 2009: 3). In this sense, a cultural foreigner differs from a racial foreigner because it is more about cultural norms than race. Thus language (a cultural marker) becomes an integral part of Korean national identity. While phenotype is commonly associated with race for white people in the U.S., for Koreans (nationals and first-generation immigrants), it is culture that defines who is Korean. In this way, emphasis on language was a recurring theme. Participants noted the pride in ethnic nationalism. Jessica plainly summed up: "But you know, that to me was always this very Korean attribute also. This like pride and, you know their language and their culture and sort of, you know, screw everybody else who didn't understand." Mina remembered a particular conversation her mother had with a friend when Mina was in elementary school. This friend was a second-generation Korean born in Hawaii, but similar in age to Mina's mother. Mina recalled that they were arguing about whether Mina was a Korean or an American:

> Well, they're not Korean, they're American. They are born in this country. And my mother was like "No! Mina, come here! What are you? Just say, what are you?" I said "I'm Korean" because that's all I knew. So I don't know if I started thinking about it more, but clearly that was a debate that existed.

This debate Mina was referring to also exemplifies how strongly the ideology of *danil minjok* continues to influence Koreans' perceptions of outsiders. In this case, whether Mina was a Korean or not was based on citizenship.

However, this type of not fitting into Korean communities existed not only here in the U.S., but also when they visited their ancestral homeland, Korea. Many participants recalled how they were made to feel ashamed for not knowing their heritage language. Dylan remembered: "We were constantly berated by people who lived there [Korea] that we didn't speak Korean." Several participants' memories of visits to Korea involved stories of taxi cab drivers. For instance, two different women related these scenarios: Jessica recounts, "Oh yeah! And there are the taxi cab drivers [who] yell at you for your Korean being so bad!" Josie says, "I remember once when we went to Korea, it was post-college and I remember a taxi cab driver was lecturing me because I couldn't speak Korean and it was like, he has a point—I look Korean, why can't I speak?" In Josie's case, her questioning of her authenticity as a Korean is very real. Her understanding of her Koreanness is based on how race and ethnicity are defined in the U.S. She does not understand what defines being a Korean aside from her looks. In a very different scenario, Wilson related an incident that occurred while he was in a summer language program during college in the early 1980s:

> Actually in Korea, in summer school walking back one night, I was with one of the Korean-American girls speaking English down an alleyway when a drunk Korean man came out. And he was like "Why are you not speaking Korean?!" and then he attacked me and we fought too. I tried not to fight but it ended up that he was very aggressive. It was a short battle pretty much. She dragged me away and he was throwing bottles around. Yeah, it was crazy!

In each of these examples, language was one of the key factors attributed to being Korean. And yet, it was their parents who did not teach their children how to speak Korean. Although not having heritage language skills put participants at a disadvantage, this represents how immigrant parents get caught in the middle between wanting their children to succeed in America and how much culture to preserve. However, we see here how Mina aptly summed up her impression regarding Koreans:

> I think Korea is very unique. It's actually, I think, one of the most homogeneous, racially homogeneous and ethnically homogeneous, countries and there probably isn't a whole lot of mixed kids in Korea and so I DO think there is an emphasis of racial purity in Korea. Their [Korean people] identity is based on who they are—has to do with blood lines or whatever ethnic purity. But I think it's really extreme with Koreans. And a lot of other countries there's so much more diversity that I don't think you can just narrow it down like that.

Many participants acknowledged that the strong sense of ethnic nationalism Koreans possess results in strong xenophobic (or ethnocentric) attitudes toward outsiders (Cummings 1997). This creates a very strong sense of in-group solidarity (Chong 1998; Shim et al. 2008). Korean immigrants retain this strong sense of ethnic nationalism, especially when confronted with other people outside "their" group.

With the massive influx of new Korean immigrants to the U.S. beginning in the early 1970s, the proportion of immigrant youth (the 1.5 generation) proliferated and soon outnumbered the very small population of American-born second-generation Koreans already living in the U.S. Zhou (1997) notes that the differences between the 1.5 generation and second generation are worth paying attention to "particularly in their physical and psychological developmental stages, in their socialization processes in the family, the school, and the society at large, as well as in their orientation toward their homeland" (64). In particular, because the 1.5 are foreign-born, they generally do not have concerns about their ethnic identity in the same way that the second generation does, although they may feel challenged in how to balance their ethnic identity with American identity (Phinney 2003). This difference may have a conscious effect on identity and may influence the experiences that each group has in relation to their place in American society (Danico 2004).

As Korean communities began to grow, the likelihood for participants in this study to encounter other Koreans increased, especially in college. As the data showed earlier, after years of being the "only" (or almost only) Asian person in their neighborhoods or schools, participants in this study had learned to blend in with the community around them. And yet, because of experiences with racism from the dominant white society around, participants were well aware of the differences between themselves and their white peers. Thus, during their college years, when opportunities arose to meet other Koreans, participants were enthralled by the idea of meeting co-ethnic peers. However, it did not take long before they felt the exclusion that was indirectly communicated to them as "outsiders" by the 1.5-generation Korean immigrants. Disappointingly, participants realized they did not fit in with their co-ethnic peers. This is clearly depicted by these participants' statements regarding their experiences with Korean student organizations in college. For instance, Dylan's reflection:

> There was a group of Korean students at Harvard, and it was nice to meet people, but it was clear that people were really actively seeking out, you know, really a Korean bond and Korean identity and wanting to just seek a connection with a lot of other Koreans. And I think that didn't seem as important to me at that time.

Josie also recalled:

> I did do a little bit with a Korean club. But a lot of the folks in that were actually from Korea [1.5-generation immigrant youth]. So I didn't totally identify with them because they all had grown up in Korea, at least through some significant period of time. Korean was their first language and I didn't speak Korean and I didn't feel like I fit in with that group. And so I did a little bit with them but not a lot. It didn't really feel quite comfortable to me. And for the most part I ended up assimilating more with sort of more American Americans.

Again, both participants expressed feelings of not fitting in primarily because of the in-group solidarity of the immigrant population and language barriers. What is interesting about both of these participants is that they are siblings who grew up in Hawaii. So as multicultural and diverse as Hawaii is, both participants felt more comfortable socializing with their white peers and more distanced from co-ethnic peers. Wilson also related his experience from college:

> There was a Korean-American group at UVA. You know they didn't talk to me. I didn't talk to them. It was the language barrier and cultural barrier, you could tell. They hung out themselves, by themselves, and I just blended in with everybody else because that's what I've always done.

Again as Jessica noted:

> You know there was a Korean student organization and there was an Asian student organization. I joined both of them but you know the Korean student organization, like [. . .] they would speak Korean at the meetings which made those of who didn't speak Korean feel excluded.

During the 1970s and 1980s, the new Korean immigrant population grew to be so large that they treated the American-born Koreans in a similar manner to how Nadia Kim's recent study of young second-generation Korean Americans were treated when they went to Korea. For this small cohort of American-born Korean Americans, not having heritage language skills in Korean created feelings of exclusion from the 1.5-generation Korean immigrant youth and the larger Korean community around them. These accounts of being excluded stem from the in-group solidarity that Koreans strongly adhere to. This also indicates that the 1.5-generation Koreans considered the second-generation Korean Americans to be outsiders. At that time, the difference in immigrant generational status (1.5 versus second) was the driving force behind this intra-group difference. It is important to note that the differences between the 1.5 generation and second generation were more blatant thirty years ago (compared to today) as the foreign-born Korean population was significantly larger than the U.S.-born Koreans at that time. However, as recent immigrants, the 1.5 generation were not being consciously malicious by their actions of exclusion towards the second generation; they were just behaving as they would have in Korea. In essence, it was more like a misunderstanding between two cultures.

Korean Language versus English-only

Prior to 1970, there were strong social forces supporting assimilation—scientific research that genetically linked intelligence to language and claimed children learning more than one language would be confused and be cognitively slower (Portes and Rumbaut 1996). This basis justified the English language as the means for social acceptance and integration into American society (assimilation). Looking back on their childhood years, participants in this study were conscious of this assimilation that their parents desired for them. Yoona remembered her parents being told by their pediatrician not to teach their children Korean because it would lead to confusion, and their children would be made fun of by other children. She also said: "So [my parents] didn't know better. At the time, they didn't know that bilingual children actually had better brains [. . .] They didn't know stuff like that and they just wanted us to do as well as possible in this country." Devin, whose mother was a physician, clearly remembered: "My parents were really very conscious not to speak Korean around me. They explained it to me later that they thought if they had exposed me to two languages, it would be confusing for me and I wouldn't really have the mastery of one over the other." This was the social and historical context that the second-wave Korean immigrant families faced, where the "English-only" emphasis from the 1950s to the 1970s affected immigrant parents' perception and manner of how they socialized their children (emphasizing English over bilingual English and Korean).

In general, many Korean parents struggled with wanting to maintain the Korean culture within the family but simultaneously wanting their children to succeed in American culture. However, because the Korean community around this cohort was virtually non-existent, no one could foresee any future benefit of maintaining heritage language skills, which is strongly associated with ethnic identity (Min and Kim 1999; Portes and Hao 2002; Portes and Schauffler 1994, J. S. Lee 2002). Instead, these Korean parents (of the second immigration wave) encouraged their children to assimilate through English usage and to experience American culture in everyday living. Many participants expressed similar sentiments. Caterina says, "I didn't speak Korean. My parents didn't teach me any Korean." Patrick recalls, "I think my parents didn't push us to learn the Korean language. They spoke to us in English. They wanted us to assimilate." All the participants were keenly aware that their parents were conscious not to speak Korean around them, and some felt that, as children, they were blocked from learning their own heritage language: Korean. Mina remembered:

> My parents did not try very hard to teach us Korean. We were not raised to be bilingual. They pretty much always talked to us in English. They would often talk to themselves in Korean. That was a decision that they made. But I do know that she [mother] really wanted us to master English and she felt that if she tried to teach us both languages that it would hinder our ability to grasp English.

There was notable frustration as Jessica commented: "It's not that I didn't want to learn Korean. I mean, you know, I was a baby and was not taught it. I had no choice!" In looking back, some participants expressed regret over how they were raised. Randy lamented: "I have regrets about this looking back on this. Great efforts were made to assimilate us and therefore essentially limit our exposure to Korean language growing up." Interestingly, because education was the driving force that brought this second wave of Korean immigrants to America, these parents were in a unique position to facilitate the assimilation process for their children by speaking English to them. The experiences early in their developmental years had a significant impact on participants as they got older because language barriers to their heritage language continued to impede their inclusion into the Korean community. These reflections from participants also illustrate the tremendous pressure on the immigrant parents to teach their children English, especially if they wanted their American-born children to succeed in the U.S.

"I'm not really Korean"

The encounters participants had with the 1.5 generation and on visits to South Korea brought them to an unsettling conclusion. There were several poignant moments during the various interviews where participants articulated their feelings on not being accepted as Korean or not really considering themselves as being Korean. Caterina displayed mixed emotions as she related to me her move to South Korea and the reception she received from the Korean community:

> And then the first shocker came when I was nine years old and moved to Korea. And then I realized that they didn't look at me as Korean at all. They called me the "American kid" even though I was from Canada. I was the "American kid." They all thought I was half Asian! None of them thought I looked Korean. So my identity there was as an outsider, of somebody with an accent who was viewed as half Korean [. . .] I did not view myself as American. But when I was in Korea, I did not view myself as Korean either. In Korea, I realized that I'm not fully Korean. And that Koreans don't view me as Korean at all.

This is a clear example of how Koreans conflate race, ethnicity, and citizenship. To the South Koreans, Caterina was an "American" citizen entering Korea. This is also a clear example of how Koreans perceive others who were born outside of South Korea. What a shock to be perceived as "half Asian." Both of her parents were full-blooded Koreans, born and raised in Korea, but who happened to emigrate to the U.S. for graduate studies and eventually return to their South Korean homeland. It may have been that her parents had not anticipated a return to their native homeland and as such, did not teach their daughter how to speak Korean or practice cultural mannerisms. Along these same lines, Josie ruefully stated: "I mean, I'm not Korean, really. I mean 'Korean-Korean.' I mean I don't speak the language, right?" Many other participants also felt marginalized from their ethnic communities because of this language barrier. They expressed regret or confusion just as Jessica articulated:

> I did not grow up speaking Korean. I understand quite a lot of it but at some point very early on my parents stopped teaching me Korean, which was a big mistake [. . .] I think if there weren't as much a language barrier and I could operate more freely like in, you know, what is a very large Korean community here and in Flushing and various other places. I probably wouldn't have the same issues, but like I don't even feel comfortable.

Or as Derek exclaimed: "Yeah it's a head trip and you can't speak to them and you really want to. You're aching to engage with them and you can't because you can't speak the language!" Derek also observed that:

> I think being Korean or being of any ethnic identity is governed by language and you access culture through language. If you do not speak that language,

then you have a very limited ability to access that culture. I don't speak Korean so I am fully aware of the fact that I can never be "fully" Korean.

This last comment was so eloquent in connecting language to culture and how that connection is used to define who is Korean. The participants in this study tried so diligently to learn English and to assimilate into American culture that it created a language barrier to their own heritage language. This language barrier, in turn, was the prominent obstacle for participants to fully accept themselves as Korean or be accepted as being a "real Korean" by other Koreans. The effect of not knowing the Korean language continues to have an impact on participants today. As summed up by Nadia Kim (2009), it is the "Korean American's inability to gain acceptance from people who look just like them [that] proves rather disappointing and disheartening" (409).

DISCUSSION

This part focused on authenticity issues as a "Korean" that this group of second-generation Korean Americans faced as they were caught between two cultural worlds that are so prominent in their lives. There are some important implications found in the data. The first is that even at an early age, participants had to negotiate their identity between trying to be white and comprehending their Koreanness. Participants' experiences with racial foreignness from their white peers only reinforced to them their Koreanness. These experiences helped participants to realize their Korean identity. Also, having two Korean parents, participants know they are genetically and ethnically Korean. However, though they understood that their phenotypical features were Korean, they were more knowledgeable about and culturally more comfortable to behave like their white peers rather than their co-ethnic peers.

For these participants, the issue of authenticity as Koreans arose primarily from not being accepted by their co-ethnic peers and community. In the company of other Koreans, mainly from the immigrant community, the "authenticity" of their Koreanness would come into question. Whenever participants were in a Korean community setting (whether in the U.S. or in Korea), their co-ethnic peers identified them as cultural foreigners, and the message was that they were not really "Korean." It seems like there was confusion from being told by their parents they are Korean but also being told by their co-ethnic peers they are not. There was confusion from differing sets of expectations, without explanations from either side as to why they were not accepted as a Korean.

Another part of the issue surrounding this idea of authenticity stems from differences in how identity is defined. In a country such as the U.S. that was founded on diverse immigrant groups, ethnicity is a strong marker for ethnic identity. Ethnic identity is also often associated with racial identity. However, the critiques around that association are better left for another conversation. Nonetheless, the racial divide between whites and blacks in the U.S. seems to be resistant to time. Today, the unresolvable question is where Asians/Asian Americans (who are neither white nor black) fit into this schema. Tuan (1999) states that the debate surrounding the authenticity dilemma for Asian Americans in the U.S. is that they are considered neither real "Americans" nor real "Asians." In this way, we can see how the U.S. tends to categorize and group people by their race or phenotypical features. However, in Korea, race is defined differently. In Korea, a country that is obsessed with purity of blood and views themselves as ethnically homogeneous, every other Asian group is considered another race. This definition of race does not focus solely on phenotypical features as it does in the U.S., but rather, it is a proxy for ethnicity and culture. Consequently, this is how race and culture plus citizenship define a national identity in Korea.

On a concluding note, there are additional thoughts to consider. One is that for many immigrants, their heritage culture seems to get "frozen" in time, meaning they bring with them the prevailing culture at the time of emigration. However, culture does not stand still and is continuously changing (i.e., in South Korea, as well as in the U.S.). Over the last several decades, South Korea has undergone dramatic changes as they moved from a military dictatorship to a democratic nation, plus the rapid economic boom. Recent liberalized immigration laws have started to change Korea into a more multicultural nation. Although the deep-rooted ideology from the early twentieth century until the late 1980s was *danil minjok*, there has recently been a shift to another discourse, moving away from the ethnic blood-based ideas of nationhood to one focusing on a democratic Korea called *minjung* (the masses) (H. Kim 2009; Shin 2006b). All these changes lead to a change in how Koreans begin to understand Koreans in the diaspora. Participants in this study might find that "newer" Korean immigrants are different compared to the Korean immigrants of the 1970s and 1980s. This is another area of future research in how these changes in South Korea are affecting the immigrant communities in the U.S. And a final note is that in recent years, there has been a growing Korean-American community within the U.S. Two excellent examples are the website titled "I am Korean American," and the KYOPO Project (2011) by Cindy Hwang (CYJO), which is both a book and a photography exhibit. All the 200+ photographs from the book were on display at the Smithsonian National Portrait Gallery in Washington, D.C. until October 2012. This is also noteworthy of more research into the meaning and culture behind the Korean-American community.

III

Three Essays by Members of the Earlier Cohort

Chapter Three

My Trek

Rose Kim

The latest incarnation of "Star Trek," the legendary science-fiction television series, premiered just a day after I was asked to write this essay describing my experiences as a Korean and an Asian American. For the first time in the history of the show that has spawned so many spin-offs, a woman—actress Kate Mulgrew—took the helm as the calm, reassuring, and commanding captain. Curiously enough, a prominent member of the U.S.S. Voyager was named Ensign Harry Kim, ostensibly a Korean.

The casting caught my attention because the television series had been the source of some of my fondest childhood memories—early Saturday evenings after dinner, with my sister and two brothers. Our parents forbade us to watch television on nights before school because they thought it would interfere with our studies. So, as soon as Friday evening arrived, we would be glued to the TV, or "the Devil's Box," as my grandmother called it.

As a child, I deeply resented my parents' prohibition on television because I missed popular shows such as "My Three Sons," "Alias Smith and Jones," and "Batman." But over time I've grown to appreciate their decision and would impose the same restriction on my own children, if I ever have any. As a result, I read more and daydreamed more often—and when I did get to watch television, I paid closer attention.

But beaming back to the Enterprise, I alternated between admiration for and infatuation with Captain James T. Kirk, the commander of the U.S.S. Enterprise. I wanted to be one of his conquests, but I also wanted "to explore new planets and new civilizations, to boldly go where no man has gone before."

The show's benevolent 1960s-ish themes of equality and respect for different cultures helped shape my social conscience—despite the constant violations of the Prime Directive to not meddle in other societies and the relegation of women to secondary roles as nurses, switchboard operators, and love objects. The show was unique in having a multiracial cast, including Uhuru, the African communications officer, Sulu, the Asian helmsman, and Chekhov, the Russian navigation officer.

The debut of a female captain in 1995 made me realize how much the world had changed since I was growing up. For though I longed to be like Kirk, when I was a child it seemed impossible, since I was female and Asian in a white, male-dominated society. For a while in my early teens, my loftiest goal was to become Secretary of State, a state office held by a Chinese-American woman, March Fong Eu, in California in the 1970s. As late as my freshman year in college, I wished to be a white man so I could achieve my dreams of being an astronaut or president of the United States.

I did hang on to my dream of being a writer, and worked for six years as a journalist for a major daily newspaper in New York City. I've grown to appreciate my Korean heritage and my gender, and feel lucky to have been exposed to two cultures. But it is an outlook that has taken most of my life to achieve. The fact that Ensign Kim was played by a Chinese actor, Garrett Wong, made me realize how much things still needed to change.

Some of my earliest memories are of suffering the degradation of being female, and for a long time I could not help but associate Korean culture with the oppression of women. I believe that my reaction was inevitable in a culture where women primarily held domestic, nonpublic roles as housekeepers, mothers, wives, and prostitutes.

When guests arrived at our house, my sister and I were shuttled into the kitchen and forced to assist in preparing food for the guests. My brothers, meanwhile, were allowed to sit with the adults in the living room. Though I now enjoy cooking, I actively resisted learning even the basics as a youngster. A virtually straight-A student, I proudly received my first D in sewing in the eighth grade. Girls were forced to learn the domestic arts, a fact that I despised. I longed to be in wood or auto shop.

As the youngest daughter in a Korean family, I often found myself on the lowest rung of the social order. My parents encouraged my brothers to attend the best universities and to become lawyers and doctors. My sisters and I were only groomed for marriage—constantly being told to look pretty, talk softly, and sit properly. A bachelor's degree was considered essential for a suitable match.

The world outside my home seemed so much more open and inviting.

I was born and raised in a middle-class neighborhood of single-family houses in central Los Angeles. The lawns were well-groomed, and fruit trees filled the spacious backyards. The neighborhood once had been predominantly Jewish, but was now divided mostly among second- and third-generation Japanese Americans and African Americans. There were also a few second-generation Chinese Americans. My Korean family stood out as new immigrants.

My father was born in North Korea, and was the only surviving member of his family. He had been a journalist in Korea, and came to the United States in 1959 on a student visa. He attended Brigham Young University in Salt Lake City, Utah, to study English, and my mother joined him on a student visa two years later. They eventually moved to Los Angeles, where I was born in January, 1962. Though they talked about returning to their homeland, they were lured into staying by the good salaries and the prospect of owning their own home. They also preferred the American schools and the higher quality of life. My mother thought that the Korean schools were too restrictive and high-pressured. She told me years later that an older brother whom she'd been close to had committed suicide after failing to get into a good university.

In Los Angeles, my father worked as the editor of the *Shin Han Il-bo*, the city's oldest Korean newspaper. It was a one-man operation. Not only did he edit the newspaper, he wrote nearly all of the articles and did the typesetting himself. Eventually, in the early 1970s, he and my mother started a lucrative wig business. My mother recently commented on how tiny the Korean community had been in the early 1960s. "There was just a handful of us," she said. "We all knew each other. Nothing like today."

Though the only family I knew as an infant consisted of my mother and father, I had two brothers and a sister in South Korea. My parents had left them in the care of my maternal grandmother and other relatives. They saved money, bought a home, and then sent for their children. My older brother, Steven, then eight, and my sister, Sophia, six, came to the United States when I was about a year and a half. My older brother, Edward, came two years later with my maternal grandmother when he was about five.

My siblings were at the forefront of the modern wave of Koreans to immigrate to the U.S., and other students teased them for their stumbling English and different appearance. I was spared such harassment because I was assimilated and able to read English when I entered kindergarten. Still, I felt the stigma of being different. While my classmates had meatloaf and fried chicken for dinner, I ate pungent, spicy foods like *du-bu chi-gae* (soybean casserole) and *kimchi* (pickled cabbage). The smells of garlic and fermented soybean paste permeated the house, and I was embarrassed to invite my friends over.

Since most of our relatives were in South Korea, we lacked an extended family and rarely celebrated holidays, neither American ones such as the Fourth of July nor Korean ones such as *Chu-suk* (Harvest Festival). When my parents visited my school on Open House nights, I felt self-conscious and ashamed of their English, a reaction that embarrasses me today. I wish that I had been more generous toward my parents, but again, as a child, there was an enormous pressure to blend in or be "normal."

In the sixth grade, I entered a lottery to attend an affluent, oceanside junior high school, and was among the ten or so winners. The school was near a college campus, and many of the students were the children of academics or professionals. The junior high school closest to my home was in an impoverished section of the city and had poor academic scores. My parents tried to send all of us to better schools outside our zoned district.

My father drove me to school in the morning, and I would catch three public buses—an hour-and-a-half ride altogether—to get back home. After saving up some money, my parents started a coat factory in Seoul, Korea. As the business took off, they became more preoccupied with their work. My mother began spending months at a time in South Korea, eventually returning to the U.S. only once a year to maintain her resident status. My father, meanwhile, often traveled throughout the United States on business. By the ninth grade, I was waking up at 6:30 AM to catch the bus to school by myself.

Except for one Chinese-American boy whose father was a mathematics professor, I was the only Asian at the junior high school. All the other lottery winners were black. Everyone else was white. Again, there was a sense of being different. While other students remained after school for extracurricular activities, I boarded the bus for the long trip home. I was in the school orchestra and lugged my cello back and forth to school each day. I was very fat and had only a few friends. Outside of a few of the others who were bussed, I hung out with Laura, the daughter of an Italian-American romance languages professor. Still, I appreciated the superior education. The school had a state-of-the-art computer system that was unavailable in the inner city.

When it was time for high school, I was uprooted again. This time my parents moved to Montebello, a middle-class suburb in the San Gabriel Valley, directly east of L.A. The neighborhood was middle- to upper-middle-class and predominantly Asian-American and Latino, with a smattering of whites. The school's academic scores were average, and there were several honors-level courses.

As awkward as my junior high school experiences had been, for some reason I sentimentalized them. Somehow, I had developed the notion that white students were superior, and felt disdainful toward my classmates. I never participated in school events, spent lunches in the school library, gained even more weight—peaking at 181 pounds in my senior year—and daydreamed constantly about going away to college. Many years later, I recognized these feelings as being the possible result of living in a society where Asian Americans were not regarded as members of the mainstream. When I read about the concept of internalized racism, the replication of racist prototypes within one's mind, I finally was able to come to terms with my past, conflicted feelings. It also occurred to me years later that I might have carried all that extra weight to obscure my gender.

Though I felt alienated from my classmates, I found friends elsewhere by volunteering in local political campaigns. As a teenager, I participated in NAACP-led marches for school desegregation, worked to gain voting rights for migrant farmworkers through Cesar Chavez's United Farm Workers, and also volunteered in the gubernatorial and presidential campaigns of Jerry Brown, the former governor of California. In my junior year of high school, I rode the bus after school to Brown's campaign office, which was on the outskirts of downtown L.A. My father's office was nearby, and he would pick me up at 8:00 or 8:30 PM at the end of his work day. We would often have dinner at a Korean restaurant before returning to our empty house. My siblings were all away at college.

Being involved in politics helped ground me, and I credit my childhood enthusiasms to my brother Steven, who was seven years older. Though my father played a strong role in my early education by teaching me how to read and grilling me on mathematics, he grew more detached as I grew older. My parents worked long hours, often six or seven days a week, so we were raised primarily by Steven and my grandmother, who lived with us until I was about eight. She fed us, kept house, and tended the garden, while Steven educated us. Under his direction, we read aloud Shakespeare's plays during winter breaks. He took us to museums, foreign films, and summer concerts at the Hollywood Bowl. During the summer, he and I used to read aloud poetry in our backyard. Another summer when I was about twelve, he made me write a college-style research paper, requiring footnotes and at least five different sources. My topic was "communal utopias," and he gave me a month to complete the assignment.

Working during Brown's second gubernatorial campaign, I formed one of my first teenage relationships with an Asian American. Cheryl, a first-generation Chinese American, was starting her junior year at the University of California at Los Angeles when we met. She had just completed a summer internship working for the U.S. Congress, and impressed me with her worldliness. Both of us worked in Brown's press office, which was headed by Bobbie Metzger, a deputy press secretary on leave from the governor's office. She was in her early thirties, and the five of us in the office, including Elise, the administrative assistant, and Holly, another college volunteer, were all female. We once calculated our average age to be about twenty-three.

Since elementary school, I had shunned Asians and girlfriends. I hated to talk about clothes, makeup, and boys, and preferred to hold discussions on politics, literature, and films. Most of my school acquaintances were guys, particularly white guys. Cheryl changed that. She exposed me to vast, unknown parts of Los Angeles—trendy restaurants, neat bookstores, and shops galore. We spent hours driving around at night, going to the beach, and hanging out in twenty-four-hour diners. I had a lot of freedom as a teenager—my parents were often away on business and my siblings were at college. My dad had bought me a brand-new, four-door Fiat sedan when I got my driver's license at sixteen.

I was a good student, and only began ditching classes in my senior year. Even then, I did harmless things like go to a matinee, browse in bookstores, or read a book at the beach. My teachers trusted me implicitly, and never questioned my sporadic absences.

When it was time to consider college, I applied to the University of Chicago, Barnard College in New York City, Reed College in Portland, Oregon, Cornell University in Ithaca, New York, the University of California at Berkeley, and maybe two others. I was accepted by all except Cornell, and decided to attend Chicago, which had been my first choice. I was attracted to the school's emphasis on the classics of western civilization and its reputation for being hard-nosed and serious about intellectual pursuits. I was the first child to attend an out-of-state college. (My sister had attended Scripps College near L.A., and both my brothers had gone to the University of California at Berkeley.)

When I arrived at the University of Chicago in the fall of 1979, I discovered the community that I had been searching for. Chicago did not attract the Ivy League crowd. The students were more middle- and upper-middle-class, serious about academics, and often emotionally maladjusted. For the first time, I felt as if I fit in. Without any effort, I shed much of my excess weight.

I formed a close relationship with my first-year roommate, Neeta, whose parents came from India as graduate students. My other friendships—male or female—were mostly with whites. I consciously and unconsciously avoided associating with East Asians, particularly Korean Americans. It was a blind effort to blend in, I think. Meanwhile, I stayed in touch with Cheryl and others I knew through my political activities.

Though the first year was exhilarating, I became discontented in the second year. I grew disenchanted with the school's rigorous ten-week quarters and harsh winters. The impoverished ghetto that surrounded the university was depressing and contradicted the college's oft-repeated platitudes regarding equal opportunity and access. I sank into a deep depression and stayed inside my room for days at a time. I had always been a responsible student, but I yearned to break loose and do whatever I wanted—to travel, to be a novelist—without any accountability to my parents. I finally dropped out at the beginning of winter quarter.

I postponed telling my parents for as long as I could, about two months, until just before the next quarter's bill was to be mailed. They were as angry and disappointed in me as I had thought they would be. They had never wanted me to attend an out-of-state college, and I had fought and begged to leave. Steven had helped persuade my parents that it was a wise move. But once they got used to the idea, they—especially my dad—were proud that I attended a prominent college. Dropping out meant losing face, and was disgraceful.

I transferred to the University of California at Santa Cruz, one of the state system's most liberal campuses. I thought a different campus might renew my interest in school, but I ended up staying for just one session. After Chicago, Santa Cruz seemed intellectually impoverished. I wrote fiction and worked as a waitress in an omelette house in Santa Cruz. After a year, I moved to Los Angeles, where I continued to write, working again as a waitress, this time in a twenty-four-hour coffee shop. The working life was exhausting, after a year I was ready to return to Chicago. I applied for loans to cover my tuition.

Returning to Chicago provided relief from the drudgery of work. I took several enjoyable classes—particularly in studio art. I became friends with Aubrey, a first-year student from Washington state and a gifted poet. School was intellectually stimulating, but it was impossible to finance a second year. The college slashed my financial aid, and I couldn't meet the college's projection of my contribution. But I wasn't too upset by the turn of events; I was restless and ready to leave. I had been developing this notion that I would return to college only when my mind needed stimulation, that I would deliberately avoid getting a college diploma, which I regarded then as an evil symbol of social conformity. My parents were increasingly dubious about my future, so it was easier and easier to do whatever I wanted. I saw them maybe once a year. I wore eccentric, second-hand clothes and shaved my head with a razor.

I moved to Providence, Rhode Island, because I had always wanted to live in the northeastern United States. I worked as a waitress in a downtown crab house and was the lone Korean in a town full of blue-blooded WASPs and first- and second-generation Italian, Irish, and Portuguese Americans. The city also had small pockets of recently immigrated West Indians, Africans, and Hmongs as well as Ivy Leaguers at Brown and art students at the Rhode Island School of Design. I became acquainted with some local writers and artists, practiced meditation, experimented with prayer, and spent a lot of time reading, writing, and exploring the city.

Life in Providence was pleasant, but after more than a year of not getting published, I grew increasingly nervous about not making it professionally as a novelist. I decided to return to Chicago to get my B.A.—a degree seemed essential for any sort of white-collar job with basic health-care benefits. My parents' ethic to be a social success had been deeply ingrained in me. I was frightened by a life of manual labor, of being a waitress for the rest of my life.

Deciding to return to school was easy, but financing it was difficult. I had unknowingly defaulted on my previous educational loans and had to pay them off in full in order to register. My scarred credit history prevented me from getting any more loans, so I decided to work full-time as a secretary in the university's fund-raising offices to get 50 percent off tuition. At $1,500 per quarter (paid out every three months), it was still a stretch on a secretary's salary. I supplemented my income by writing for a variety of local newspapers and magazines. Working during the 1980s for the gay weekly, the *Windy City Times*, stirred my interest in journalism. So much was happening in the gay community—gays and lesbians were gaining historic and legal rights, while at the same time being ravaged by AIDS. The *Windy City Times* played a vital role in informing the community about all of these events and fueled my interest in journalism.

Obtaining my college degree was exhausting, but the upside was that it taught me a lot about self-discipline. For three years, I took two classes a quarter, the maximum number allowed an employee. Though I had always shunned rituals, I attended the graduation ceremony at Rockefeller Chapel and was happy to receive my diploma from the college president Hanna Gray in December, 1990. The photo of that moment sits near my desk even today.

Since I enjoyed working as a freelance journalist, I decided to seek a full-time position at a daily newspaper. One of the newspapers I had been freelancing for was the English section of the *Korea Times* in Los Angeles. My sister was an assigning editor at the paper, which was edited for some time by K. W. Lee, a pioneering Korean-American newspaperman. Both of them encouraged me to become a journalist and stoked my interest in covering the Korean-American community. Journalism seemed like the perfect way to combine my interests in writing and public service.

I was in the process of accepting a summer internship at the *Tacoma News Tribune* in Tacoma, Washington, in the spring of 1991, when I learned that I was one of ten finalists in the *Los Angeles Times*'s Minority Editorial Training Program (METPRO). I was the first Korean American to be accepted into the program, and struggled with the decision of whether to accept. In recent years, Korean Americans had figured prominently in the news with the Brooklyn boycotts of 1990-1991 and the fatal shooting of Latasha Harlins in Los Angeles in 1991. The lack of Korean-American journalists had resulted in a distorted, incomplete picture of the Korean-American community. I wanted to fill that void, but also wondered whether being affiliated with a minority advancement program would stigmatize me. Ultimately, it was an offer that was impossible to decline. METPRO provided the graduate-level training in journalism that I lacked, as well as lots of hands-on experience; after one year in L.A., interns were placed at one of six Times Mirror newspapers across the country. A permanent job was assured at the end of the second year, if you didn't screw up. Entering METPRO was a decision that I never regretted. It was exhilarating to work for my hometown newspaper, even for a year, and my subsequent assignment to *Newsday* in New York was just as exciting.

More than 120,000 Koreans and Korean Americans live in New York City, and more than 350,000 in the New York metro area. It's the second-greatest concentration of Korean Americans in the country, following Los Angeles, and newspapers, as well as other businesses, are trying to tap this market. With my cultural and language skills, I was able to break stories and to obtain exclusive interviews within the Korean community. For years the only Korean-speaking news reporter at a mainstream daily in this city, I regularly included Koreans in a variety of stories and suggested covering little-known aspects of the local community, such as second-generation voter-registration drives. I also spoke out when my paper misrepresented or stereotyped Korean Americans. One of the most egregious examples was an article that covered the raid of a Queens brothel. The brothel was run by a Korean woman and the article quoted police sources who claimed that *ah-joom-mah*, the Korean word for aunt or older woman, was the Asian word for a brothel madam. It was mind-boggling that someone would think in this day and age that there was a pan-Asian language.

My fears of being stigmatized did not materialize, but more than once I have felt self-conscious about being a product of a minority advancement program. In recent years, the newspaper industry and journalism in general have undergone corporate downsizing and reorganization. After *Newsday* closed its city edition in 1995, the staff shrank considerably. With such economic pressures, there seem to be undercurrents of resentment toward ethnic and racial minorities and the suspicion that we were somehow second-rate and robbing others of their rightful jobs. The reduction in staff no doubt negatively affects the depth and variety of news being reported. It also threatens the diversity of the newsroom by the sheer reduction in staff.

In a recent interview, the newspaper's chief executive, Mark Wiles, said he was trying to build up readership in minority communities. He suggested that quoting more minorities and using their photographs more frequently would win their loyalty. I think that in-depth reporting on minority communities, through bilingual reporters who are sensitive to different cultures, is a better strategy.

In the summer of 1998, a few months before the publication of this book, I decided to leave my full-time reporting job to seek a graduate degree in sociology. I was growing disenchanted with the quick processing of facts required by journalism, and wanted the chance to do more in-depth research. I am interested in further exploring questions and issues raised in this essay and this book. As a child, for so many years I denied my ethnicity. Now here I am planning to devote years of study to it.

Though there may not be a common language uniting all of Asia, there definitely is a pan-Asian identity taking shape in this country. Korean

Americans on their own form a tiny subset, yet, coupled with Japanese, Filipino, Chinese, and Indian Americans, they can achieve a significant political mass. In this country, we share a physical or geographic resemblance, whether we think so or want to. I participate in the New York City chapter of the Asian American Journalists Association, and am well acquainted with other minority journalists, especially blacks and women. My friends are of diverse backgrounds, but recently I have grown to know more Asians and other ethnic minorities.

I used to tutor two Korean boys, ages fourteen and twelve, who immigrated to New York City in their early teens. The older one once chastised me for owning a Honda Accord, a Japanese car. He said he preferred American or Korean cars, and evoked Japan's brutal occupation of Korea as the reason for his position. I admitted that Japan and Korea had a violent and tragic history, but chided him for regarding one nationality or race as being morally superior to another. There are good and bad Japanese, I told him, whether he understood or not.

We have this illusion of shaping or directing our lives, but, just as strongly, life imposes its circumstances upon us, requiring us to adjust. As I have attempted to explain, my perception of my ethnicity and identity has undergone many permutations and it is difficult to predict how I will feel in another thirty-six years.

I'm grateful to have been exposed to two cultures. Some of the Korean or Asian ideas that have influenced me are a respect for elders, a reverence for scholarly achievements, and an appreciation for formality in social interactions. I love all sorts of international cuisines, but still rank Korean as one of my favorites, and have introduced it to many of my non-Korean friends. But American meals—broiled meats and tossed salads—are more convenient to prepare and eat on a daily basis.

American influences, meanwhile, seem to be my belief in the importance of self-reliance and public service, as well as the virtually limitless possibilities of the individual. I always have been thankful that my parents immigrated to this country. America, despite its setbacks, has offered me opportunities that would have been virtually impossible in Korea.

My parents were at the beginning of a massive emigration of Koreans, and I consider myself to be a transitional generation, marking that jump. To a great extent, they have retained their Korean culture. Though my mother's English skills are weak, she embraces this country. My father, on the other hand, is more fluent, yet he longs to return home. I cannot ever imagine leaving this country, as my parents left theirs. Yet, neither do I feel comfortable or fully accepted here. I expect that my children will feel far less conflicted than I do about their ethnicity, and I hope they will assimilate more effortlessly.

When I tell them stories about my life, perhaps they will seem as strange and fantastic as the stories of my parents—of living in a war-torn city, of dodging gunfire, and of hiking across mountains and jumping on railroad cars to visit friends in distant villages. Korean Americans, after all, have been making enormous advancements and popping up in the most unexpected places. Comedian Margaret Cho had her own TV sitcom, and former presidential candidate, Senator Phil Gramm (R-Texas), is married to a Korean-American economist. As a transitional generation, settling into a new land, I must say that I sometimes feel like a space traveler, boldly going where no one has gone before.

Captain, out.

NOTE

This chapter was originally included in *Struggle for Ethnic Indentity: Narratives by Asian American Professionals*, published in 1999 by Alta Mira Press, edited by Pyong Gap Min and Rose Kim. Rose Kim is now assistant professor of Sociology at the Boroufh of Manhattan Community College.

Chapter Four

A Handicapped Korean in America

Alex Jeong

Any Korean parent taking a look at my resume would want me for a son-in-law. I'm twenty-nine, single, and an assistant district attorney in New York City. I'm a graduate of Colgate University and George Washington University Law School. But if they were to meet me in person, perhaps they might feel differently. A traffic accident six years ago left me paralyzed below the chest, and irrevocably altered the perception of most Koreans of not only my eligibility as a husband, but also my most basic identity as a man.

In all societies, the physically handicapped are subject to some prejudices and discrimination. Yet the bigoted attitudes I have encountered in the Korean community far exceed anything I have encountered in American society at large. In Korea, individuals with disabilities are shunned and locked away. Unlike America, there are no laws ensuring equal access and opportunities. Many Korean Americans share this prejudice. When strangers see me on the street, they pity me without even knowing who I am. They think that I deserve their pity just because I cannot walk. Even my own parents have told me that they would rather see me as an able-bodied ditch digger than as a disabled attorney.

When I became disabled, my status within the Korean community suddenly diminished. Before the accident, I served as a Sunday school teacher and as the president of my church's students' association. Church members viewed me as someone who could make valuable contributions and often consulted me on ecumenical affairs. After the car accident that disabled me, they treated me more like an infant than a grown man. When church members approached me after Mass, they would only discuss my physical condition. "How are you doing, Alex? I hope you improve soon." I stopped attending church because of the closed minds of some of the parishioners. These days, I remain reluctant to attend any Korean social function because of the uneasy reception I'm bound to receive. It's a pity that people make such assumptions about me without even having a clue as to who I am inside.

In 1976, when I was nine, my entire family immigrated to New York City. I am the only son and have two sisters. We lived in a high-rise apartment building on a relatively quiet stretch of Kissena Boulevard in Flushing, Queens. My cousins lived in the same building and we spent a lot of time together, along with other Korean kids in the building. Flushing—where I still live today—has the second largest enclave of Koreans in the U.S., following Koreatown in Los Angeles. Even in 1976, there was a sizable Korean population, with several Korean markets and stores, many with signs posted in Korean. In my class, there were four other Koreans. Although there were also Chinese and Japanese Americans and a few African Americans, at least seventy to eighty percent of the students were Caucasian, and of Italian, Irish, or Jewish descent.

Some of my most vivid childhood memories are of the hardships that my parents endured when they first came to this country. My father, a graduate of Korea University, worked in real estate before emigrating. In Korea, we owned our own home; in America, we didn't even have furniture or carpets. I was embarrassed by our living conditions and resented my parents' decision to leave Korea.

My parents came to America for the reason shared by so many immigrants: more economic opportunities, a higher quality of life. We were misled by false perceptions, I think. Several of my uncles already lived in the U.S.—two were doctors and the third, a pharmacist. We imagined that we would live as they did. Instead, my parents held an assortment of manual labor jobs. As soon as my mother recovered from her jet lag, she got a job as a seamstress in a garment factory. She left for work early in the morning before we left for school and came home when it was dark. Her ankles swelled like balloons from pressing the pedal of the sewing machine ten hours a day. My father endured similar struggles, driving a taxicab and hauling boxes in a warehouse.

Despite the physical labor that consumed their lives, my parents never forgot the importance of a good education. Like many other Korean parents, they strongly believed that America provided a higher quality of education for their children. I was given a lot of freedom as a child, but never strayed into delinquency. For as long as I can remember, my parents impressed upon me the fact that I had to take care of them when they grew older. Being successful in school and becoming a professional, white-collar worker were essential to achieving that goal.

My parents suffered many financial ups and downs, but they always managed to find money for school-related activities. I belonged to a number of sports teams and they made sure that I had the uniforms and athletic equipment I needed. Seeing how hard my parents worked motivated me to do my best in school. I concentrated on my studies, more or less continuously attending school from the third grade until my graduation from law school.

When I started the third grade shortly after my arrival in America, I didn't even know the English alphabet. A Korean boy was assigned to serve as my interpreter, but he was rather aloof and we never really got along. I recall sitting through entire lessons, not understanding a word of what was going on. There were a few Korean girls in my class and they were much more helpful. In and out of school, I mingled only with other Koreans. It was convenient, because they all knew Korean, but my exclusive association with them hindered my acquisition of English.

Two years after we emigrated, my family moved to Alameda, California. One of my father's friends asked him to manage his liquor store, and he accepted, hoping the change would bring better economic opportunities. I loved living in northern California. Alameda was a predominantly white, upper-middle-class suburb outside of Oakland. Though there were a few Asians in the neighborhood, most were native-born Filipino or Chinese Americans. Suddenly thrust into a very different environment, I was nervous about being teased and harassed by the other kids for not speaking English perfectly. However, few kids teased me, perhaps because of my bigger-than-average size. In fact, I made friends easily. Kids were more athletic than in New York and I enjoyed playing sports. I was a sprinter in junior high school, and also played a lot of baseball. Dating, however, was a problem. There were enough Asian-American girls, but the good-looking ones often paired off with non-Asian guys. Approaching white girls, meanwhile, was difficult because I was not among the school's social elite. I used to attend school dances in junior high school, but eventually quit going when I started high school.

When I entered the tenth grade, my parents moved back to New York City. I didn't want to move, but the liquor store went out of business and my dad had difficulty finding another job. We moved back to New York and lived in Co-op City, a huge complex of apartment buildings in the Bronx. It was a depressing change from California. The local high school, which was predominantly black, was considered a rough school—the type of place where you could get killed over a leather jacket—and had a poor academic reputation. My parents decided to enroll me in a private Catholic school they picked out of the phone book. There were fewer than 800 students at the school, most of them from blue-collar, Italian- and Irish-American families. I caught a public bus to and from school every day. Unlike me, most of the students did not even think about going to college. I participated in soccer, but had only a few acquaintances from school. I developed other friends through a Korean church. On weekends, my church buddies and I would attend Korean parties at local colleges. The first time I attended one of these affairs, I was stunned and exhilarated by the sheer number of Koreans.

Back in New York, I discovered that I spoke better English than a lot of other Korean kids. I even knew more English than some kids who had immigrated at a younger age than I. If I had remained in Flushing, I suspect I would never have gained my current mastery of English, a skill that is essential to my job as an assistant district attorney. The trade-off, however, was that my Korean language skills lagged behind those of my Korean friends.

Most of the Korean I know today is the result of being forced to speak it at home. My parents never punished me for not speaking Korean, but I had no choice since my mom didn't speak any English. When I was a child, I was embarrassed that she was unable to converse in English. Today, I consider it a blessing, as it has helped me retain my native tongue. Though I feel most comfortable speaking English, I'm glad to have some Korean.

By the eleventh grade, I had settled on becoming either an attorney or a doctor—the only two careers that most Koreans seemed to know about. I just knew that I wanted a job with social prestige, and that I had to earn enough money to take care of my parents as they grew older. A Korean priest I knew from my church encouraged me to become a lawyer. He was an activist priest, and often talked about how the knowledge of law could empower the Korean community. My father had majored in law in college, but never became an attorney. Perhaps that also influenced my decision.

I had my doubts about becoming an attorney. My greatest fear was that I didn't write or speak English well enough, a skepticism echoed by my twelfth grade English teacher. She was a good, sensitive teacher, but thought I simply lacked English skills. The absence of Korean attorneys to serve as role models or mentors didn't make it any easier to imagine myself holding such a position. Despite these doubts, I graduated from law school and passed the New York State Bar Examination in November 1993.

As an undergraduate, I attended Colgate, a small liberal arts college in upstate New York; for my law degree, I went to George Washington University Law School in Washington, D.C. Like many Koreans, my parents equated going to a prestigious university with getting a good education. So, with little regard to my family's financial situation, I chose the best schools possible. Today, I would do it differently, focusing on practical considerations such as financial aid and scholarships. Unlike in Korea, people in America can graduate from top-ten law schools with mediocre grades and still end up unemployed, while others who graduated from mediocre schools with excellent grades can make close to six figures right out of school.

Life in law school was miserable. I lived with two college friends in the Foggy Bottom section of the capital, a yuppie neighborhood near George Washington University. There wasn't much of a life beyond going to class, reading casebooks, and taking tests. I was just waiting for law school to be over.

The car accident that paralyzed my lower body occurred at the end of my second year of law school. It was the first day of summer vacation and I was driving with a friend to Texas, which was where my parents were living. Four or five hours into the trip, in Virginia, just miles from the Tennessee border, it happened. A car cut me off, and to avoid crashing, I drove into a grassy median. I hit a ditch and the car flipped over. My injuries were severe and emergency crews transported me to a local hospital, then airlifted me by helicopter to an even larger hospital. For five months in 1991, from May until October, I underwent rehabilitation at New York University's Rusk Institute. The Institute was a premier rehabilitation center and a relative of ours worked there.

In the summer of 1993, I completed my final year of law school at Queens College. My first full-time job out of law school was as an assistant district attorney in the Kings County District Attorney office in Brooklyn, New York, a position that I have held now for approximately five years. My job involves all aspects of criminal prosecution, from interviewing crime victims and witnesses, negotiating plea bargains with the defense, and preparing for trial to ultimately trying cases in court. I enjoy the legal profession and feel lucky to have chosen a career well suited to my personality. Despite the moderate income, I am fulfilled by my job, particularly because of its potential to make an impact on society.

My parents did the best they could to offer me a bright future, but little did they realize that the traditional Korean family structure—the only one they knew—might sabotage my future in the American workplace. While my parents emphasized and practiced a strong work ethic, they paid scant attention to developing the social or conversational skills that can be so crucial to advancing in the workplace. My job evaluations always have highlighted my strong work ethic, and I think that's an edge I have over most of my colleagues—nearly all of whom are non-Korean, native English speakers. But if I am competent on the job, it's a completely different story when it comes to mingling with my colleagues outside the office.

I feel uncomfortable and often tongue-tied at work-related social gatherings, whether it's a formal office party or an informal get-together at a local bar. At the last office Christmas party, an executive assistant district attorney approached me. After our initial hello, I couldn't think of anything else to say. We silently sipped our drinks, then went our separate ways. On such occasions, the ability to banter and tell humorous stories is far more important than the ability to formulate brilliant legal arguments. Though I keep up with current events and am an avid sports fan, I have always had a hard time shooting the breeze.

My lack of communication and social skills is the result, I think, of the Korean cultural patterns that prevailed within my family. We rarely talked with one another. Dinners often lasted less than fifteen minutes since we never uttered an unnecessary word. We loved and still love each other very much, but, unlike Americans, we did not physically or verbally express our feelings. In traditional Korean society, a child was considered virtuous if he or she was silent and obedient to his or her parents. Because of my parents' own experiences in traditional, authoritarian families, they lacked the knowledge of how to create a warm, familial atmosphere where open verbal exchanges flourished. In fact, we were discouraged from pursuing any type of discourse. I remember that my sisters and I once overheard our parents discussing a juicy piece of gossip about a relative. When we inquired about it later, my parents reprimanded us for being nosy. Nosiness was not an attribute of well-behaved Korean children, they told us over and over again. Because of the way I was raised, I have difficulty talking with my parents even today.

My inability to banter has also caused difficulties in my relationships with the opposite sex, especially during college. There were few Asians at Colgate or in any of the neighboring towns. Social activities revolved around fraternity parties and two downtown bars; no other social outlets existed. At a party or over cocktails, the ability to tell a funny story is crucial.

Korean social situations were easier to navigate. When I hung out with my Korean friends, we often went to Korean parties at local colleges. It was easy to meet Korean women. They often found me attractive and, for some reason, small talk was unessential. A lot of Koreans I've known feel more comfortable among one another. One Korean friend of mine doesn't have any non-Korean friends.

Though I am often quick to find fault with some aspects of Korean or American culture, I realize that I am the result of both, and feel, all in all, culturally assimilated. Sometimes the Korean and American characteristics are so intertwined in my personality and identity that they are impossible to separate. I feel fortunate to have been exposed to two different cultures, and I strongly believe that diversity breeds tolerance.

Racism, I have come to believe, is something that exists outside of us. It only begins to become a problem when one starts internalizing racist concepts and develops feelings of inferiority. Being a Korean immigrant has caused me to feel insecure about myself at times, but I have developed my self-esteem, first by excelling in sports, and then later in other endeavors. Superior skills make race—and physical condition—a non-factor.

I plan to open my own law firm in the future. I want to provide Koreans with reliable, effective legal services at reasonable costs. I am particularly interested in helping Koreans because of the difficulties my own parents faced. As newcomers to this country, Koreans can be taken advantage of easily because of their inability to speak English and their unfamiliarity with the American legal system.

If I lived in Korea, my opportunities, no doubt, would be restricted by the ill-informed perceptions that most Koreans have about the disabled. By functioning effectively as an assistant district attorney, I have helped to alter the perceptions of many Koreans.

NOTE

This chapter was originally included in *Struggle for Ethnic Indentity: Narratives by Asian American Professionals*, published in 1999 by Alta Mira Press, edited by Pyong Gap Min and Rose Kim. The Honorable Alexander Jeong is now a judge for the New York City Criminal Court of Kings County.

Chapter Five

Reflections on a Korean-American Journey

Ruth Chung

COMING TO AMERICA

I peered out the oval window of the 747 jumbo jet as it made its final descent to Los Angeles International Airport. Tired and dazed from the long journey, I wondered what this new world would hold in store for me. My mother, brother, and I, then eight, came with high hopes and expectations, but on that autumn day we had not even begun to imagine how profoundly our lives would be changed by our transpacific migration from South Korea.

America was a bewildering place at first. As we entered the terminal reception area, a strange man rushed up to me and smothered me with hugs and kisses. This stranger turned out to be my father, whom I had not seen in three years. I felt so dwarfed to be in this new place. From my father to the freeways, the buildings, and even the facial features of Americans with their big eyes and big noses, everything loomed large and strange. Such a strange place with strange people, I thought. And this was to be my new home. Even the trees didn't conform to a Korean child's notion of what they should be. I thought palm trees were telephone poles until I looked up and saw the strange, featherlike protrusions on the tops.

One aspect of living in America that I looked forward to the most was having our own car. I was so proud that my father owned one. In Korea, only the wealthiest families did. As he drove us to our new home, I failed to notice that it was an old, faded blue Rambler with cracked plastic seats that had tufts of browning foam oozing out from the fissures. I sat proudly in the rear right seat, the seat of honor in Korea, and imagined that I was a little princess being chauffeured to my new home.

My father came to America on a visitor's visa with only twenty dollars and the dream of studying in America and then returning to Korea. When the visa expired, he lived the fearful life of an illegal alien until he managed, eventually and miraculously, to get a green card. He then sponsored us to join him. Now, when I hear negative sentiments expressed against illegal aliens, I think of my father and what he must have experienced. It is difficult to reconcile the stereotypes and images of illegal aliens with him and to think that not so long ago, he was perceived in the same way. The faces of illegal aliens now may be different from his, but their hopes and dreams for a better life are not. It seems that the best of what America stands for is in the hearts of those who come to its shores.

I THOUGHT I LOOKED LIKE A CAUCASIAN

By the time my mother, brother, and I arrived, my father had paved the way so that we could bypass the usual stopover in L.A.'s Koreatown and settle directly in the suburbs. Growing up in a predominantly white environment forced me to learn the language and adapt quickly. It also didn't take long before I became painfully conscious of being different. I quickly experienced the consequences of being a minority in America. One day in the second grade, I looked wistfully at the blond hair of a classmate who was sitting in front of me, wondering why couldn't I have been born in America to white parents, why couldn't I have blond hair and blue eyes like her, and a "normal"-sounding name like Smith. Instead, I was subject to a litany of well-intended but humiliating questions such as "Where are you from?" and "How come your eyes look different?" "What do you eat at home?" There were also the taunts, pairing my last name Chung to some form of sing-song rhyme that was derisive of the Chinese. It failed to impress my tormentors that I was Korean, not Chinese.

As I grew into adolescence and entered high school, the impact of being a minority and being different became more complex. I had acculturated rapidly and was thus able to disguise the more obvious tokens of my difference. I had mastered American language and culture enough to act like a typical American teenager when at school and with my white friends. But the reality was that I lived a double life. At school, I was an outgoing, all-American teenager, but at home I was a good, quiet Korean girl who spoke Korean and ate Korean food. The shift from one to the other was immediate and automatic as soon as I opened the front door of my house. It was also largely unconscious.

My family was financially established and lived in a nice house in a middle-class, suburban neighborhood by the time I started high school. Still, I was ashamed to bring my friends home. I felt as if I had some deep, dark secret to hide. I was afraid that my friends would find out how different I really was. I didn't want them to have to take off their shoes at the door, to notice the smell of *kimchi* that lingered in the air, and to ask questions about the Korean wall hangings and calendars that adorned every room. I was ashamed of my Koreanness and anything that hinted at my difference. I believed that I had to reject my culture and deny who I was if I wanted to be accepted by my friends and American society. No one ever said this to me; no one needed to. The message oozed in through my pores in the faces and images that represented America and its notion of female beauty. There was little there that was reminiscent of me. By virtue of being non-white, I was excluded from society's perceptions of beauty and value. And yet I tried desperately to be white and actually came to believe that I was successful, until one day during my sophomore year.

I was walking down the mirror-paneled hallway of my high school, talking and laughing with a group of friends. For a brief moment as we walked past the mirrors, I caught my reflection in the midst of my friends. What struck me at that moment was how visibly different I was from them. Because most of the faces that I saw around me were white, I had come to believe that mine was too. In that devastating moment of truth, I was confronted with the reality that no matter how much I tried to deny it, I was inevitably who I was and that it was useless and foolish to ignore that fact. I recognized that in my desire to belong and fit in, I had been deluding myself to the point of thinking that I was actually white.

This incident served as a catalyst for painful soul-searching and marked the beginning of an inner journey toward greater self-acceptance. Until that point, my struggle with ethnic identity and the denial of my Koreanness had been largely unconscious, but I began to see that the cost of my denial was too high a price to pay. I accepted the reality of my biculturality, that I was inevitably both Korean and American, and that I had a unique opportunity to learn from both cultures, rather than rejecting one for the other. For the first time since that moment in the second grade when I wished I was a blond-haired girl with the last name Smith, I began to see my bicultural experience as a blessing and an opportunity rather than a curse.

College provided different issues and challenges as I continued to come to terms with my ethnic identity. Going away to college and living in the dorms made me confront my previous dualistic life: now my home and school environments were the same. I found that while the culture of high school was that of conformity to a narrowly defined notion of what is socially acceptable and desirable, the culture of college was that of finding and expressing one's individuality and uniqueness. I consciously tried to be more integrated and culturally balanced. And in my friendships I sought out the company of Korean Americans as well as that of whites. I experienced new-found enjoyment and pride in my ethnic heritage. However, echoing my earlier dualistic life, the two cultural worlds remained unintegrated, not because of my own design but because the two spheres were so distinct.

Most of my Korean friends associated with other Koreans, and my white friends socialized among themselves. When I spent too much time with my white friends, I worried that my Korean friends would think that I was too good for them or that I was trying to assimilate. On the other hand, if I spent too much time with my Korean friends, I was afraid that my white friends would think me too cliquish. As I shuttled back and forth between my two segregated worlds, trying to maintain a balance, I was painfully reminded that I resided in the crevice between two worlds, not fully belonging to either. The cost of complete belonging would be the surrender of one for the other. I knew I did not want to do this, nor could I. I realized that I had to create a new space, a unique place of my own, forged by selecting and integrating the best of both worlds.

My awareness of this hybrid and hyphenated nature of my in-between existence left me with a profound sense of alienation and aloneness. It made me wonder if anyone else would share that peculiar space with me. Would I find someone to share my life who would understand this part of me? At that point, the prospect seemed dim. I had yet to encounter anyone else who seemed to be struggling with these issues. My fellow Koreans, who tended to be more recent immigrants, seemed content to be just Korean, and obviously none of my white friends seemed to struggle with their ethnic identity. I wondered why I was the only one grappling with these issues, and if there was something wrong with me. Eventually, I learned that many other 1.5- and second-generation Korean and other Asian Americans struggle with these issues; but, like me, they maintained an exterior that belied that inner struggle. I appeared to them as unaffected as they did to me. Only later, after the fact, would we give word and voice to that which we had kept hidden.

Defining my ethnic identity is an ongoing process. I operate from two basic principles of balance and integration. I try to maintain a balance of my two worlds and to integrate what I deem to be the best of both, but this is easier said than done. When I graduated from college, I thought I had resolved my "ethnic identity crisis," but then I realized I had other related questions to consider. No sooner had I achieved a comfortable state than I was confronted with still other unexplored dimensions and challenges. How would my ethnic identity affect who I would marry—would I marry a Korean American as I was told to, or marry a non-Korean, as I was inclined to do? Once married, how would I negotiate gender-role expectations within the marriage? How far would I go to instill Korean culture and identity in my children? I realized that the questions were endless and varied, according to the tasks and issues particular to a specific stage of life. I was forced to abandon the notion of a static ethnic identity and to reconceptualize it as a dynamic process that I would address on an ongoing basis.

In talking to some of my Korean- and Asian-American students, I realize that, while we share similar experiences, they—separated by a decade or so—have grown up in a different environment. The broader American society, at least in Southern California, is now more culturally diverse and tolerant than when I first arrived. Because of this, there is less of a stigma attached to being a minority. Even the Korean-American community is more open than the one I grew up in.

When I returned to Korea for a visit, I made the surprising discovery that the Korean-American culture I grew up with was much more conservative than the one in Korea. The Korean culture practiced by the first generation of immigrants tends to be the one that existed at the time of their migration. For many, culture is frozen at this point in time, preserved with great passion and determination and increasingly idealized. Unfortunately, just as *kimchi* that is pickled and buried in jars in autumn turns sour and unpalatable as the winter wears on into spring, so does a static, preserved Korean culture appear to the next generation, particularly if it is rigidly imposed upon them. In my experience of working with Korean-American families, parents who enforce Korean values without any regard for the different reality in which their children live can cause tremendous pain and suffering for their children and themselves. And children who are devoid of a sense of their own history and background often fail to appreciate the sacrifices that their parents have made and the values that they have imparted. Better communication, openness, and a desire to understand each other can go a long way toward achieving reconciliation and harmony.

I WAS TOLD THAT I COULDN'T MARRY A NON-KOREAN

As I entered adolescence, my parents began to tell me how important it was to marry a Korean. Even without their direct prohibition, I was already fully aware of the shame and stigma associated with out-marriage. The price would be ostracization for me and the loss of face for my family within the Korean community. The problem was that I was more attracted to white men than Korean men. This was due in part to my resentment of what I deemed to be oppressive patriarchy within Korean culture. It seemed that most of my Korean-American male counterparts favored traditional gender roles (not that American culture is immune from this). This is understandable from their perspective: they are privileged in this system and stand to benefit from it. As I observed the inequality between men and women in Korean culture, I was determined not to perpetuate the pattern. When I was thirteen, I was given the dubious title of a "women's libber" by my brother when I refused to get up from the dinner table and get him a glass of milk. I believe the precise phrase that proclaimed my liberation was "Get it yourself!"

Another reason for my attraction to white men had to do with my ethnic identity. During my I-want-to-be-white phase, dating white men symbolized my arrival as an American, and proved that I could fit in. Dating was one thing, but marriage was quite another. Even as I was more interested in white men, I found it difficult to ignore the deeply ingrained script of "don't marry a non-Korean." Thus, I would inform any potentially serious prospect that our relationship could not continue beyond a certain point. In retrospect, I think the warning was more for my benefit than theirs. Despite this, one relationship did get serious enough to test the boundaries of the out-marriage taboo and the limits of parental love. Needless to say, my father was quite displeased when I asked for permission to marry a non-Korean. He bombarded me with all the familiar arguments against interracial marriage that I already knew: whites were not as committed to marriage as Koreans, thus more likely to divorce; cultural differences would doom the marriage to failure; our "half-breed" children would be rejected by both cultures; other Koreans would look down upon me (and my parents).

When these arguments didn't achieve their goal, my father uttered the worst sanction that he could think of: he threatened to disown me. The threat of being disowned meant not only separation from my family, but also from Korean culture. It seemed as if I were being forced to choose, once again, between the two cultures. Even without this ultimatum, I knew that I would inevitably drift further from Korean culture if I married a non-Korean. Furthermore, while I could "pass" to a large extent in his world, he couldn't pass in my Korean world.

I eventually ended the relationship for reasons of interpersonal incompatibility, but parental objection and the fear of losing my culture were undeniable factors in the decision. I still wonder sometimes if my father really would have carried out his threat if I had married a non-Korean. I'll never know for sure because I eventually met and married a second-generation Korean American who shares with me that in-between place of biculturality. He was the second Korean that I had dated. In contrast to my past relationships with non-Koreans where I felt like a cultural tour guide, I found it refreshing not to explain so much of myself. I also appreciate the fact that my parents can easily relate to him and, vice versa, even if he doesn't speak Korean fluently.

In retrospect, a powerful factor in my lack of interest in Korean men had to do with negative stereotypes. Just as I had internalized a white standard of female beauty that made me resent my "mongoloid" (the technical term used to describe the Asian race) features, I also bought into the prevailing image of masculinity that precluded Asian-American men. In keeping with stereotypes about them, I dismissed Korean guys as passive, wimpy, nerdy, and socially inept.

Stereotypes about Asian Americans not only affected my attraction to Korean men, but also my own self-perception and self-esteem. Without knowing it, my brother and I had actually bought into the stereotypes, and appropriated them to salvage a positive sense of self. For example, my brother didn't know anything about martial arts when he was in Korea, but not long after his arrival in the U.S., he began to develop a real interest in it and became quite skilled at it. I don't think it is coincidental that the only positive Asian male role model at the time was Bruce Lee—or that he was the only Asian male I found attractive. As for myself, I wanted to fit the "Suzie Wong" China-doll image. Unfortunately, I was tall, not short and petite. I also had frizzy, curly hair that wouldn't lend itself to a short, blunt, face-framing cut; to no avail, I slept each night with big plastic curlers in my hair, trying to straighten it. And no matter how hard I tried, I was never very convincing at the shy, demure act. Both my brother and I bought into the externally defined and static notions of what an Asian American should be to gain greater acceptance. Left with limited alternatives and few positive role models, we did the best we could by appropriating the few, seemingly positive images available to us.

Stereotypes also had an interesting and contradictory impact on my social life. On the one hand, there have been white men who have been interested in me only because I am Asian; on the other hand, there have been those who excluded me from their realm of possible relationships for exactly the same reason. In both cases, my race—and stereotypical notions about my race—prevented them from knowing me as an individual and not just as a member of the Asian race. Those who were interested because I was Asian (commonly known as Asian woman fetish) seemed to operate from their own preconceived notions. Their ideas of me were based on common stereotypes, such as those portraying Asian women as demure and passive. They became somewhat puzzled and eventually lost interest when I didn't live up to their expectations.

I never doubted that it would be ideal to marry within my culture—I was simply skeptical and distracted. Not that I believe in any of the arguments against interracial marriage, nor do I oppose it, but to the extent that one is steeped in a particular culture, marrying someone who shares that culture would, all other things being equal, ensure a greater degree of commonality and compatibility. While I preferred to marry a Korean American, I'm not so sure that it will matter as much, nor should it, for the next generation. I know that I will not brainwash my child with the same expectations with which I was raised. Intermarriage cannot help but be a critical issue between first and second generations. It is the contested ground upon which our identities and our hopes and dreams are played out. My research on Asian-American families confirms this, revealing that the issue of dating and marriage is one of the greatest sources of conflict between college students and their parents.

For immigrant parents, intermarriage may symbolize the ultimate loss of their children to America. While they immigrated with hopes and dreams for a better future for their family, they failed to realize that an unintended consequence is the Americanization of their children. As they work hard to provide a stable financial base for the family, their children rapidly acculturate. Parents see all too late that acquiring the house in the white suburbs with the good schools also means that their children want to become like those around them—like whites. Immigrant parents fear not only the loss of Korean culture but also the loss of their children. Outmarriage may be perceived as the final step in this process. On the other hand, for teenagers and young adults who grew up in this culture and accept it, it can be difficult to subject matters of the heart to the artificial constraints of race.

"ARE YOU SURE YOU DON'T WANT TO BECOME A DOCTOR?"

Being a Korean American has certain advantages. For example, your life is neatly laid out for you. All you have to do is just follow the prescriptions and you are rewarded with approval. Your parents get to brag about you to their friends; they, in turn, use you as their comparison standard when they turn to their own children, saying, "Why can't you be more like so-and-so?" We are expected to aspire to one of the few clearly identified status professions: doctor, dentist, lawyer, or engineer. The problem arises when you don't want to or can't enter those fields.

As a female, I was under less pressure than my older brother; if I couldn't become one of the above, I could always marry one. While I was encouraged to strive for academic achievement and to pursue a high-status career, I also received conflicting messages that led me to believe that my education and career were a pretense to make myself more "marketable" as a wife and to add to my dowry, so to speak.

My parents supported me and encouraged me to choose my own career. However, upon hearing that I wanted to major in psychology, they were immediately skeptical. They were the first to ask the often-repeated question, "What are you going to do with that degree?" Needless to say, there were no role models for me and I had only a vague notion of what I would do as a psychologist. My mother in particular encouraged me to go into nursing, if not medicine. She said it was a good, respectable profession for a woman and a "safe" one because I would be able to support myself if anything should happen to my husband. I knew she meant well, and that security and stability were the most important values for her, but they were not the determining ones for me. As uncertain as I was about my career path, I was certain of a few things. I wanted to have a career of my own, regardless of my marital status, and I wanted it to be meaningful and fulfilling.

I must confess, there were many times when I considered more traditional careers like medicine and law, especially because most of my Korean-American friends were committed to that route. They seemed to have the benefit of a clearly defined path while mine was not so clear. I had only a vague notion of what I wanted to do and a little better sense of what I didn't want to do. But as I continued in the general direction of my chosen path, things became clearer to me and I experienced greater intrinsic confirmation that I was indeed on the right track. At times I felt out of place and less valued within the Korean-American community because I didn't aspire to one of the more recognized careers, but I felt compelled to find my own way. I suspect that my parents' friends stopped using me as a positive model in their comparisons and may have even used me as a negative model of what not to become. Eventually, despite my own doubts and fears as well as those of others, I obtained a Ph.D. in counseling psychology. Ironically, now that I'm a professor, I've been revived as a role model—educators are highly respected in Korean culture and somewhat rare in the immigrant community.

My overriding motivation to pursue a career in psychology directly relates to my bicultural experience. I saw that immigrant families faced many difficulties in the dislocation and adaptation process, and had few avenues of support. There were few trained mental health professionals who could speak their language or understand the nuances of their culture. Cultural and intergenerational differences, exacerbated by a language barrier, caused many immigrant families to lead separate and alienated lives. Given the importance of the family and its tremendous impact on both the individual and society at large, I felt that I could have the greatest impact by promoting healthy families. As a Korean-American psychologist and as a member of the 1.5 generation, I see my role as being a facilitator and educator for the first and second generations, bridging the gap to help each better understand and accept the other.

In my educational process, I struggled as an Asian-American woman to speak out and be assertive. In college, I wanted to participate in class discussions, but felt that unless I had something truly profound to say, I shouldn't waste other people's time. But many of my fellow classmates, particularly white males, didn't hesitate to speak up, even when what they had to say wasn't particularly insightful or profound. In graduate school, I realized that, contrary to my socialization, I needed to be more assertive and expressive if I was going to survive in academia. The social and behavioral skills that I eventually acquired to help me succeed were not only those of the predominant white culture, but also those traditionally seen as masculine. It is a challenge to maintain femininity in an environment that sees it as a weakness. While for the most part I value the newly acquired behaviors, I resent the cultural and gender hegemony in academia and the fact that I had to transform myself in this way to survive.

Being an Asian-American woman professor has its advantages and disadvantages. Because there aren't many like me, I get more attention. This helps bring notice to the issues I fight for, such as the establishment of Asian-American studies and the challenge to institutions to be more inclusive. But I also have received some unwanted scrutiny in the form of racial and gender stereotypes. I have been referred to as "a nice, Oriental lady," and asked, "How did you learn to speak English so well?" I also have received unwelcome comments about my appearance in professional settings; despite the fact that they were complimentary, they undermined my intellectual qualifications. My assertiveness and articulateness seem to surprise and threaten some because I don't fit their stereotype of an Asian woman. Others ignore these traits altogether and treat me in a condescending and paternalistic way.

I find that I have to compensate for my race, gender, and age, and have to prove myself in ways that my fellow white, male, older colleagues do not. While they are automatically given a certain level of respect and authority, I have to earn every bit of mine. I am often mistaken for a student or a staff member on campus and treated accordingly. A few times when checking out books from the library, I had to ask for faculty borrowing privileges even though they should have known that I was a faculty member by the type of ID that I had. In another situation, I went to get my photo ID upon arriving at a new campus. They mistakenly gave me a student ID even after I told them twice that I was a new faculty member.

Despite these challenges, I enjoy my profession immensely. One of the most rewarding aspects of being a professor is serving as a role model. For most of my students, I am the first Asian-American woman professor they encounter. Many Asian-American students have told me how refreshing and empowering it is for them to see me in front of the classroom. I can only hope that my presence gives them a sense of possibility for their own dreams and aspirations.

FROM A STRANGER TO AN AMERICAN

Ron Takaki, in his book *Strangers from a Different Shore*, refers to George Simmel's notion of being a "stranger" as a central motif in his historical overview of Asian migration to America. I arrived in America almost thirty years ago, a stranger from a distant shore. Just as I was seen as a stranger, I, too, found this to be a strange place. Now I call this place home; that which was strange has become familiar and comfortable. The personal experiences that I have shared chronicle key moments in the transformation process.

I call America home not because it is a perfect place, but because there is enough space and freedom here for me to define my own version of America—a Korean America, an Asian America. Although many people may still regard me as a stranger, and may continue to do so, my very presence is helping to reconceptualize what it means to be an American. I am contesting the narrowly defined notion that only white Americans are Americans, and striving to establish a new national identity that includes all those who have come and will yet come to its shores, regardless of race and skin color. In doing so, I feel that I and others like myself exemplify the true spirit of what America stands for.

NOTE

This chapter was originally included in *Struggle for Ethnic Indentity: Narratives by Asian American Professionals*, published in 1999 by Alta Mira Press, edited by Pyong Gap Min and Rose Kim. Ruth Chung is now an associate professor of clinical education at the Rossier School of Education at the University of Southern California

IV

Four Essays by Members of the Later Cohort

Chapter Six

Growing up Korean American

Navigating a Complex Search for Belonging

Brenda Chung

I sat down at the kitchen table across from my dad, expecting a scolding. There was a span of silence, and I stared fixedly at the table, wishing I were upstairs in my room. Finally my dad spoke. "We are not inferior," he said, "we have ability." Part of me was incredulous while the other was captivated and inspired. I snuck a quick look at his alert, almond-shaped eyes and saw a vitality and confidence there. Despite his slender frame, calm demeanor, and accented English, his words had an authority that stuck with me. Later that week, as I walked down the hallways amid catcalls and jeers, his words echoed in my head.

These were my high school years. Like the adolescence of most, this time in my life was fraught with socialization issues and punctuated with a heightened search for belonging. I was painfully aware that my ethnicity set me apart, but chose to downplay my race. Instead I sought my own niche, one that might celebrate my minority status while still being distinctly American. It seems that this is a common path for Asian-American kids who grow up outside of the safe bubble of their respective cultural communities.

I am the child of Korean immigrants, and I love my family. I am immensely proud of each one of them, not necessarily for their individual accomplishments, but for the people they are. Their personality traits are ones that I equate with being Korean: they are hard-working, creative, kind-hearted, conscientious, intelligent, resourceful, and strong-willed. I think it's safe to say that I'm proud to be Korean.

SEEING THE WORLD THROUGH SLANTED EYES

But it wasn't always that way. I first became aware that I was different in elementary school. In a classroom full of blond- and brown-haired children, I was the only kid with straight black hair and slanted eyes. Other kids would ask me why I closed them when I laughed. It was such a small thing, but to me it was huge. They were singling me out for something that I couldn't change, something that would forever mark me as someone who was not like them. I would come home crying at first. I remember telling my mom that I hated my eyes and wished they were the same as everyone else's. She would tell me to ignore them, and after a while that's exactly what I did. I quickly learned to dislike emotional displays of weakness and, instead of tears, I would respond with either stony silence or jokes. Still, I was a talkative, cheerful child. My early school years were mostly uneventful and I enjoyed a relative amount of peace.

It wasn't until I got a little older that I began to experience a more barbed discrimination. Most comments were easy to brush off, as they were the products of plain ignorance. What was harder to get past was the intent. When I was in high school, one kid said to me, "My daddy killed a bunch of you guys in the war." I laughed and explained to him that South Korea and America were allies in the Korean War, and that he would have a hard time finding any North Koreans in the U.S. to heckle. But on the inside I was irked by his malice and couldn't help but wonder why he would say something like that to me. The jab I heard most frequently was more playful but equally hateful. The silly, sing-song noises used to mock Asian languages were a constant reminder that foreigners were looked upon in a derogatory fashion. I dealt with these occasions the same way I dealt with the comments about my eyes when I was younger—I laughed them off or ignored them. Somewhere along the way, I also began to ignore the fact that I was Korean.

There was another kind of stereotyping happening around then that I wasn't entirely hurt by. When people see Asians, it's usually assumed that they're studious. I had already grown accustomed to being teased by other students on a daily basis, and usually kept to myself. But when it came time to do a group project, other students would immediately pick me to be on their team. I knew they were only picking me because they were hoping I would do most of the work and they'd be guaranteed a good grade, but I felt a sense of accomplishment at the same time. Despite the fact that I was excluded socially, it was generally recognized that I was a person of ability. I started to see that maybe there wasn't necessarily anything wrong with me or with being different—I began to see my exclusion as a compliment.

Opportunities for alienation weren't limited to school. Some of the most emotionally reactive moments I can recall occurred at my parents' store, which had a predominantly black customer base. I found out from working there that being the target of discrimination is much different than observing it. It's easy to ignore a haphazard comment that someone throws at you when you know you're being goaded. Watching your loved ones being ridiculed for no apparent reason, however, is nothing short of enraging. It was terrible to see customers lash out at my parents, the two people I looked up to as pillars of ability and resilience. To me, the angry taunts were attempts to dehumanize my parents, to reduce them to mere merchants who spoke English as a second language, as though their English language skills were any indication of how intelligent they were or what kind of people they were. Even after all this time the old feelings are quite vivid. I recall a customer's smug attitude as she walked up to the register and asked, "Anyone sprake Anglish up in here?" I quickly learned to laugh it off, but I remember the profound effect it had on me. My anger served as a catalyst. It made me want to learn English well enough to be mistaken for an American native, but more than that, it made me want to express myself in a way that was correct but also respectful. Looking back, I see the immense power of words; they not only convey thoughts and feelings but have the capacity to deeply affect others. Maybe I should thank that woman for motivating me to seek basic human dignity.

There were many more instances of discrimination, both at school and at the store. Sadly, there are too many to list or even to remember. What I do recall is that I grew up with a reluctance to bring any undue attention to my ethnicity. It's not that I was ashamed to be Korean, but rather that calling myself Korean seemed to invite negative interactions. It is said that people determine their self-worth based on the reactions of others. It is also said that self-esteem is directly proportionate to the gap between a person's inner self and the way others perceive that person. If these statements are true, then those who are consistently misjudged by their outward appearances have little chance to develop a healthy self-image. I believe that it's important for youngsters to know that adolescence is a crude mirror at best. So, while it was tempting to believe the negative feedback, I fought against developing a poor self-image. What happened instead was that a longing to be truly understood by others was born. I think this was a large part of the allure of the internet for me. There was anonymity there, and I grew to like being judged by my words and actions rather than my gender or my race.

THE HERMIT KINGDOM

When I was in the fifth grade, I visited South Korea for a month with my mom and my brothers. It was a summer vacation filled with visits to different family members' homes, outings in the country, and trips to shopping malls and other tourist attractions. What sticks out most in my mind isn't really the culture itself. Most of my memories are sensory: I remember the smells of animals from the country, the colorful graphics and music of the video arcades, the hot summer weather minus air conditioning, and the multitude of refreshing frozen treats. Other random details come to mind. I remember the Coke cans having a different shape than the ones in the U.S., the Cheetos tasting much different, and the hamburgers from Wendy's being a lot smaller. Houses and rooms were smaller, and so were the bath towels. The roads seemed narrower and more crowded and I recall that people would hang dry their clothes instead of using a mechanized dryer. Hot water was limited. It was about efficiency and making the most of things while trying to use the smallest amount of resources possible. The whole trip was a far cry from the oftentimes ridiculous excess of the U.S.

Despite my encounters with the daily details of living during that visit, my perception of Korea remains almost mystical. When I think of Korea, I think of the Hermit Kingdom. Imagine a quiet grassy mountaintop with old-style, picturesque architecture, complete with tiled roofs and swirly clouds dotting the sky. My mental picture of Korea is similar to one of those calligraphy watercolor paintings with small accent drawings on it.

Not all of my recollections are lighthearted though. I also experienced a different type of discrimination than I was used to. Although I was quite young, I became acutely aware of my lack of Korean language skills. During an excursion to Lotte World, a cleaning lady asked me what my father's name was. When I answered, it must have been painfully obvious that Korean was not my native tongue, and she began laughing at me. It was then that I decided that discrimination was not a white or black or yellow problem, but a human problem. My sense of isolation deepened.

LOST AT SEA

Since I never learned to feel completely comfortable amongst the Korean community, it's no surprise that the social circles I traveled in were normally made up of American kids. The neighborhood I grew up in and the schools I went to had a white majority ratio, so that was the environment in which I felt the most natural. Growing up, I had more positive encounters with white kids and their families than with people of other ethnic groups. There was a family that lived up the street from us that my brothers and I would occasionally visit. I remember that when we'd go over there to play, there would be cool things sitting out in their garage that I'd never seen, such as a rock tumbling machine for smoothing rocks. The parents were not only polite and well-educated, but also tolerant and kind. In my head, I could imagine that they all sat on their couch and watched movies together, and went on family camping trips. It seemed like the ideal life and I remember thinking that my friend was a really lucky kid. It's childhood memories like those that most likely caused me to lean towards white Americans for belonging, and conditioned me to think of them as the default group.

As I got older, the kids I identified most closely with were the misfit types who, despite being born here, had endured similar experiences of feeling ostracized or misunderstood. From my earlier childhood brushes with discrimination, I had developed the disposition of a loner. But I also feel that some of my loner tendencies were inborn traits. Although I loved to have fun and laugh with friends, I also disliked frivolous conversation. I was especially wary of overt shows of conformity—the type of actions made not for the sake of group solidarity but for the sake of squashing the quirky parts of human nature, the qualities that make us all unique. In retrospect, I was somewhat introverted and required less social stimulation than others, but when I did have interactions, I wanted them to be worthwhile and real. I suppose I was in that stage in my life where I was very critical. I saw something wrong with every high school clique that I encountered and with society as a whole. It was a disharmonious period in my life where I sought to understand my place in the world by watching others interact rather than interacting myself. Since I had memories of being regarded with disdain by most kids I met, white or black, friendships were few and far between. I neither sought out nor avoided people of other minority groups. Instead I valued a close few. It seemed other kids who were disgruntled with the status quo were the only ones I could make a connection with. We naturally gravitated towards each other, perhaps on the basis of being on a similar wavelength rather than any outward circumstances or conditions. Despite all this, I retained some sense of stability mainly because of my strong relationship with my family, who I now recognize as a great stabilizing force and the source of my inherent sense of worth.

Although I did have some contact with other Korean kids earlier in life through Korean school and church, the relationships that resulted were mostly short-lived or somewhat superficial. Especially in Korean school, I encountered more prejudice from other Korean kids than I did from white American kids. I didn't think much of it back then, but in retrospect, we were going through many of the same pressures; the difference was in the way we chose to resolve those pressures. Being the immigrant children of a homogeneous people who have a hierarchical social structure meant that there was an expectation of conformity. In the Korean community, it seemed that everyone knew all the details about everyone else. It was hard to have a conversation that didn't involve what musical instrument someone was taking lessons for, whether or not someone was making good grades in school, what type of business someone's family ran, or even what kind of car someone's parents drove. The level of scrutiny was enormous. Although back in Korea it may have fostered a feeling of village togetherness, transplanted to the U.S., this scrutiny resulted in a feeling of competitiveness. And in conforming to what would become the Korean-American ideal, many kids became increasingly status and class conscious. My preference for privacy and inclination towards individualism automatically placed me on the outskirts of the herd in terms of group mentality. I didn't blend in, and maybe because of my rocky social experiences with non-Koreans, I didn't particularly know how to. Although I could function and be friendly with other Korean kids, I never tried very hard to make lasting friendships. Somehow I felt that I fell short of the expected ideal and assumed their parents would not approve of me.

Parental approval was not a priority when it came to dating, however. It was unspoken for the most part, but I knew my parents expected me to marry a nice Korean guy from a good family who was college-educated and had a stable job. Perhaps unintentionally, the guys I dated were nothing like that. I was drawn to artistic, volatile people who, for one reason or another, existed at the edges of society. In contrast, the type of partner my parents seemed to want for me was someone who was practical, utilitarian, steady, and emotionally stoic. The differences in these two sets of expectations would resolve themselves over time, but this period of my life was tumultuous, to say the least.

I did date one Korean guy. It was nice in a lot of ways, since he had experienced many of the same things that I had. We were also able to do things such as watch Korean-dubbed cartoons together, and tell Korean-English puns without having to explain what made them funny. When he visited, he was able to speak to my parents in Korean. You would think that all this understanding would have stacked the odds for a successful relationship in our favor. The irony was that our shared culture was one of the obstacles. Much more so than with American couples, traditional Korean marriages require the families to mesh well. Although the eventual breakup involved other factors, one of them was our families and their lack of acceptance.

Naturally, after a certain time, my parents stopped openly showing approval or disapproval of the guys I dated. They probably figured that regardless of what they said, I was going to make my own choices in the end. Looking back, I realize that a lot of my past choices were partially reactionary and partially a search for identity. I regret the grief I put my parents through and hope that others in a similar situation make their decisions from a more grounded, sincere place.

IDENTITY CRISIS

It amazes me how things that are undeniable to others can be taken for granted by the self. For instance, I am clearly Korean and female on the outside, but have managed to go through much of my life accepting neither on the inside. I feel that the two "conditions" are closely linked. I've noticed that the socialization of Korean males and Korean females differs. This must be largely due to the stark differences in their respective gender roles. Here in America, we refer to women as the "fair sex." My perception of the Korean role was that women were the weaker sex. Korean women were expected to be dutiful, subservient daughters and wives who excelled at cooking, cleaning, and anticipating the needs of their family members. American women, on the other hand, were expected to stand up for themselves and know what they wanted in life. It's laughable to expect an American woman to make her important life decisions based on the preferences of her family, yet a Korean woman would be looked down upon for failing to do so. The predominant emotion I remember feeling was confusion. Was I supposed to behave like a soft-spoken, obedient Korean female or an aggressive, independent American one? Could I behave like one at school, and then switch to the other when I was at home? Which was the real me, and did switching back and forth mean I was faking it? The huge rift that existed between these ideals was nearly impossible for me to navigate with any sense of continuity.

Instead, I responded by rebelling against being Korean *and* being female. With no clear map showing the way towards a liberated, fulfilling existence, Korean-American women are left to negotiate an identity of their own. As I tested those waters, I gravitated towards hobbies and interests that involved the intellect, or ones that were not traditionally feminine, in an attempt to escape those binding roles. Although you may see a lot of Korean-American girls who are well put together and place a lot of importance on their appearances, there are also some out there who would rather be smart or successful than attractive. Sure, everyone wants to be attractive, but if it means being objectified and not taken seriously as a real contributor to society, some might choose to err on the side of plain-looking. It's hard to take pride in and celebrate being female when it seems to carry negative connotations. Men and women have had equal rights for some time now, but I can understand if there is still a fight going on in the hearts and minds of women. The rest of the country may see them as equal to their male counterparts, but inside, they struggle to do something meaningful and prove to themselves that their worth is separate from their looks.

There's an audio clip out there that very accurately satirizes the interplay of Korean gender roles. The narrator is a Korean guy, speaking English with an accent, who is monologuing to his wife. He's trying to explain what he expects of her in terms of Tae Kwon Do. The husband is the right leg, and his role is to have power. The wife is the left leg, he says, and stays home while the right leg goes out and does its awesome kicking work. The right leg has power, but it can't kick unless the left leg stands and supports it; therefore the wife's role is support. Had I heard the clip when I was growing up, I would've been adamant that I was not going to be the left leg. I find the clip hilarious now, with a little perspective.

ROOTS

Having a dual-national identity caused a lot of social frustration and confusion during my childhood and adolescence. Traces of those feelings remain in my adult life, and they return to me momentarily when I walk into a room filled with Korean people. As I greet fellow Koreans, my bow is a little stiff. My greeting is blurted out quickly to disguise my American pronunciation. I may look and sound unnatural, but the warm intentions I feel inside are real. They come from the recognition that I am amongst my parents' people. And despite how Americanized I may be, they are my people too.

Sometimes I mourn my lack of Korean language skills. I can speak well enough to say some basic phrases, but a real conversation is over my head. I can read typed Korean characters from a page in a book, but will only be able to comprehend bits and pieces of it. If the characters are scrolling across a screen, chances are they'll be moving too fast for me. Handwritten Korean usually has an individual flair to it that I find hard to distinguish. As for my Korean handwriting, I may as well be sitting next to a kindergartener. When writing Korean, proper sentence construction doesn't come naturally. And due to the subtle vowel sounds, spelling is especially challenging for me. Sometimes I think of doing self-study or even taking a college course in Korean. It doesn't come to the forefront of my mind until I'm driving my grandmother somewhere. Although I can understand a large percentage of what she says to me, I find that I can't think of a single thing to say to her. I hope that a proper greeting and an attentive ear make up for my silence. It's a little sad but it seems that Korean language deterioration is common for 1.5- and second-generation Korean Americans who are not actively involved in the Korean community.

Korean food is something that seems to stay with the younger generation, however. There may be a gap during which kids will forgo Korean food in favor of American or other nationality foods, but in time they return to their roots. To my knowledge, no other culture has a love of spicy pickled vegetables, sauce-drenched leafy herbs, marinated roots, and seasoned legumes that can compare to Korean *banchan* (side dishes/small plates that are served at virtually every Korean meal). Many of us grew up eating soybean sprouts with our rice, and think fondly of seaweed rolls and Korean barbecue short ribs. They remind us of the comforts of home, even if that home has a U.S. zip code. My personal favorite is *dduk* (sticky rice cakes), and I'm proud to say that I like the same *shiru dduk* (rice cake with sweet rice, red bean, and dates) that my dad does. Genetics are a funny thing.

BECOMING ME

In general I like being me. There were times growing up that I felt like a tiny object caught in a huge chaotic storm, but I feel that it's been a tremendous learning experience. They say that adversity is life's way of making a person stronger, and that it builds character. I'm a firm believer that people don't just come into the world set on the path they were intended to take; people live and experience hardship to become who they were meant to be. Sometimes it's a rough process, but that doesn't mean that it isn't worth it.

I have two beautiful half-Korean children, and I feel blessed that they get to grow up in such close proximity to their Korean grandparents. My son loves the different noodles and soups that his *halmuni* (grandmother) makes, and my daughter can be seen running around the house with a baked *goguma* (Korean sweet potato) in her hand, asking her *halmuni* for more *kimchi*. They both speak by blending random Korean words in seamlessly with their English. With medium brown hair and a fair cream-colored skin tone, they could both be mistaken for white Americans from the back. No one could make that mistake from the front, as they have both inherited my dark brown eye color and clearly have an Asian eye shape. Although at times I worry about their inevitable struggles, especially once those rough teenage years begin, I find it hard not to be proud of them. In my opinion, they exhibit positive qualities from both American and Korean culture. Maybe it's parental pride speaking here, but I can already see their future talents growing. I strive to instill in them the high standards that are a hallmark of Korean upbringing, while preserving their strong sense of individualism, which is necessary to succeed in American society.

I recognize that my ethnic identity is still not fully formed. I have identified more closely with outcasts most of my life, and it seems that I've classified my struggles as inherently human struggles rather than ones of a particular ethnic group. My life experiences so far have reaffirmed an empathy for the underdogs of the world, and underscored the importance of compassion.

This is not to say that I don't have any sympathies with the Asian community. I have an immense pride in being Asian, and see the valuable contributions they have made everywhere I go. I enjoy watching martial arts movies, and take pride in the prowess of Asian action stars. Also, I view the many disciplines themselves as practices deeply entwined with Asian culture. When taught as a life tool, I feel that martial arts have a lot to offer in the ways of self-discipline, confidence, and respect for other people. Anime, though not entirely accepted by the mainstream, has a huge niche following and is well-loved by hordes of Americans. The art style has a flair that is unmistakable, and the storylines are often adaptations of Asian history or mythology.

In reference to Korea specifically, I have a Kia, an up-and-coming manufacturer of well-made, reasonably priced, fuel-efficient cars. They have some of the best warranties around and are making USB ports standard in the dashboards of their vehicles now. The cellphone sitting on my desk is a Samsung Galaxy S II, a great smartphone made by a Korean company known for its innovative and high-quality electronics. There are even a few PC games out there that I am proud to say are released by Korean developers, who have a reputation for immaculate graphics. Their games utilize the modern micro-transaction based model, which savvy gamers know will soon be replacing the subscription-based model, to fund their endeavors. Ever sit through the credits at the end of cartoons? Be surprised and amazed to see that the lists of animators contain a large number of Korean names. Korea's image on the world stage has definitely changed over the years, and it is one that I am not ashamed to be associated with.

If I had to pick one thing that has cemented my appreciation of my ancestry, I'd have to say that it's been the process of having a family of my own. Becoming a mother has made me much more comfortable in my own skin. It has helped me see the good in the softer aspects of being female, and it has also shown me the upside of a strict Korean upbringing. That which once brought me great sorrow and embarrassment has been assimilated into my identity in such a way that I feel great contentment about who I am. I attribute this new-found peace to God. I no longer feel the need to prove anything with my looks, intellect, profession, or income. At this point in my life, I would choose wisdom over everything else. It's funny, as an adult, I find that my values are somehow parallel to the very ones I sought to distance myself from as a youngster. In my mind, Korea stood for being family-oriented, focused on education, conscientious, morally upright, and concerned with the welfare of the group. Somehow this monolith stood unnoticed all these years in my subconscious, silent and inconspicuous, but wielding a heavy influence over my life.

Although my children are half-Korean and are living in a time when they'll be subjected to less racial prejudice than I faced growing up, it's naive to think that they will be completely exempt. Regardless of that, I feel it is important that they maintain their connection to their Korean roots. It is my sincere hope that my kids and other Asian-American kids out there make it through the rocky parts of their personal journeys and come through each experience stronger, kinder, and wiser.

I understand that, as minorities, we have contended with a generous portion of suffering and bias. But rather than leave it at that, I believe that we were meant to find the lessons embedded in that suffering and allow it to change us in a positive way. If we are to live and thrive as a transplanted, reinvented culture, we have to find a way through our painful experiences that focuses less on bitterness or resentment and more on the bright future ahead. It is my wish that my peers and the generations that follow come to see our ethnic background as the gift that it is.

Chapter Seven

How to be a Korean

Sun Park

GOLDEN BRICKS

Park Dae Won was a good man. He was born in Chun Yun Dong, a poor village outside of Seoul, Korea, amongst a hungry and uncompromising line of five brothers and two sisters. Dae Won's father had passed when most of the children had not yet reached their teen years, leaving his widowed mother to raise the seven children alone. She was thankful for having to bury only one child, which was a comparatively fortunate number in their paltry village. Dae Won, like all good sons, wanted to make up for his mother's suffering. It was a tense childhood, growing up using sticks and rocks for toys, and fighting with his siblings over the last few grasshoppers they had caught to appease their hunger for a moment. Dae Won proved his worth by serving his required time in the military, exercised his values during the protests and riots of his college years, and guided himself to church and became a Christian. Church was also where he met his future wife, Kim Ok Young, a wide-eyed, warm city girl. Park Dae Won promised her and their children a good life. However, Dae Won had dreams of something bigger and better for his family.

America hovered like the luminous sun over the distant Korean mountains whenever Dae Won thought of his family's future. Despite humble beginnings, Dae Won attended a renowned college in Seoul University and landed a high position at a reputable trading business. His family would live comfortably if they stayed in Korea. America, however, was a gamble, with the promise of riches and happiness on one end, and the risk of the unknown on the other. Even as he slept, he dreamt of America, the images of happy Korean families living in grand houses, and their faces took the likenesses of his colleagues and friends who had taken the voyage. Dae Won decided to prove himself yet again. So, like many others, he worked relentlessly and saved for years (pooling family money together with his siblings) until it was his turn, until he could afford to send his family to America.

Dae Won had a plan. One of his elder brothers, who had left a year prior, had already set up a business with money Dae Won had saved on the side. "When my family lands," Dae Won thought, "they will land with both feet running into the streets lined with golden bricks." He reminisced of his life as a small farmer boy, and as a troublesome teen who drove his mother to smoke cigarettes when no one was watching. To make up for her hard life and her illnesses, his suffering had finally paid off. His work had just begun.

As was the case for many immigrants, America started as a nightmare instead of a dream, and the streets were lined with concrete and dirt, marked with words and symbols he did not understand. His older brother had spent the family savings on booze, unable to deal with the bare truth after only a year of the Great America. There was no business and nowhere to live—there was nothing. At the time, my mother was pregnant with me. Like much of the Korean population in America, my generation was born under the heavy hearts of a disgraced and homeless people, who had to start from scratch to fend for the lives of their children. And so my life as a second-generation immigrant began.

STEP 1: THE MAN IN THE MIRROR

I am a second-generation Korean, born and raised in Queens, New York. By definition, I am labeled as a "second-generation Korean American." I had difficulty accepting this label at first, because of some of the negative stigma and stereotypes attached. There are, however, generalizations that are unfairly assigned to every nationality, but in this instance, I will explore some of those that pertain to being an American-born Korean, and the effects they have had on my ethnic identity throughout my life.

Somewhere between working the register at my mother's deli on the weekends and taking Korean 101 in college, it seemed that I had given up on being Korean. I stopped singing church hymns in Korean, and trying to keep my unsure pronunciation with the tempo; I no longer cared about the reproachful gaze of other Koreans when they realized I couldn't speak the language; and I reveled in the fact that I had no Korean friends. It was during my second year of college, when I signed up for Korean literature, history, and language classes that SUNY Buffalo offered, that I began an effort to make up for my earlier apathy of my ethnic identity. At times I had doubts, showing up only for the tests and doing enough to get credit, both on paper and in my head. It was a slow and steady process, one that began with the resentment of being born as the second generation of a people that I couldn't seem to connect to. I've had just a few Korean friends over the past few years that weren't part of any particular crowd growing up in New York City, and they seem to have eventually found their place in their professions, a comfortable group of friends, or a significant other, and the patches of their identity seem to have fallen into place. I, on the other hand, am still sorting out the pieces, figuring out why things don't fit.

I do not display most of the characteristics normally associated with second-generation Koreans, some of which include having a number of Korean friends, watching Korean dramas, speaking fluent Korean, and having visited the country—none of which apply to me. I believe being a Korean is not defined by these specific behaviors, although they would surely help in categorizing someone into a social group. In this respect, I was always behind the curve in what most would define as displaying attributes of "being Korean," whether it was as a first-, second-, or 1.5-generation, and the classifications these numbers tend to represent. From my childhood to teen years, I associated these traits as defining characteristics of being not only Korean, but any nationality. I was confused and miserable that I harbored such resentment against my own people, and eventually, my own family. It was only when I had reached my twenties, in the middle of my college years, that I began accepting and embracing my heritage. It is only now, in hindsight, that I can explore the reasons behind my personal feelings of displacement growing up as a second-generation Korean American.

The evidence for my "Koreanness" is in my love for my family, my enjoyment of a satisfying Korean meal, and even when I occasionally glance at what my parents watch during their Korean TV sessions. When I see a Korean fighter in the ring or cage (the one father/son activity that endured— watching combat sports, including boxing, kickboxing, and Mixed Martial Arts), I root for him. If there is a Korean player at bat during a baseball game while I am flipping through the channels, I remain watching to see if he gets a hit. When the Korean soccer team is doing well and all the Koreans in Flushing (a community populated heavily by Koreans and Asians) are wearing red soccer shirts (I often hear people grumbling and whispering in a racist manner that the "Be the Reds" shirts are Communist-pride shirts instead of a display of Korean nationalism), I wish I had worn the color red too (I always forget). I make my own definitions of what it is to be Korean, and for me, I am as Korean as they get.

I can't speak the language fluently and I haven't been to visit the country. These are two dilemmas that I hope to rectify within the coming years. At the moment, focusing on family and my professional career have more pertinence in regards to my current circumstances, but taking my family to visit Korea is a goal for the near future. I have realized that my inability to speak Korean has become a barrier between me and other Koreans outside of my family. It is not merely the lack of being able to communicate; it is the preformed conception in the opposing person's mind that I simply do not care enough to learn the language of my own people. Before even saying a word in English (mine fluent and theirs broken), they have already formed their notion of what a "bad Korean" I am. These notions are untrue, but to disprove these misconceptions, I need to do my part in studying the language comprehensively. A Korean who is different from the norm can still be just as "Korean" as others.

I am proud to call myself a Korean American now, something I couldn't say ten or twenty years ago. The majority of that time I spent staying away from Koreans, being antisocial when I was forced to interact. There was a period of time where I moved out of the house and refused to say a word to my parents, and even to my sister, who were trying to reach out and understand why I became so unhappy and distant. It was only just these past few years, as my parents became an elderly couple and I've come to watch and care for them more often, and when I finally experienced life outside of New York City and experienced not only Koreans, but other second-generation immigrants who've longed for a connection to their nationality while embracing their individuality as Americans. Although I am still working on being a Korean, I am proud to call myself a Korean American.

STEP 2: COME OUT AND PLAY

I am fortunate to have been raised in New York City—an urbanized jigsaw puzzle of nationalities and ethnic communities attempting not to overlap, but failing miserably. This type of environment breeds a network of funky, open-minded people, some old-school first-generation parents, and everything in-between. This is the atmosphere I've known growing up, and though I was the minority Asian in most cases, I always had a group of Orientals somewhere in the playground to fall back on and disappear into. Our weakness was also our main strength—we all looked the same to bullies, and they treated us as such.

Bullying was rampant across all nationalities, but Asians appeared to be considered one of the weakest, despite their usually large numbers in school in comparison to other minorities. We clung together like a herd of deer in the hallways, and bullies would target the weak link (the skinny straggler with the overstuffed bookbag and thick-framed glasses, running late to class). I had one fellow Korean friend, Lee, whom I had met in second grade, but by sixth grade, he had become one of the main bullies of our school. It was particularly uncomfortable because our parents knew each other, and I'd often be sent to their vegetable store which was two blocks away from our house. I'd have to bow to his mother, who would tiredly smile at me from behind the register, and who reminded me of my mother in so many ways.

She always let me go if I was short on money, not having any idea that her son was the reason I was two dollars short for the apples.

My first year of high school, I went to Bronx Science, a specialized school in a rough part of the Bronx. Across the street was the notorious Clinton High School, which was known for having metal detectors and gangs. The students from Clinton used the 4 Train as their de facto "office," mugging many of the nervous-looking Bronx Science Asians huddled together by the poles in the middle of trains. I had hoped that being Asian was only a hindrance as a child, and that high school would be another fresh start. Instead, I found that Asians were the most common victims of muggings on the train. The white population of Science was large enough to protect one another, and many of them could afford to take buses that shuttled them to and from school. Other minorities that weren't able to blend in with the predominantly African-American and Hispanic population of the area were forced to endure an unnerving fifteen-minute walk across the bridge to the train station, which merged with the entrance to Clinton, where the Clinton kids would enter the herd of bustling students like hunters scattering prey. The first year was about surviving. Instead of wanting acceptance, I wanted to withdraw and again felt resentment towards the curves of my eyes and the fairness of my skin, and it manifested when I would come home to my family and would eat dinner without a saying a word, or during church services when I refused to sing the hymns.

Bullying is present in all schools, even in the most prestigious schools in the city. Stuyvesant High School was located in Manhattan, and it was a competing high school to Bronx Science. The student body was roughly half Asian and half white, with a small percentage of other minorities. At Stuyvesant, there was not physical bullying. Instead, there was a clique mentality that ostracized those who didn't fit in, which is as harmful to a child's mental health as physical bullying. I saw division within the Korean community, as well as in other nationalities. Hispanics were divided into Dominicans, Puerto Ricans, and Mexicans, while the South Asians were divided into Indians, Pakistanis, and Bengalis. It was ludicrous, but everyone seemed to be caught up in belonging somewhere, and that seemed to measure the success of one's high school career. Even within the Korean student population at Stuyvesant, there were the "cool" ones (those who congregated around the fourth-floor lockers and wore matching black clothes and donned the same highlighted hairstyles) and the "uncool" ones (those that congregated in vacant spots in the hallways or empty classrooms and wore oversized clothes their parents were waiting for them to grow into, their brooding faces hiding behind books).

I avoided the Korean packs like the plague. Their eyes were like those of hungry predators, watching for freshmen and loners. I would quickly walk past the fourth floor wall, usually going the long way, which meant passing through either the football hangout or the senior bar, but I was willing to risk it. The feeling of being looked down on by your own kind was more hurtful than being physically bullied by anyone, as I had learned several times before. Many of Stuyvesant's kids were picked on themselves growing up. Though I was never physically threatened by another Korean, high school was all about innuendos, and they didn't need to endanger me to make it clear I wasn't welcome in their group.

When I worked at my mother's deli, my mother would sometimes sleep in a reclining chair wedged in the back whenever she had a chance (she didn't have much time to sleep at home) while I watched the front, stealing cigarettes and drinking beer in the walk-in refrigerator. When customers entered, I would serve them as quickly and as painlessly as possible, so I could resume my time-passing. Whenever a group of Asian teenagers entered, whether I recognized them or not, I tried my best to avoid them. I was unfamiliar with the "in" Asian/Korean crowd in high school, and could rarely tell their age, or even recognize which ones were in my grade. I wanted to avoid any possibility of confrontation, afraid they may poke fun of me in my stained t-shirt and oversized cap, eventually dragging out the fact that it was my own mother's deli. I would watch them from behind the glass doors of the refrigerator for as long as possible, which had enough room for me to sit on a milk crate and sip my beer until I was forced to exit and ring them up from behind the register if Jose, my mother's lone Ecuadorian employee, was unable to do so. I avoided all eye contact, and the teenagers actually seldom said anything. They would mostly eye me curiously, this fellow Asian teen running this small, shabby deli himself, and reeking of smoke and alcohol. I would reflect for a moment after these groups left, watching after them as they crossed the street laughing and smiling, wondering if I should have just extended my hand and introduced myself instead of giving in to paranoia. By that point though, it would be too late, and then someone would order an egg sandwich and my mother would wake to the sound of scraping pans and splattering grease.

After college, I worked for a number of years running a bagel shop in an upscale Italian neighborhood called Howard Beach. I became rather comfortable working in the neighborhood, though it was rare to see any other Asians. My regulars were neighborhood Italian Americans who would greet me and ask how I was doing whenever they came in because they knew that I ran the place. However, when I took my family to the neighborhood fair one year, they all avoided eye contact with me. Even the Italian girl I was seeing had to hide our relationship. Outside of the store, I was a ghost, and inside, I was known as "the Chinese Kid who runs the Chinese Bagel Store," though I'm not Chinese and most of my employees were neighborhood kids.

I haven't had much traveling experience outside of New York City. I have mostly been to small church retreats in upstate New York or in nearby states.

When I do venture outside of the familiar, however, I am often greeted with culture shock. In certain upstate towns, some of which were less than a two-hour drive away, Asians are nowhere to be found. During these retreats, some of which included other church members, while other times I was only with my immediate family, the group would often make rest stops during the particularly long drives. Occasionally, at these local spots, I would encounter lingering looks, mostly from young children, who were not used to the sight of an Oriental face. It still surprises me, partially because I have been spoiled by small luxuries, such as the Internet, and having lived in predominantly Asian-American communities in an extremely diverse city for the majority of my life. It rarely ends up being anything more than a long stare, but it is a constant reminder of how lucky I am and that I shouldn't take my comfortable atmosphere for granted.

STEP 3: THE SOCIAL NETWORK (KOREAN-AMERICAN VERSION)

Most of my interactions with Koreans were through church, which was the one thing I dreaded more than school. In school, I was able to avoid interactions with other Koreans, but in church, I was placed in youth groups with other children my age, children who mixed their Korean and English smoothly and had no problem belting out Korean hymns. Having been so young at the time, it's difficult to differentiate whether it was my interactions in school or at church—or a combination of both—that triggered my insecurities around other children, particularly Koreans. I realized that I found rejection by my own people even more painful than being teased or bullied at school.

My lack of Korean was an obvious barrier. I usually got by with a nod and a hello. *Ahn nyung ha sae yoh* (Korean for "Hello, how are you doing?") was one of the few phrases I forced myself to enunciate in the mirror. That single phrase has gotten me out of many uncomfortable conversations. The parents of other children in the youth groups would ask my parents why I wasn't taught Korean. In reality, they had—several times. There was always a language class for the second-generation youth groups who were beginning to forget their Korean, who began to call their parents "mommy and daddy" instead of "*um-ma and ap-pa*." The language class wasn't difficult—it was usually a review of the Korean alphabet or basic words—I simply refused to take the time to memorize the material or complete any assignments. In contrast, I was one of the top students in my elementary and junior high school. My parents couldn't understand why I was so against learning the language, but they eventually gave up on worrying about it too much and settled for the check marks and A's I was receiving in English and math.

It was during my college years that I began to make an invested effort in embracing my culture. Having forgotten nearly all of my Korean, I gave it another shot by taking Korean 101. It was one of several Korean-based classes I signed up for, but surprisingly, Korean language was still the most difficult.

When I was forced to have a conversation with a Korean adult, or was at least present while parents were having the conversation, the talks usually circled around the same topics. These topics included, but were not limited to, the child's academic standing (which high school or college they were attending and the grades they were receiving), the child's level of Koreanness (an ideal level would be a Korean child who enjoys an occasional hot dog but prefers a home-cooked Korean meal), the child's attentiveness towards their parents (like a good boy, lil' Sun never seemed to disobey his parents, isn't that right, Son?), and the child's overall level of sharpness and "*heem*" (Korean for "strength"), as judged by the onlooking Korean elder. It was usually a painful situation, as I usually could not fend for myself because of my lack of Korean communication skills, and relied on my parents to tell little white lies about how good my grades actually were and how respectful I actually was towards them—even during the years when I was a moody, angst-ridden teenager. I had no interest in being my parents' type of Korean or the fourth-floor type of Korean.

Ironically, my first girlfriend was Korean. Her name was Jane, and she was flat-chested, walked with her back too straight, and had small, lazy eyes that appeared in a nervous half-smile, accentuating her unassuming Asian face. She mournfully referred to herself as "Plain Jane." She clung to individuality in the form of punk rock shirts, cheap bracelets from underground thrift stores around her home in Greenwich Village, and a lone, bright pink streak she kept in the front of her hair for years. It was a stark contrast to the dark orange highlights that other Korean girls fashioned, and they would stare at her pink patch of hair like a bald spot. I disliked the pink streak, the pulsing mark that I saw no purpose for other than to brand her as different. I wasn't the type to draw attention to myself, always lingering on the outside of things, and always searching for a spot without asking anyone to move. The unique way in which we each exhibited a rebelliousness to the norms of our culture was what drew us together. We hid ourselves away in alcoves underneath the staircases instead of going to class, shared a pair of earphones while we listened to a Nirvana album; went to our first concert together, full of teenagers on ecstasy. The spiky-haired Koreans in black clothes who gathered on the fourth floor could recruit every Korean in New York for all we cared.

We broke up after a few months, and she promptly started going out with the editor of the school newspaper, a lanky white boy who looked like the lead singer of Weezer (her favorite band). He had his own circle of school newspaper crews and punk rockers, which mingled at the points of creativity and pot smoking. She seemed happier during that last year of high school; her back seemed to ease up a bit when she walked (she bought a smaller book bag), and her eyes looked a little more sure when she walked the hallways with her boyfriend. She kept the pink streak until the last few weeks of school, when we were scheduled for our yearbook photos. I actually got mad when I saw that she had gotten rid of it because she hadn't stuck with it until the end.

STEP 4: LAVA LAMPS, TWINKIES, AND COLLEGE

My perception of Korea and what it meant to be Korean began to take shape during my college years. In my competitive high school, going to college was not enough; most of the kids in school were aiming for Ivy League or top universities, and a majority of those top students were Asian. I shrugged off going to a state college while most of my friends got in to at least one of their top three college choices. I told myself that my parents couldn't have afforded it anyway even if I had been accepted, that all I wanted was to get away from home. I spent most of my time at my prestigious high school wondering about what floor to hang out on, and hadn't really focused on grades. It may have been for the best, as attending a state college provided me an eye-opening experience about myself and others, which I may not have had time for if I had had my nose buried in books.

I went to SUNY Buffalo, a ten-hour drive upstate near the border of Canada. There's only two to three months out of the year that Buffalo isn't skin-numbingly cold or buried underneath snow, so there wasn't much to do besides drink or waste time away in someone's dorm room. My most illuminating experiences, however, weren't from staring at lava lamps or nights spent at house parties; it was the time I spent with other second-generation students like me. Most of them were born here in the States but retained— and, in fact, celebrated—their ethnic identity by organizing Student Ethnic Association groups. Funded by the Board of Education, groups such as the Bengali Student Association (BSA), the Filipino Student Association (FSA), and the Korean Student Association (KSA), among dozens of others, allowed a meeting place for people of the same nationality, as well as anyone who was interested in the culture. For the first time, I experienced nationalities congregating within an institution not because of clique mentality or as a symbol of social status, but simply as a way to celebrate heritage, values, and customs. It was a quality I had not realized so many of the new generation carried, and I found it beautiful.

Being introverted, and especially self-conscious towards other Koreans, I wasn't quite ready to jump into a cultural revelation headfirst. I never ended up officially joining the KSA, though I did have a Korean girlfriend who was an ongoing member (she liked to call herself "Twinkie"...not my best days). As a result, I attended meetings and met other Koreans that felt as displaced as me growing up, only they didn't grow up in New York City, and didn't have a group of Asian faces to fall back into. I did join my friends' clubs, being one of the only Koreans in the aforementioned BSA and FSA. Besides the social aspect of developing my ethnic identity, I also tried to connect with my Korean roots by enrolling in the variety of Korean classes they had to offer (SUNY Buffalo is the second-largest State University of New York). I enrolled in Korean Language 101, Korean Literature, and Korean History, my efforts to be a Korean, to make up for the resentment I felt growing up. I learned that I could be a Korean without fitting into any particular mold or fitting any certain criteria. I loved and missed my parents, Korea is where they were born, and in my eyes, that was Korean enough.

STEP 5: WILL THE REAL KOREAN AMERICAN PLEASE STAND UP?

Until recently, I have spent most of my post-undergraduate career making cold, hard cash at a bagel store. It disappointed my parents to see me working in the same type of business as them, especially after I had finished college. My parents may have felt guilty because of the many hours I had spent in their own deli store, thinking they had pushed me too hard, or that they hadn't done enough themselves. I had finally decided to look for something else besides the bagel store after six years, with the realization that my family had been waiting for me to do it on my own all along.

Growing up, the idea of "Korea" signified many things—the unfriendly stares from a familiar pair of eyes of the kids in Sunday school, the judgmental critiques from Korean parents, and the rejection from my Korean peers in high school. It was difficult to separate the negative from the positive, and they blended and distorted into resentment and anger. I wasn't merely annoyed by my culture—I had despised it, wanted nothing to do with Koreans (though other minorities, including other Asians, seemed not to bother me), and for most of my childhood, I wished I had been a white boy on television.

My perspective changed as I grew older and experienced the world through college, friends, the Internet, etc. I listen intently whenever my parents are willing to retell a piece of their history or a tale from their childhood, even though their stories often involve a great deal of sacrifice and suffering. Now, their struggle is something I embrace rather than shun. Though I am still currently finding my own path, I know for certain that I am not alone in my journey. Along with me and my family, all of the stereotypes that we represent, including "the Korean Pastor" father, "Korean Deli Owner/Nail

Shop Working" mother, and "second-generation Korean American" are going through it together. The struggle to find my identity and to come to grips with my heritage has been a driving force throughout my life, both professionally and personally. It is still hard for me to sit down with my parents and have dinner at the apartment without the television on. My father is old now, and he's forgotten more English than he remembers. My mother quietly hums a hymn while preparing dinner in the background—a tired angel I cannot imagine my life without. When I was little, my father and I used to pretend that we were pro wrestlers. The days of body slams and elbow drops are over, but I would someday like to reminisce with him about those fun times, about how he would rub my face in his armpit against my useless squeals to imitate the wrestling move "The Pit Stop." I treasure those memories more than he knows, before the combination of cultural differences and my growing up made the gap between us more apparent.

As for my grandmother, the hard, tight-lipped, four-foot-something old woman was the last of my father's side to make the trip to America, seeing off all of her five sons and two daughters before she made the trip herself. She spent the final years of her life bedridden, taking turns being cared for by each of her children before passing. My father conducted the services for her funeral.

Sometimes I imagine all of us in Korea, living in one of those checkered huts like the ones on Korean period drama television shows. I imagine us inside the hut, sitting cross-legged on the floor around bowls of rice on a low table, in the traditional Korean fashion. Other times, I imagine that a "Korean" version of me would dream about sitting around a dinner table with the television on, like on the American television shows, just like me and my parents in real life.

Chapter Eight

Too American to be Korean, Too Korean to be American

A Second-Generation Outsider's Account

Thomas Chung

I can't remember the exact moment when I realized I was Korean. I have some vague memories of children calling me Chinese or Japanese. These taunts didn't register with me at first, probably because I didn't know what Chinese or Japanese meant. In fact, someone probably had to point out that I didn't look like everyone else in my neighborhood. I do recall my mother getting upset though. "We are not Chinese or Japanese," she would say, her tone uncharacteristically serious, "we are Korean." At a certain point, her saying that over and over again must have registered in my head, and from a very early age, I began repeating her words to others who dared to misidentify my ethnicity.

My name is Thomas Chung, and I am the first-born child of Korean immigrants. I was born in Atlanta, Georgia, in 1976, a few short months after my parents had moved to the States from Asuncion, Paraguay. My father had migrated to South America from South Korea after his tour of duty in Vietnam, hoping that it would serve as a jump-off point to the United States. Even with the liberalized Immigration Act of 1965, it was still somewhat difficult to procure a visa directly to the States from Korea. Thus, my father purchased a small grocery store in Asuncion, and quickly picked up Spanish. Prior to the Vietnam War, he had been a middle-school English teacher in Seoul, so he was already familiar with the Roman alphabet, Latin roots, and western sentence construction. After living in Paraguay for a year or so, he sent an airplane ticket and a letter to Seoul, asking my mother to marry him. My mother, who was eighteen and fresh out of high school at the time, accepted his proposal, and left her homeland for the first time in her life. It must have been frightening and exciting to be so young and to uproot her life to move to a strange, equatorial land on the other side of the globe. Judging from pictures, their wedding looked beautiful. I noticed that some of the bridesmaids were Paraguayan, while others appeared to be Korean. According to my folks, there was a significant Korean community in Paraguay, even in the 1970s.

MOVIN' ON UP

After my mother became pregnant with me, she and my father decided that it was time to head north to the United States. There were several reasons behind their decision. They wanted their first-born child to have American citizenship and all the perks that go along with it. My father also thought that there would be more opportunities for upward mobility for all of us in the United States. Last but not least, my pregnant mother had a difficult time dealing with the tropical climate and humidity. They left Paraguay, which they had come to like despite their grievances against it, and hopped on a plane headed north.

I was born in Atlanta around Thanksgiving of 1976. I wonder if my parents had known about the racial history of Atlanta and the Deep South, especially since they had moved there in the years just following the Civil Rights Movement. My father worked at a warehouse during the day as a forklift operator, while my mother stayed home with me. We lived in Lakewood Homes, low-income apartments in south Atlanta, not far from Hartsfield International Airport. After working a full day at the warehouse, my father would come home for dinner and a brief respite before starting his nighttime paper route. He would sometimes take me and my mother along to keep him company while he delivered newspapers. According to them, I would sit on top of the piles of newspapers in the backseat. I don't have any recollection of this, but it sounds like a nice family activity, and I bet that I probably enjoyed it.

After burning the candle at both ends like this for a few years, my parents saved up enough money to purchase a wig store from another Korean couple in Decatur, a nearby suburb of Atlanta. I was two years old when they bought the store. I have a vague recollection of being somewhat frightened by the army of mannequin heads. I got over that pretty quickly, and I proceeded to spend much of my childhood and formative years playing and working in the store.

GROWING UP AND CALIBRATING MY ETHNIC IDENTITY

My level of Korean ethnic retention has had peaks and valleys in my life. For the first few years of my life, Korean was my first language, and Korean cuisine was my primary source of sustenance. Before I started attending school, my parents and I exclusively spoke Korean at home. However, I had learned some English from watching *Sesame Street*, *Electric Company*, *CHiPS*, and other American television programs. I didn't have many problems in terms of language and comprehension when I started kindergarten. Years later, my parents admitted that they had initially worried about my language skills in school. Little did they know that English would quickly replace Korean as my first language.

Once I had become accustomed to the routine and structure of attending an American public school, my true assimilation into American culture began. An unfortunate side effect of my rapidly improving English was a concomitant decrease in my Korean fluency. I would not realize until years later that by letting my Korean language skills fall by the wayside, I was unconsciously building a barrier between myself and my Korean roots. After only a year or two of being in school, I found myself speaking only English with my parents, even when they spoke to me in Korean.

Our home life was a melting pot of Korean and American cultural ingredients. We took our shoes off at home, greeted older Korean visitors with a ninety-degree bow, ate nori and rice rolls as after-school snacks, and wore Korean underwear and socks (usually brought or shipped to us by Korean relatives) underneath our American department and discount store clothing, which were distinctly Korean cultural characteristics. However, like the other kids at school, we watched American cartoons and sitcoms, and asked our mom to buy us American toys. We rode bikes and played basketball, soccer, and baseball with the other kids in the neighborhood. My mother prepared a mix of Korean and American food at home, but aside from *bulgogi* (marinated barbecue beef) and dumplings, we quickly grew to favor American food. Looking back, our food favoritism served as an apt metaphor for our muddled sense of ethnic identity. As a child, I hated *kimchi*, the most Korean of Korean dishes (I have since acquired a taste for it). I also loathed the smell of *doenjangjjigae* (fermented soybean paste stew), salted fish, cow neck soup, and other decidedly un-American dishes. At the time, I thought I was simply experiencing sensory revulsion. However, in hindsight, I can now see that my dislike of Korean dishes was some sort of subconscious, symbolic rejection of my ethnicity. Even though my palate had indeed grown accustomed to standard American fare, such as hamburgers, fries, and pizza, the Korean dishes that my family ate at home separated and distinguished me from my American classmates and friends. I already realized that I looked different from everyone else in my school. Although we were retaining a few of our

Korean cultural characteristics, we were also beginning to stifle and stunt that part of our identity, without even realizing it.

My mother, sister, brother, and I began attending the first large Korean Presbyterian church in the metropolitan Atlanta area around 1981. My sister and I had problems with it from the outset. For a while, we tried in earnest to be good, obedient, Christian children. I feel somewhat guilty in admitting that our disdain had more to do with social reasons than anything religious or spiritual. We were relentlessly picked on and harassed by the other Korean-American children. In Sunday School classes, we learned about the virtues of Jesus. Even at a young age, I understood that one of the prevailing messages of Christianity was love. We were taught to honor and respect our neighbors, yet as soon as we were out of class, the other Korean kids would try to beat me up and would make fun of my clothes. If I had possessed the vocabulary at that point, I would have called them hypocrites. I still don't know why we were treated so badly by the other kids. At that point in our lives, we weren't very different from most of them. Most of their parents also owned small businesses (mostly wig shops, liquor stores, dry cleaners, grocery stores, etc.), and we all had pretty similar backgrounds.

I believe that my bad experiences with the Korean Church were some of the most significant factors that led to my subsequent (albeit subconscious) rejection of my Korean identity. Even though I occasionally had to put up with white and black kids calling me "ching-chong" or making their eyes small and slanted, I was appalled to endure such treatment from people who were supposed to be just like me. This seemed much worse. We looked the same, spoke the same language, ate the same food, and our parents had taken similarly difficult paths to get to where they were. My sister and I actively stopped attending church as soon as we had the gumption to put our collective foot down. I must have been around ten when I decided that I would rather help my dad at the store on Sundays than go to church with my mom.

After visiting South Korea for the first time in 1989, my brother, sister, and I began attending The Korean-American School of Atlanta. I was twelve years old at the time. The school was in session from 9:00 AM until 1:00 PM every Saturday. Even though I wasn't particularly thrilled about having to wake up early on a weekend (which also meant missing Saturday morning cartoons), I was actually excited about learning more about the motherland. One of my two uncles who lived in the U.S. had taught me the basics of *Hangeul* (the written Korean language), but my reading and writing skills improved drastically upon attending Korean School. In addition to reading comprehension and grammar classes, we were also offered electives, such as music, history, tae kwon doe (which I was thrilled about), and drama. I actually was picked to play the wicked brother Nolbu in a dramatic adaptation of the Korean folktale *Heungbu and Nolbu*. Having to memorize tons of lines in Korean was a challenging-yet-rewarding exercise for me. It was also pretty entertaining and therapeutic to yell my lines and chase the other kid actors around with Nolbu's props, which included a bamboo fan and a smoking pipe made of metal. Although I enjoyed the educational and cultural aspects of Korean School, I still felt somewhat different and alienated from the other kids. At times, I felt like I was destined to be an outcast forever. In a way, the future proved me right and wrong.

RACISM 101: AN INTRO TO PREJUDICE AND CORRUPTION OF INNOCENCE

Despite growing up in a Korean household, my brother, sister, and I had little trouble fitting in at school, at least early on. I believe that racism and xenophobia are learned and conditioned behaviors, and most young children are unaware of who they should or should not be hanging out with until someone tells them otherwise. Sadly, we had an easier time fitting in when we were younger because the other kids had not yet learned how to be racist. As we later learned, it was only a matter of time.

A black family moved into the house across the street from ours right around the time that I started helping my parents at their wig shop. Coincidentally, my parents' clientele had gradually shifted from affluent, old white ladies to lower- and middle-class black women. Although I was aware of the existence of different races beforehand, this time period marked my first real encounters with different racial dynamics. We quickly befriended the two young black boys who lived across the street. George was the older brother, and he was my sister's age (two years younger than me), while Charlie, the younger brother, was the same age as my brother (three years younger than me). Aside from their complexions, they didn't seem different from anyone else in our neighborhood. They too rode bikes, watched *Thundercats* and *Transformers*, played with the same toys that all the other kids liked, and enjoyed eating pizza, ice cream, and Cheetos. My brother, sister, and I were rather confused when our maternal grandmother (who had come from Korea to live with us right around the time that I started kindergarten) would yell at us in Korean about hanging out with black people. We could not comprehend why she cared who we played with. After all, we did the same things with George and Charlie that we did with our white friends. If anything, we were less inclined to get in trouble hanging out with them because we tended to stay closer to our own house. Although thinking about her words makes me cringe, I try to understand where those words came from, and I don't resent my grandma for feeling the way that she did. Her views were the product of living in a racially and ethnically homogeneous country, something that I cannot even comprehend as an American. I bet that most Koreans in the 1980s (and even now) feel the same way about black people.

Although my siblings and I were color-blind when it came to hanging out with George and Charlie, our experiences at the wig shop were not so harmonious. I have some vague recollections of being threateningly harassed by black kids. I couldn't figure out why I was being picked on. However, I began to notice that most of this bullying was usually accompanied by comments about my being Chinese or Japanese or Bruce Lee. I didn't even know who Bruce Lee was because my mom thought his films were too violent for us to watch at such young ages. I had a sickening revelation one day. A customer had gotten upset because of my parents' no-refund policy at the store. Her voice began getting louder, and I started hearing her calling my parents Chinese and ching chong. Finally, she screamed, "Go back to your country!" and huffed and puffed as she left the store. I could not believe that adults were capable of such hateful and childish behavior. However, I was even more shocked that this lady had used the same sorts of Chinese/Japanese taunts towards my parents that I had endured from children. I began to think that black people, for whatever reason, did not like people who looked Chinese, Japanese, or Korean.

I was only half right. I soon learned that many white people also didn't like people who looked like me. As I got older, I began hearing similarly infuriating things from white kids. What made it even more confusing was that I heard racist remarks from some of the same kids I had played with when I was younger. Why had they tolerated me only a few short years before? I had not felt so different from the other kids when I was younger, but age was making me more conscious of being Korean, even though I felt rather American. Suddenly, the white team captains during recess started picking me last, even though I was just as athletic and coordinated as the kids who were picked first. In an ironic twist of pan-Asian vindication, two confident and athletic Southeast Asian students (one was Cambodian and the other was Laotian) transferred to my school in fourth grade. They were immediately recognized as being the most athletic and charismatic boys in the schoolyard, and the two of them replaced their white successors as team captains. Touch football was the game of choice during physical education, and the two Southeast Asian boys noticed my propensity for catching a football. In an unintentional act of racial solidarity, the Laotian captain (the captains would also play quarterback for their respective teams) began picking me first or second, which pleased me to no end. I became one of his favorite targets on the field, going on to score countless touchdowns that school year.

After becoming conscious of racism, I began noticing it everywhere. It seemed that hostile confrontations between my parents and black customers were becoming more frequent. I could not understand why most of these interactions ended with the customer telling my parents to go back to their country. I failed to see the correlation between buying wigs or hair supplies and my parents going back to Korea. I continued working at my parents' store through high school. As my teenage hormones raged, I grew tiresome of what I thought were unwarranted attacks on me and my family because of our race. I found myself engaging regularly in shouting matches with customers after hearing racist remarks. I think that my retorts were especially heated and venomous, because unlike my parents, English was my first language. I had the luxury (or misfortune, depending on how you look at it) of comprehending veiled, subtle racist comments. Unlike my parents, I also had a fully-stocked arsenal of American obscenities, which I utilized frequently. I eventually adopted a decidedly defensive disposition at work, ready to erupt at the first mention of race. Even though my parents didn't enjoy such treatment from their customers, they also didn't condone or encourage my frequent profanity-laden outbursts. "You're being as bad as the customers," my mother would say to me. "No I'm not," I would reply, "they started it."

One day at the store, I found a small pamphlet with a Black Power fist and offensive caricatures of slant-eyed, buck-toothed Asian people on the cover. In big block letters, the pamphlet read, "Boycott Korean Businesses." I opened it up to find a list of grievances against Korean-owned businesses in black neighborhoods. Although I was enraged, sickened, and hurt by what I saw, for the first time, I realized that the verbal racist attacks on my family were, though a bit misguided, not totally unwarranted. Even with my Korean bias, I could understand why any group of people would be upset at the prospect of outsiders coming into their neighborhoods to sell products. The pamphlet said that Koreans did not support the black community because they didn't hire black employees and didn't give back to the community by supporting community organizations. Although my parents had hired a few black employees over the years, our store was usually staffed by family members, exchange students, or new arrivals from Korea. I was more confused than ever.

Although I was deeply troubled and affected by the prejudice I experienced from black people, as I got older, I began noticing the widespread and comparatively more subtle nature of white racism. In fifth or sixth grade, I was selected to represent my school in a county quiz bowl. As soon as I walked into the room, the white students on the opposing team seemed intimidated. I overheard some of their parents pointing out the "mature-looking Oriental boy." I was already quite accustomed to having other people point out my race. At times, it didn't faze me very much. However, I didn't like being made to feel so conscious of being different. I felt as if people didn't see me as an individual. On the contrary, as an "Oriental," people just assumed that I was adept at solving math problems and playing a classical instrument like violin or piano. They also assumed that I was respectful towards my elders and polite and disciplined. It didn't help matters that all of the above were true at that point in my life. During the quiz bowl, every time

I answered a question correctly, I could see the shoulders of my opponents slump ever so slightly.

As I grew older, I began to see some of the many different faces of racism. As a college student, I took a trip to Savannah, GA with my girlfriend at the time. We went to a bar to have a mid-afternoon vacation drink. As we sat sipping beers, I noticed an elderly white Vietnam veteran staring at me. I tried to ignore him, but he kept glaring at me in a very unfriendly way. Finally, he pointed his finger at me and said, "I fought your people." I was more irritated than scared. I responded to his comment with the question, "Really? What people did you fight? My people are allies with the U.S. military." He replied, "Asiatics." I stifled a laugh at his anthropological description of "my people," but he was dead serious. He then pointed at my girlfriend and said, "I fought your people too." His second comment was even more ridiculous, because she was Irish American. We decided not to indulge this man any further, finished our beers, and promptly left. Since that time, I have read quite a bit of literature about the Vietnam War, including history books and autobiographical accounts of the traumatic war. Many Vietnam veterans who suffer from symptoms of post-traumatic stress disorder experience anxiety and anger upon seeing Asian people, which, given the circumstances of that particular war, is understandable. However, I was not feeling so sympathetic or forgiving during that particular incident at the bar, especially since I knew that my father, a Vietnam veteran himself, had fought side by side with American troops and had even been shot during combat. For some reason, I don't think that this man would have even comprehended or believed what I had to say. Once again, I felt persecuted and unwelcome, simply because of my Asian physiognomy.

PUNK ROCK AND SOCIAL NETWORKS

By the time I had started attending kindergarten at a public school, my family had moved into a four-bedroom house in a nearby suburb of Atlanta called Stone Mountain. At the time, Stone Mountain was predominantly middle-class and white. My brother, sister, and I quickly became friends with our white neighbors and schoolmates, which would more or less set the tone for our formative years. At the time, we were the only Koreans in our neighborhood and at Rockbridge Elementary School. Aside from having a few black friends (including our aforementioned neighbors George and Charlie), most of our friends were white.

In high school, my sister and I discovered punk rock. We had finally found something to latch onto. Punk was a musical genre and lifestyle that was started by a motley group of degenerate-but-artistic outcasts in New York City in the early to mid-1970s. Its fast, shocking, aggressive aesthetics and anti-authority messages really spoke to us. It also didn't hurt that punk style, with its proclivity towards brightly colored hair, black leather, and metal accessories, really seemed to irk parents, teachers, and other kids. When we were younger, we had tried in vain to fit in with other kids and the status quo, but to no avail. Punk offered us the option of celebrating our outcast status. Not only that, it also allowed us to do so on our own terms, with the added bonus of getting to listen to fast and fun music that made us feel vital. We quickly adopted some of the other outcasts in our school, some of whom were also into punk rock and skateboarding (the two seemed to go hand in hand). However, we also befriended other kids who didn't fit in. Although there were some black and Hispanic bands and artists in the early and contemporary punk scenes, punk was a movement that was largely started by white art-school students, misfits, and hooligans. Although we knew a few black and Hispanic punks, the majority of our friends during this phase of our life were indeed white.

Identifying with punk had some strange, unforeseen side effects. Though we were initially attracted to the more cathartic and rebellious aspects of punk, it also helped open our eyes and ears to the world. I felt that most of the other kids in school blindly accepted anything and everything that was shoved down their throats, including clothes, music, and overall attitudes. On the surface, punk seemed to encourage bad behavior, and in a way it did. However, punk also encouraged us to read more books, to question authority, and to seek out unusual and obscure films, writers, art, and music genres. In a strange, circuitous way, punk opened me up to interests and ideas that I still treasure to this day. I became interested in existentialist writers like Albert Camus, Samuel Beckett, and Jean-Paul Sartre, which led me to American Modernist writers like Ernest Hemingway, F. Scott Fitzgerald, Virginia Woolf, and William Faulkner. I started watching foreign and independent films, and my musical interests expanded exponentially. I discovered Mississippi Delta blues, German kraut-rock, Jamaican music, and post-punk (which was a more angular, cerebral, and less angry art-school incarnation of punk). My thirst for anything outside the contemporary status quo was insatiable. Forging my identity through the medium of punk gave me self-confidence, a sense of worth, and a sense of individuality. At long last, I didn't feel bad about not being like the other kids. In fact, I took pride in it.

I also met my first girlfriend because of punk. Most young people who identify with a sub-culture tend to immerse themselves in the aesthetic sensibilities of their chosen genre/medium. I could spot another punk in the same way that my mother could spot other Koreans. In a way, the conspicuous fashion characteristics of punk were as salient and infallible as the physical features of a particular ethnic group. My first girlfriend was a beautiful and rebellious white girl. Her father was a pharmacist in a large Atlanta hospital, and her mother was an eccentric artist who practiced Wicca. To my pleasant surprise, they accepted and embraced me, and rarely mentioned my race.

I knew that my parents wanted me to date a Korean girl, but given my history and interests, I think that they knew it was a long shot. Additionally, there were not any other Korean people in my school or neighborhood, and my access to other Koreans was severely limited because I did not attend Korean church. Throughout high school, college, and beyond, I almost exclusively dated white girls. I did not feel that I was consciously making this decision to exclude Korean, black, Hispanic, or other minority girls. In hindsight, I realize that I had become so assimilated into white America, it felt more like a natural progression than a choice.

I experienced an ambivalent revelation about racial hierarchy and perceptions one evening during my high school years. I had been pining for a pretty white girl named Susan who sat next to me in French class. We became friends and started spending a lot of time together, but I could tell that she just wanted to be friends. Regardless, we became very close, and her grandparents (whom she lived with) really seemed to like me. I think that they assumed I was dating their granddaughter. One evening, I received a phone call from the girl's grandmother. She was clearly distraught, and I asked her what was wrong. She said that Susan had gone on a date with a black boy, and she wanted me to talk some sense into her granddaughter, and went on to say that she wished that Susan was with me instead of the black guy. I had very mixed feelings. On one hand, my feelings were hurt because the girl I liked was hanging out with another guy. On the other hand, I felt sad that her grandmother was unhappy about the situation merely because of the guy's race. And for the first time, I realized that, for better or for worse, as an Asian, I was more accepted than blacks by the white status quo. In the past, I had heard white people say somewhat complimentary but condescending things about Asian people. I have even heard some people refer to Asians as "honorary whites." Apparently, we were hard-working, clean, intelligent, and respectful people. It was my first experience with the model minority myth.

As I mentioned previously, the vast majority of my dating partners have been white. However, after finishing college, I briefly dated a Korean girl. She was getting her PhD in English from Georgia State University, and she had moved to the States from Korea primarily to get a higher education. Aside from our ethnic backgrounds, we actually had a lot in common. She was deeply moved by literature, enjoyed writing and acquiring knowledge, and even liked a lot of the same obscure music that I liked. Even though she had moved to the States as an adult, her English was perfect, and she barely had any trace of a Korean accent. We spoke to each other in English. Occasionally we would speak Korean, but those instances were rare. Needless to say, my parents were thrilled when I brought her to their wig shop one day, but they didn't have too much to be excited about, because our relationship didn't last long.

SUMMER CAMP IN KOREA

When I was fifteen or sixteen years old, my parents sent me to an educational summer camp for overseas Koreans at Seoul University. They didn't have to twist my arm or anything. I actually wanted to go, especially since I had only been to Korea once when I was younger. Even though I had begun to forge my identity through the medium of punk rock, European art films, and expatriate writers, I thought it was important to stay in touch with my Korean roots.

After a brief stay with my aunt and cousins in Seoul, they dropped me off at Seoul University. The majority of the kids were Korean American, but there were also Koreans from Germany, Guatemala, England, Australia, and a few other countries. I had never seen people who looked like me speaking perfect German before. Since it was the middle of summer, university was not in session, so we stayed in dorms. My roommate was a nice kid from Bayside, Queens. However, most of the other kids were not so nice. I immediately became the target of taunts and finger-pointing. Keep in mind that I had invited this kind of attention by flying my freak flag. I had long hair with the sides and the back shaved, and I wore punk rock t-shirts and combat boots. I was also one of the only kids from the Deep South, so I had a southern drawl (which has since faded away). Punk had given me a tough skin, and I had learned to revel in being different, so it didn't bother me too much, but at the same time, it was somewhat disheartening. I felt like I was reliving my younger days at the Korean church.

I mostly hung out with my roommate or kept to myself. Luckily, the camp program included lots of cultural field trips, which I actually found very interesting. We visited Buddhist temples, old palaces, famous mountains and parks, and well-known neighborhoods and commercial districts in Seoul. I eventually spotted another lone wolf on one of these excursions. He was sitting by himself on the bus listening to a cassette through headphones. He was wearing a t-shirt depicting The Tick, a comic book that I liked (comics had become one of my decidedly low-brow interests). I commented on his shirt, and he proceeded to ignore me. He later admitted to me that he thought I was mocking him. We eventually started hanging out, and realized that we liked a lot of the same music, including his favorite band, the Pixies. Our shared interest in music and comic books was only the beginning. He also disliked going to Korean church and felt alienated from other Koreans. We quickly became best friends, and over twenty years later, we are still best friends. It is somewhat ironic that we became friends based on our mutual feelings of being marginalized by Korean and Korean-American society. Friendships and relationships work in mysterious ways. That summer was wonderful and eye-opening for me. My Korean had improved drastically from spending time with my extended family and wandering around various parts of South Korea. I also felt closer to my Korean roots, and it strengthened my desire to explore and cultivate that part of me. After returning to the United States, things quickly returned to normal. I continued feeling confused about my ethnic and racial identity. However, I had made my first bona fide Korean friend.

OBERLIN COLLEGE, PURSUING MUSIC, AND ADULTHOOD

There is somewhat of a gap in the chronology of my quest for my Korean self. I went off to a small progressive liberal arts college called Oberlin, which is in northern Ohio, thirty or so miles from Cleveland. For the first time in my life, I was surrounded by like-minded people. I saw stickers of my favorite obscure bands on dorm room doors. There were film, art, and postmodernist theory students who knew far more about those subjects than I did. People accepted and even welcomed me just as I was. While I had been one of the odder-looking kids in my high school, I blended in fairly well among the myriad hippies, punks, anarchists, art students, young Communists, Foucault worshipers, and assorted weirdos—not only that, people didn't look at me like a freak when I spoke in class or stated my views about a current event or a film. Although I had some inkling of what I was getting into when I had applied to Oberlin, I was shocked and ecstatic that I had landed in what seemed to me like a liberal, alternative, intellectual utopia. Nobody at Oberlin persecuted or harassed me for being Korean or punk. For the first time, I felt like I could just focus on being me without worrying about being different. It felt liberating to finally be accepted by my peers.

I decided to major in creative writing, which was no surprise. My father had instilled his love of reading and writing in me at an early age. During high school, I had even self-published a few issues of a small literary magazine, simply for fun. Out of curiosity, I enrolled in a few African-American Studies courses; Oberlin, which was the first college in the United States to admit female and black students, has a well-known African-American Studies department, with some distinguished and celebrated faculty members. I felt that taking African-American Studies classes would perhaps offer some insights into my own status as a minority in America, and also the conflicts between my family and our black customers. In the intro course, I learned about institutional racism. Although I had never heard those words together before, I already knew exactly what it was and how it felt. It is so deeply ingrained in the foundation and day-to-day logistics of American life, I am sure that every person of color in the United States knows what it feels like, even if they don't know exactly what it is called. I thought back to the pamphlet I had found as a youth about boycotting Korean businesses. I was beginning to understand why black people seemed to have such a chip on their collective shoulder. While there are huge differences in the experiences of blacks and Asians in the U.S., there are also lots of similarities based on being people of color in a white-dominated society. I took some Asian-American Studies courses as well. My mind was blown because I hadn't even known that such a thing existed. I learned about early Asian immigrants, the model minority myth, and middleman minority theory. I had started to think about my ethnic identity again, but I now had a new and more refined set of tools to work with.

In 1998, I returned to Atlanta, after two years at Oberlin and a brief-but-exciting stint in Brooklyn, NY. Oddly, I had missed living in the Deep South, despite its history of racism, Jim Crow laws, segregation, and conservatism. You can take a boy out of the South but you can't take the South out of the boy. I spent thirteen years there trying to figure out what I wanted to do. In lieu of having people tell me to go back to my country at my parents' wig store, I procured a job at Criminal Records (which had been my favorite independent record store for years), dabbled in freelance journalism, continued reading and writing fiction, started a rock band with some new kindred spirits who had moved to town, and watched tons of Hitchcock and French New Wave films. After contemplating the seemingly aimless trajectory of my young adult life, I decided that I wanted to become a public school teacher. However, on the cusp of commencing the teacher certification process, my band unexpectedly started attracting some positive attention, and I decided to pursue a long-time dream of being a professional touring rock musician, which I did on and off for ten years. I would talk more about my life as a musician and its many adventures and ups and downs, but I could probably write a whole book about that. This essay is supposed to be about my attachment to my Korean identity, not what an awesome bass player, singer, and driver I am.

"BE THE REDS": A LITERAL AND FIGURATIVE RETURN TO KOREA

A few years after moving back to Atlanta, I made my third visit to Korea. My brother, a couple of friends, and I had procured tickets to the 2002 World Cup, which was co-hosted by Korea and Japan. We had even gotten tickets to two matches featuring Korea. We attended South Korea's first match, which pitted them against the presumably superior Polish team. I must say, I had never felt so proud to be Korean. From the moment we set foot into the crustacean-like stadium in Busan, my American friends and I were quickly and completely swept up in "Be the Reds" fever ("Be the Reds" was the slogan of fans of the Korean national soccer team; the fans referred to themselves as "the Red Devils"). I was surprised at how readily I adopted South Korea as my team. Although I had lived my entire life in the States, I even rooted for Korea when they played the U.S. On my last night in Korea, we attended the South Korea vs. Portugal match. The Reds upset the powerhouse Portuguese, which advanced the team to the playoff round. Pandemonium swept the entire nation that night. People paraded, chanted, and wept with joy. I felt like I was walking in a dream world. As I marched and chanted alongside the countrymen of my parents and ancestors, I truly felt proud to be Korean.

My perception of South Korea has changed as I have gotten older. When I was a little kid, I always thought of Korea as a small, humble, underdog nation. Hyundai and Samsung seemed like second-rate versions of Japanese brands like Honda and Sony. The Korean movies and dramas that my mother had watched in the 1980s and early 1990s had poor production values and looked like they had been shot on home camcorders. Compared to the iconic American sports juggernauts I had grown up watching and admiring (Michael Jordan, Bo Jackson, Mark McGwire), even Korean athletics seemed ramshackle and amateurish. The 2002 World Cup changed all that. I feel as if the success of the South Korean national team during that World Cup was symbolic of South Korea's rise to international prominence in all of the aforementioned areas. After the overthrow of the military dictatorship in the 1980s, Korean censors seemed to relax a bit. Suddenly, South Korea began releasing thrilling, provocative, visually stunning films and art. I do not doubt that such artistic visionaries were working under the radar during Chun Doo Hwan's regime—I just never had any access to it. Additionally, Korean electronics and automobile companies seemed to undergo a massive and extensive transformation in the 1990s and 2000s. Suddenly, Korean products were no longer looked upon as being inferior to Japanese products. If anything, it appears that Korean products have become even more ubiquitous and popular than those of their formerly dominant East Asian counterparts, in the United States and beyond. I no longer look at South Korea as "the little country that could." I feel like it has become a "grownup" nation, on par with the United States, China, Great Britain, Russia, and other superpowers.

There is no tidy Hollywood ending to this story. After returning to the States and coming down from the high of the World Cup, it was business as usual again. It is easy to feel warm and fuzzy and nationalistic whilst wearing a "Be the Reds" shirt and chanting alongside thousands upon thousands of my fellow Koreans. However, when I flew back to the States and finally took off the red shirt, I once again felt like a marginalized, hyphenated demographic component, neither Korean nor American, but some strange mutation or hybrid that neither nation seemed to want to claim as its own. If you think about it, doesn't Korean American kind of sound like potassium carbonate or some other chemical compound? I have read and heard many accounts from other 1.5- and second-generation Korean Americans about how they feel caught between two worlds. We are too Korean to be American, yet too American to be Korean. Even though I have American sensibilities, and speak English with a thoroughly American accent, I will always be perceived as exotic or foreign to most Americans because of my Asian features and complexion. It doesn't matter that I practically worship Ernest Hemingway, baseball, the Ramones, John Ford western movies, Charlie Parker (for the record, I think that jazz is far and away the United States' greatest cultural contribution to the world), and other quintessentially American ideas, inventions, movements, and people. Nor does it matter that I curse in English when I stub my toe or miss a subway train by two seconds. And it certainly doesn't matter that I hold a U.S. passport or that the United States is the only nation I have ever had the pleasure of calling home. To a stranger on the street who has no idea how I speak, I am no different from the fresh-off-the-boat Chinese guy from Fuzhou who stands on East Broadway, hawking roasted sweet potatoes on cold days, and shouting in Fujinese-accented Mandarin. After thirty-seven years on this planet, I have come to accept and expect that kind of ignorance, willful or not. However, that doesn't mean that I have to like it.

In 2010, after retiring from my musical endeavors (spoiler alert: I didn't become the next Mick Jagger), I moved to Brooklyn, New York, thirteen years after my initial brief stint there in 1997. I currently work part-time as the English-language editor, multi-purpose writer, and web manager for the Research Center for Korean Community at Queens College. In a strange way, the job works nicely as a metaphor for my existence as a Korean American. At least now, I can use my decidedly American skills to learn about and help the Korean and Korean-American communities. I have learned so much already, and I know that I have only scratched the surface. I am also surrounded by Koreans and Korean Americans at my job, and I actually feel comfortable and accepted by them. After lying dormant for many years, my Korean-language skills are actually getting some exercise. It helps to have some fellow Koreans around who don't ridicule my middling-but-improving grammar and vocabulary; rather, they correct me and understand why my American English brain would translate words and thoughts into the pidgin Korean that I speak. While I still feel conspicuously American around most Korean immigrants or large groups of Koreans, I have come a long way since the days of feeling alienated and rejected at church and Korean School. My quest for some sort of resolution or reconciliation between my two identities will continue. People in the United States will continue to ask me where I am from and compliment me on my English, and people in Korea will continue to comment on my American-accented Korean and Western body language, mentality, and tastes. Some who were born on that small peninsula in East Asia will accept me as Korean, while many others will think of me as just another ignorant and indulgent American. This will continue until I am no longer of this earth. But to paraphrase the words of a wise poet or sage, it's all about the journey, not the destination. However, on my particular journey, I get to experience the best from both worlds.

Chapter Nine

The Way I See

Post-Ethnic Formation of Identity

Bora Lee

"Where are you from?" This is a question that initially pops up in everyone's mind when they first meet me, almost without exception. I can't say that I really blame them, because I've asked the same question (sometimes even out loud) about myself and others, although it's always been to feed my curiosity about other places and to allow people to share their experiences. However, others don't generally ask this question for the same reason. The intention is never simply to ask, "Where are you from?" In actuality, they are asking, "What are you?" I reply with, "What do you mean? Do you want to know where my parents are from? If I'm Chinese? If I was born here? If I'm a citizen? If I'm good at math?" Knowing the answer they're searching for, I say, "My parents are from Korea, but I was born here." The curious look on the questioner's face quickly disappears and is replaced with satisfaction, as if my response answered all of the questions floating in their mind. Now, they think they understand.

"My parents are from Korea, but I was born here" has become a sentence that regularly rolls off my tongue these days. Growing up, I don't recall ever having to say something along those lines. Gluing those words together in order to quickly explain the ethnic part of my identity has been a process. I can hear my parents in my head saying, "Remember, you are Korean." What exactly does that mean? As a child, that definition was solely based off of what my grandparents and parents taught me, which was to negate everything else in my life as American or "other." They said it with such certainty and conviction. My parents can't comprehend what it's like to be both Korean and American, just like I can't understand how it feels to live in a foreign land, not knowing when you'll be able to go back home.

OBLIGATIONS WITH NO EXPIRATION DATE

In Korea, being the oldest son means that you take care of all responsibilities in the family. Somehow, being Korean American, "son" was crossed out and was replaced by "child." Not only was I the oldest of four, I was also the oldest daughter of my grandparents' only son. To explain it in plain language, I took more and more responsibilities in my family because my father, by default, was the oldest son, and I, by default, was treated like the oldest son too. I never questioned it as a child. My parents worked seven days a week at their grocery store, from sunup to sundown, which was pretty typical (and stereotypical) of Korean immigrants. We lived in Park Slope, Brooklyn, which was a different neighborhood from the upscale community it is now. As children, when my siblings were hungry, I would grab a chair, stand on top of it, turn on the stove, and start cooking. I would get off the chair and move it towards the opposite end of the counter to check the rice cooker, making sure there was enough rice to feed them. The thought of this being dangerous did not cross my mind, nor did I expect positive words of acknowledgement from my parents. I did my part, following my parents' motto: "No work, no food." I never thought my responsibilities as a child would make people say, "Wow," or look at me with plain shock, until I got older.

We moved to Flushing, Queens, when I was in fifth grade. While my grandmother took care of household chores and cooked meals for my family as she had always done, I continued to take care of my siblings as I always had. I was the middleman between my siblings and the elders, translating as best as I could. My parents were limited English speakers and my siblings could barely speak or understand Korean at all. With my vocabulary being limited and having difficulty putting together grammatically correct sentences, conversing with my parents has always been somewhat of a challenge for me, but I have always understood Korean very well.

I thought that I would be relieved of my family duties once I finished high school and moved on to college. I had planned on going away to attend college, but not too far away. However, my plans fell through. At the time, my family lived in Plainview, Long Island. We moved in the middle of my sophomore year of high school. When I started receiving acceptance letters from different schools, my parents asked me to stay close by. They asked me to take care of my grandmother by getting an apartment with her while attending Queens College. During this time, I was also expected to commute to Brooklyn to help out at their store on the weekends. Once again, I was stuck with first-child duties, assisting my father in his role as the oldest son. How could I say no to taking care of the woman who had raised me and traveled the world to settle in an unknown land of promised hope, just to secure the future of her grandchildren? I shrugged, knowing full well that I wouldn't say no. I thought to myself, "Only four years and I'll be free." I said those words to myself seven years ago. I'm twenty-four now, and I still haven't quite reached that point.

THE FOREIGN LAND CALLED KOREA

South Korea, or the Republic of Korea, is the southern half of the Korean Peninsula, divided by the 38th parallel. To put it in perspective, it's between China and Japan, with North Korea (officially, the Democratic People's Republic of Korea) above it. The geography and the fact that the majority of my family is either there or from there was all I knew about it as a child. I knew more or less about it than any other country, with the exception of the United States, the country I call home. My parents called Korea "our homeland," but to me, the word "home" means a place that is familiar, a place with memories, and a place of origin. Korea didn't mean any of that to me. It meant a familiar place to my parents, a place where they had memories, a place of their origin—not mine.

I was expected to understand the culture, rules, and social norms of our culture; a culture that I never lived by other than at home. It was also a culture that was never explained to me by history books, teachers, or peers. As I grew older, I started questioning my parents about the culture I followed at home. Did they not understand that the definition of culture changes over time, or that they themselves hadn't experienced or lived in Korea's culture for the last twenty-five to thirty years? I don't think that they realize how much Korea has changed in the last couple of decades since they immigrated to America. What they know of Korea is what it was like a whole generation ago. During that time, Korea went from being an underdeveloped country to a first-world nation through industrialization and technological advancement. The government turned into a republic, hosted its first summer Olympic Games and World Cup, and opened its doors to the west. That's the Korea my family missed out on, which is comparable to missing out on the Civil Rights era in the United States!

The actual perception that I have of Korea is tied to economics, technology, and history. With Korea going through drastic economic and technological changes and being more and more recognized throughout the world, it has become an example of what underdeveloped countries can become. Most people would assume that I watch Korean dramas or listen to Korean music, but I hardly identify with Korea's popular culture at all. However, I do see my own morals, life choices, preferences, and personality being shaped by Korean mannerisms and cultural norms that have been practiced throughout history, albeit with some alteration due to generational gaps and technology.

THE KOREAN-AMERICAN FORMULA

Mix a little bit of church here, piano lessons and Korean language school there, a pinch of Tae Kwon Do and fan-dancing lessons at the end, and you've got a full-fledged Korean-American child. When I asked why we had to do all of these things, my parents always answered, "Because you're Korean." I was never given any other explanation. My parents believed that this formula would lead to a path of success for me and my siblings. Korea is a heavy class-based society, due to a history of strict Confucian philosophy. Religion has always played a major role in society, and though the predominant religion in Korea has changed, religion's influence on Korean society has stayed constant throughout history.

I learned all of those aforementioned activities through the church. The church, especially within the New York City Korean Christian community, is an integral part of life for almost every Korean, especially for first-generation Koreans in the United States. Prior to immigrating to the States, many Koreans were considered to be well-educated, and had economic, social, and political autonomy. After immigrating to America, all of that was lost. They would use the church to gain higher social status within the community in order to regain some of the lost status they once had in Korea. The church, being a social institution, is heavily inclusive, and follows a strict hierarchical model. It serves as a fundamental gateway for networking within the community and it can also serve as an easy jump start towards regaining social autonomy.

For my parents, church was a free babysitting service, plus more. For my mom, it was about God, but for us, it was more for the sake of community. I found God much later in life, during college, after years of struggling to understand my faith. At the time, the church was my only connection to the Korean-American community. Since my parents worked all the time, they didn't have many friends who weren't business partners. I wasn't exposed to many other Korean-American children other than my own siblings or cousins. I didn't connect with the other youth in the church and I didn't have many Korean-American friends in school, even though I lived in a neighborhood that was heavily populated with Koreans.

I felt like I had to belong to the church in order to be connected to my community. In spite of this, I didn't feel connected at all. I tried to find similarities between myself and other Korean Americans in my youth group, but other than our ethnic background, there wasn't much I could relate to. I envied the attention others received from adults because of their parents' social status within the church's hierarchy, their fluency in both Korean and English, being part of the youth group's praise team or cabinet, and being able to connect with each other. Since I felt no connection, I thought that maybe God didn't love me, and that I didn't belong in his world. I was mad and blamed God for many years until I realized that it was due to my lack of understanding about my own self.

Even in terms of Korean cultural practices, I was different. I can speak the language conversationally, but my Korean-language skills have been described to me as "a child speaking to their grandmother." I can't go a week without eating at least one Korean meal, but does that show that I'm Korean enough? Apparently not, in the eyes of other Koreans. Also, within the Christian community, my family was different because my family practices *Chesa* (a traditional Korean memorial ceremony for an ancestor's death) and *Charye* (memorial services for the family's ancestors on Korean Thanksgiving and New Year's). These ceremonies go against the ideals of Christianity and Catholicism, so many Koreans and Korean Americans no longer practice them. Fellow peers would look at me as if I had three heads when I would tell them that I bow to my ancestors, who sit behind an enormous table garnished with fresh fruit, nuts, and specially prepared food, or that I celebrate my grandfather's death day.

I had a similar experience in college, where again, I attempted to be a part of the Korean-American community. Queens College has a lot of Asians, especially Koreans. It was my first exposure outside of church where Koreans knowingly sought each other out in order to create bonds and friendships in an unknown sea of people. I made a friend that I instantly connected with, and she just so happened to be Korean American. She talked about joining a Korean Christian club on campus and I immediately agreed, thinking that I could attempt to connect again, from the beginning. No matter how much I tried, it didn't happen as planned. I forced myself to stay connected, and I even started listening to some popular Korean music and watching Korean dramas. Eventually, I got tired of forcing myself to associate with people I clearly did not relate to. I started separating myself from the group, stopped talking to the friends and acquaintances I saw every day, and focused more on school work and my many part-time jobs.

This second attempt at trying to connect with the Korean-American community failed, which made me re-evaluate who I was. I kept asking myself, "Am I not Korean enough? Why don't I fit in with my own community? Am I so different?" As a teenager, I was naively certain that I knew who I was. It was during this time that I started to challenge everything in order to change, redefine, and reassess my identity. Being Korean was only a sliver of who I was, and it was by no means the most important part of my identity. My gender, age, and class also affected my identity. I view identity as how one defines his/her own sense of self. It's not one factor, it's multiple factors and experiences that shape an individual. It was a struggle piecing together the puzzle; I was attempting to clearly define my identity as being ethnically Korean, my nationality being American, and overall, being Asian American.

Thus, my identity has been shaped and influenced by my family, my peers, and how I connect with the social networks surrounding me.

A BOX OF CRAYONS

When you're young, you can see but can't yet comprehend what makes people different. It never struck me as odd that the girl on my right could speak Russian, that the boy on my left could read Hebrew, and that I could understand Korean. I was a transfer student, the new girl from Brooklyn. To my new Queens classmates, Brooklyn seemed like another world, a place that they had only heard of. When I think of it now, my classmates didn't ask me about Korea, they asked me about Brooklyn. People, especially other Koreans or East Asians, tried to talk to me and befriend me, to be a part of their group, as if it was by invitation only. Even in elementary school, I never felt that connection with the general Korean-American crowd. They would talk to me about K-pop, Asian actors, and a whole lot of random topics I didn't know anything about. I was asked questions about Brooklyn, why I had moved, and what toys or new gadgets I had, as if they were trying to label me into one of their categories.

Randomly, a girl came up to me, introduced herself, and simply asked if we could be friends—nothing more. Her name was Gladys, and she was Guatemalan. I had never even heard of Guatemala before I met her. She had no idea where Korea was on the map either, but who could blame us? I ran to a map, looked for something vaguely familiar (trying to cover my bluff until I found China), and moved my finger slightly to the right of the map, and showed her where Korea was. This was the beginning of a life-long friendship, with a person I didn't know I'd have a world of connections with.

Queens is the most diverse place in the world, with residents that collectively represent over a hundred nations and roughly two-hundred languages. My fifth-grade classroom was a microcosm of the population of Queens. We were a box of crayons, different shades comfortably nestled in the same room, the same school, and the same neighborhood. We were all different, but in some ways, we were the same, and we all knew that too. In the end, we were all crayons.

At school, we were all the same. We primarily spoke English (minus the non-native English speakers), had the same teacher, and loved similar books. But at home, it was another world. As soon as school was over, we lived our other lives. We'd come home, shut the door behind us, and the rules and social norms changed. Some of us spoke a different language, and/or practiced a different culture at home. Some ate different foods, and had different routines. Whether our families were Korean, Russian, African American, Spanish, or Caucasian, home was a different place entirely. While many of our families shared similar socioeconomic statuses, our home lives entailed very different cultures.

Junior high wasn't so different from elementary school, at least in the beginning. As we started getting older, cliques started forming. Old friendships were broken as new ones formed with people we thought we had more in common with. The cliques were divided by those who were academically ahead, on sports teams, and by ethnicity. Race had not become a factor yet. Still, I felt most comfortable with my random grouping of friends. My best friends included a Chinese-American male, a Filipino-American male, and Gladys, my Guatemalan friend from elementary school. I never felt out of place with them, and the mentality we had in elementary school about race and ethnicity hadn't changed for us. It was a mutual understanding that held us together. Plus, since I went to church, I thought that was enough of a connection to the Korean community for my parents to be content.

My parents never pushed me to make Korean friends and never judged the friends I had made. They also never favored my Korean friends over my other friends. My parents always talked to my friends, were generally courteous, and asked how their parents were doing. My mom, being more limited in English than my father, did speak to my Korean-American friends in Korean, but asked the same questions she would ask my other friends, usually not much more, unless she happened to know their parents. Even then, the conversations were short, and could be answered with a nod. This is something I truly cherish about my parents. Talking to my father now, I know that we were just a box of crayons in his eyes. He understood that the difficult process of assimilation that he had dealt with didn't quite apply to me since I was already American.

Even as I grew older, my father understood that the likelihood of me dating a Korean male was about the same as me dating males of any other ethnicity. Of course, they preferred me to date a Korean male for obvious reasons. Either way, it would have been shameful if they couldn't eat my grandmother's *ggakdugi* (spicy pickled radish kimchi) or eat my mom's *dduk mahndoo gook* (chewy rice cake and dumpling soup), Korean language notwithstanding. Unfortunately, my grandmother didn't see eye to eye with my parents, and definitely didn't want to understand. Being a teenager, I had to rebel against someone or something. That something was my grandmother constantly insisting that my boyfriend must be Korean. My first boyfriend was Korean-American, but that was merely coincidental.

NON-MINORITY MINORITY

Have you ever seen an ad for a social club and thought, "Yeah, that's me?" Then you go to the first gathering, excited to be meeting people that you're sure you'll be able to connect with, only to find that you clearly don't belong. Isn't it embarrassing and awkward when the room just turns and stares at you? Let's take that same scenario, but replace "social club" with "minority." I am Asian American, specifically a Korean American. I should feel connected to other minorities, but because of the model minority myth, the word "minority" doesn't exactly apply to me in the eyes of other major minority groups.

Like most stereotypes, the model minority myth was developed to label and separate groups based on assumptions. It labels groups who, on average, achieve higher success in comparison to other ethnic or racial groups. Asian Americans have been profiled as the model minority in order to justify the uneven distribution of assistance for those in need. Asian Americans are not seen as a problematic minority group, meaning that we don't need help. Such an assumption cripples those who are in actual need of critical assistance.

Its role in society was to be used as an example to push other minority groups to a "path for success"—to shadow Asian Americans. However, various factors were ignored, including our different political and historical backgrounds. The model minority myth was created in order to take the blame off racism, prejudice, and terrible policy decisions, and was used to redirect escalated frustration and anger from years of oppression. To other minority groups, Asian Americans are not seen as a minority in a general sense because of this. We are a non-minority minority group; we are a minority group in terms of population size, but to the general population, we are identified as a community not "in-need." People have difficulty fitting Asians into the black-and-white world that they're accustomed to.

When people ask me if I have ever experienced racism, I have some trouble answering the question. I have definitely experienced racism, but the situation is a little complicated, and it's not what people typically think about when they hear racism being mentioned. I don't just experience racism from those in power, but from both the privileged and the oppressed. I'm in a sort of limbo. The larger minority groups don't see Asians being affected by white collar crimes or prejudice, while the privileged don't think my community is in need, therefore we don't get affected by policy. I have always felt this way. When I first heard someone use the term non-minority minority, I automatically connected to it, because the term encompassed everything I had ever felt.

Even though I grew up in the same neighborhood as some of my Puerto Rican friends, they still have this notion in their heads that my family was well-off while theirs weren't. But they themselves are a mix of lower and lower-middle class, and weren't all living in heavy poverty. Just because I was Asian, I still "didn't understand how it feels to be poor." To them, I was more privileged simply because my parents owned a grocery store. If only my friends knew how many hours my parents worked and how little they made, while their parents had set wages, salaries, and even healthcare. But I was young at the time and didn't know how to respond. I couldn't make a good enough argument, no matter how much I tried. I didn't understand why they couldn't see that I was in the same economic bubble as them. I knew it was more of a race factor than anything else, but I couldn't put my finger on how to explain it in a way they would understand. If anything, their parents had more of an advantage over the system than mine; my parents didn't speak English well, were immigrants, and didn't know how to navigate the system.

I also felt like a non-minority minority in college. You would think that people in a public university, especially professors, would be more conscious and aware of certain social contexts. In fairness, many were socially conscious, but I had many minor and a handful of major negative encounters during college, which might have been the case because I was double-majoring in sociology and urban studies. Common ones included having professors confuse me with other Asian female students, fellow students asking me for help with their homework because they thought I was smarter than everyone else, and everyone in class looking at me when any Asian topic came up in class.

When I spoke to some of my peers about these incidents, many of them told me that they were common, unintentional, and harmless mistakes. Apparently, I was overreacting, and to them, we all looked alike. Other friends who are children of recent immigrants tell me they can relate to me. Some of my other friends don't perceive me as being Asian, but as American. Queens College has a lot of Asians and immigrants in general, and a large population of students with visas. My friends would often ridicule their sense of style, inability to speak English, and other factors involved with their being immigrants. That always made me feel uncomfortable.

BEING AMERICAN KOREAN

In the middle of ninth-grade computer class, my teacher informed us that the Twin Towers had fallen thirty minutes earlier. Soon after, our principal announced over the loudspeaker that all students and faculty were to report to the auditorium for an emergency assembly. Everyone was confused and in shock. One girl immediately started crying. I later found out her father worked at one of the towers. As we walked down the stairs and into the auditorium, there was an odd but obvious mix of silence and low commotion. Gladys and I immediately sat next to each other as we watched the auditorium fill up with students and staff. The principal announced that two airplanes had crashed into the World Trade Center towers, causing them to fall, and in the process, killing many people.

Almost as soon as he had finished his sentence, Gladys started crying at the top of her lungs. I was shocked and I held her, thinking she must have known someone in one of the towers. I asked her if she knew anyone in the buildings, but she shook her head. I learned that she was crying because she had seen the Twin Towers as symbols of freedom and hope. She had immigrated to the United States from Guatemala when she was in second grade. She had lived through the terrible and slow immigration system on the path towards gaining citizenship. She took being a citizen very seriously, whereas I took it for granted. To Gladys, the World Trade Center was a symbol of being American.

I wondered why I wasn't as sad as her. After all, I was American and I was also thankful for freedom. Was I not American enough? But how could she possibly be that sad, seeing as how she was an immigrant? Yes, she considered America to be her home after living here for so many years, but I had lived here longer and I was born here, so why wasn't I as sad? Why didn't those thoughts cross my mind when I first heard about the incident? I realized later that it was because her family had fought for citizenship and experienced a long road of hardship to gain it, something I would never understand. I realized all of this much later. I remember at that point I felt ashamed of my emotions and reactions, confused about my identity and what it meant to be American, and unsure of how to console my best friend.

I questioned my Americanness, but I think I questioned my Koreanness even more. I didn't feel like I belonged with the other Korean students. I never did and I didn't think I would now. I couldn't talk to them about Korean pop culture or what the new Korean dramas were, I couldn't share which church I went to, because, at the time, I had stopped attending church regularly. I couldn't compare new designer handbags because I didn't have any, nor could I go shopping with them because my parents didn't have money to just throw away. I could never relate to that materialistic middle-class Korean-American mindset and day-to-day lifestyle. I don't know if their families were rich, but I knew that my parents were barely making it and still working seven days a week. I began to resent the middle-class Korean Americans that I was exposed to and the materialistic lifestyle they chose to live. So, what now? I'm apparently not American enough and now, I'm not Korean enough? What am I?

I know I'm Korean American, which is the social label used to describe American-born children with Korean parents. I know Korean American sounds much smoother than American Korean, but it doesn't make sense to me if I identify myself that way. American Korean is a more apt description because I identify myself as being American first and Korean second. I am American by birth, and being Korean is something I biologically inherited from my parents. I don't fully connect to everything in both American and

Korean culture because I live in two worlds and never fully got the chance to explore both because culture is constantly changing. I just can't keep up.

People think it's ironic that I work at a non-profit organization serving Korean Americans, given my rocky past with my co-ethnics. My friends and peers knew that I resented the middle-class Korean-American population that I grew up with, yet I was working to help them. It didn't make sense to them, and I myself wasn't so enthusiastic when I first walked into the office. Just to clarify, I didn't have a choice, and I had to take the internship at the organization for a fieldwork class or I couldn't graduate from college. I don't regret it because it ended up changing my life and my career path.

The organization opened my eyes and made me aware of a much larger Korean-American and Asian-American presence in New York City. I saw elderly Korean Americans living in poverty, and young Korean Americans struggling with similar issues and responsibilities as I had. I was exposed to only a fraction of the Korean-American community growing up. Without realizing it, my resentment for the middle-class Korean-American community faded and was replaced by shame, even for my own parents. The feeling of shame came from the middle class's lack of acknowledgment of the lower class. I wasn't sure if it was from pure ignorance, pride, or selfishness. Nevertheless, that feeling quickly faded, knowing that there wasn't a quick fix for the Korean community because there isn't much of what people would define as a community to begin with. I wasn't surprised. Korean Americans tend to care about their immediate families and not for the larger community. Many immigrant groups have a shared sense of community formed through common experiences from struggle, immigration, language, culture, and so on, but the Korean community in New York City lacks that and it's clear through the lack of representation in local government. I do acknowledge that this community is still growing and the process takes time.

After serving for two years as an AmeriCorps volunteer, my identity reshaped itself again as I started to think more progressively and became more aware of certain disparities around me. In my mind, I started piecing together the mental puzzle of inequality, discrimination, and poverty, in contrast to what I had previously been taught. And I worked not only with Korean Americans but also with many Asian Americans and non-profits that served Asian Americans. I realized that I had started thinking in a post-ethnic perspective, in the words of renowned psychologist Phillip L. Hammack, encouraging "awareness of the multiple identities that individuals inherently embody as they negotiate the discourse of their surroundings." I am now an advocate for the pan-Asian community, and my responsibilities include seeing commonalities among the needs of all Asian Americans. A lot of my identity has been shaped by community engagement and has allowed me to reflect on my life choices and how I was raised.

I also think it's ironic that my partner of the last six years is Korean American. I would have never seen this coming. I think it's ironic because of the nature of my relationship with Korean Americans prior to starting my career. However, it's not so ironic because his sense of identity (although it may not fully align with mine) and mentality regarding, race, ethnicity, and the idea of being a non-minority minority are similar. I think for the most part it's because he wasn't part of the New York City Korean community that I'm used to seeing. Being from Delaware with a smaller Korean-American community, his experiences, friendships, and identity were formed much differently than my own. You're probably wondering if he speaks Korean and likes Korean food. To clarify, he understands Korean very well but when he speaks, he sounds like an American who took an elementary Korean class in college. Our ability to speak and understand Korean does come in handy when I need to ask him an embarrassing question in public. When it comes to food, who doesn't love *galbi* (marinated beef short ribs)? But to answer your question, he prefers a good steak or a burger over rice with pickled side dishes. Does that make him any less Korean-American than me? I don't think so.

THE WAY I SEE

Being Korean is only a fraction of what makes up my identity. Although it's an integral part, being female, an advocate, educated, and American are as important, if not more important than my ethnic background. Who I should be to my family versus who I need to be are two completely different avenues that don't cross paths often. Being Korean isn't what is important to me, but wanting to understand my parents' culture, history, and language is. The main reason is so that I can understand them and their story better. That's the case even more so now because of my current career choice dedicated to advocating for underserved immigrant communities, including the Korean community.

The lens through which I see the Korean community now is different from before, but I would have never perceived it that way if I didn't have the experiences I lived through. The hardships and challenges the Korean-American and pan-Asian communities face are caused by political, social, and historical obstacles that are different from other minority groups. Although the Korean community is very different from other Asian communities, their needs are very similar. Adults who are limited-English-proficient need language assistance and education from the government and their agencies, while the youth need the basic tools in order to gain a higher education and have a more political and social conscience in order to be key leaders for the future of this nation. I see my parents' sacrifice for economic advancement through other immigrant parents, and I see youth struggling to understand themselves as I did. I would have never seen through this lens if I hadn't engaged with the community and learned about the many disparities that directly affect them or lived through my personal experiences. My identity would not be without the application of my past to the present, and my re-involvement with the Korean community.

V

Three Essays by Members of the Later Cohort

Chapter Ten

Miyeok guk for the Korean Soul

Helene K. Lee

In a series beginning in 1993, *Chicken Soup for the Soul* offered collections of stories designed to inspire readers by emphasizing the power of positive thinking and personal strength to overcome difficult struggles. Translated into over forty languages, they are sold around the world, spawning over two hundred titles tailored to a wide range of identities including children, mothers, fathers, teenagers, pre-teenagers, grandparents, college students, and teachers, as well as runners, cat-lovers, dog-lovers, sports-lovers, Christians, and even NASCAR enthusiasts. Noticeably absent are books targeted at communities that are at the margins of our society. I received one of these books as a high school graduation gift, but when I finished, I felt that the stories, while uplifting, didn't really reflect my own experiences. By focusing solely on the self-help doctrine of using individual solutions for problems in the world, this series ignores the systemic discrimination embedded in our society that shapes our encounters with racism, discrimination, poverty, homophobia, sexism, and nativism.

A critical look at the stories of second-generation Korean Americans offers a better way to understand how we make sense of our ethnic identities as individuals as well as a community more broadly. Stories passed down from generation to generation form the bridge between Korean Americans and the homeland and preserve what it means to be Korean, especially in the face of assimilation pressures in the United States As Korean Americans, we also tell our own stories about our experiences and struggles as first-generation born-and-raised Americans, whose experiences are qualitatively different from those faced by our immigrant parents. This paper analyzes stories of my own experiences with race, nationality, and gender that helped me navigate multiple identities as "American," "Asian American," "Korean," and "Korean American" at different periods in my life.

COMING TO AMERICA—MY PARENTS' PAST STORIES

"Oh, you're a buckeye!" said my friend's father when he heard that I was born in Ohio, a place I have no memories of since I've lived in California since I was five. I remembered thinking that was really cool because I imagined a buckeye was a graceful deer (I was cruelly disappointed to find out much later that a buckeye is actually a type of tree common in Ohio). I try to imagine what my parents must have felt, both younger than my age now, coming to this new, strange land with one small baby in tow and another one who would come along the next year.

Before immigrating to the U.S., my parents told me stories of how their families were lucky to be on one of the last boats that left North Korea for the South during the Korean War. Many family members were separated forever, like my grandfather who never saw his parents or brother again. After they married, my parents came to the U.S. with few financial resources, but with the hope that a better life could be made in this land of endless opportunities. The immigration story is important for second-generation Korean Americans like myself whose roots in the U.S. are fueled by an unerring faith in the economic, political, and social upward mobility that are hallmarks of the "American Dream."

I was the first in our family to be born in the U.S., the first "real" American. Even as our family settled into their new American lives, they still imparted a strong sense of Korean pride in my brother and me. Even if being different meant that we needed to work twice as hard to prove that we were just as good as anyone else, we were expected to do what it took to succeed. While we dutifully learned English in school and were encouraged to be as "American" as the other students, we could not forget that our blood and our family's roots were Korean. At home, we spoke Korean, ate Korean food, and played with friends whose parents were college classmates of my parents.

OF "FOBS," "TWINKIES," AND OTHER TERMS OF RACIAL OUTSIDERNESS

As a teenager, I often felt that I was in the no-man's land between Korean and American, left to carve my identity between the two paths of assimilation defined by the terms "twinkie" and "FOB." Twinkies, like the popular Hostess snacks, were "yellow on the outside, white on the inside." In other words, becoming American meant assimilating to a dominant U.S. culture rooted in whiteness. All traces of ethnic difference were downplayed or avoided. The social networks of twinkies were largely white and they avoided being associated with Korean Americans and other Asian Americans. Twinkies had very limited knowledge of Korean and were perceived negatively by other Korean Americans as being "too white" or "too American."

The other path also offered little hope. "FOBs" were "fresh off the boat," meaning their foreignness marked them as "too Korean" and inassimilable. In contrast to twinkies, the social networks of FOBs were 1.5-generation or fellow immigrants. Their accented English betrayed their foreign roots and they often spoke Korean with friends and family. FOBs were up-to-date on the latest K-pop sensations and Korean dramas, and FOB girls were overly interested in Hello Kitty and other Sanrio creations featuring cutesy animated characters with enormous eyes. Needless to say, twinkies and FOBs did not interact.

I never really felt like I had membership in either group, or maybe more accurately, I had elements of both of these identities. In some ways, I felt like a twinkie because I wasn't involved in the Korean church community in L.A. and had a lot of friends who were not Korean. My brother and I were reluctant attendees of Korean classes at our church to work on our reading, writing, and speaking skills, but our abilities never improved noticeably and we eventually joined the ranks of Korean school dropouts. But I also felt like a FOB, especially when my public and private worlds intersected. As a child, I squirmed with embarrassment when my parents would talk to my friends, teachers, or coaches, their accents and pronunciation so different from the standard diction of "real" Americans, which marked them as immigrants. I remember being self-conscious that our home smelled "weird"—of *kimchi* and *duenjang jjigae*—and we ate strange things like dried squid, seaweed, and fermented bean products.

The FOB/twinkie binary also spoke to the ways I understood the penalties of being non-white in the U.S. in the face of indirect and direct racism. From an early age, I learned that being too ethnic came at a large social cost, because popular kids were never FOBs. Public displays of Koreanness were to be avoided at all costs. During my teenage years, when image meant everything, I started to feel like expressions of ethnicity were safe only within the private realm of the home and family. Because of this heightened awareness of difference, my elementary, junior high, and high school social networks gravitated to other second-generation Asian Americans who understood the struggles of being both proud and ashamed of the differences that set us apart from "real" Americans.

Later, when L.A. exploded into violence in 1992, I realized that regardless of the degree to which we had assimilated into the dominant culture as FOBs or twinkies, Korean immigrants and Korean Americans could also instantly become a third status in the U.S., the "inassimilable outsiders."
Korean Americans as Public Enemy #1

I remember feeling a sense of panic and cold, hard fear when I saw the plumes of smoke around the city concentrated in the heart of Koreatown.

During a press conference, Rodney King, the victim of police brutality that sparked the uprising, said in a broken, tired voice, "Can't we all just get along?" With the acquittal of the four, mostly white LAPD officers, L.A. answered this question with a resounding "no." What I didn't expect was the central role that Korean immigrants and Korean Americans would play, and the ways that I felt implicated in the attacks and vulnerable as someone who didn't fully belong here.

As a city and as a nation, we watched images of looting and violence that reinforced the image of blacks and Latinos as instigators and Asians as victims. I remember a detached part of my brain noted that it was the first time that I saw Korean Americans represented on TV, but we were not glamorous, beautiful movie stars. We were armed, scared, and emphatically and undeniably foreign. Within the immigrant Korean community, I remember hearing rampant anti-black sentiments and racist ideologies, deflecting blame onto "poor blacks and Mexicans" rather than systemic racism. Up to this point, I had been largely protected in my bubble of class and race privilege. The L.A. Riots/Uprising planted the seeds of doubt in my mind about the American Dream, the bedrock of my parents' immigration stories. Instead, I started to see how this dream could be tarnished by patterns of structural racism in the U.S.

Who are You Rooting For? Are You Korean or American?

As avid soccer fans, a friend and I had gone to a local bar to watch the World Cup Soccer game in 2002 between the U.S. and South Korea. Rather than enjoying the close game between the two teams, we started to find ourselves dealing with blatant racism and nativism produced by the mix of alcohol and a packed, nearly all-white environment with American flags painted on people's faces. When it was apparent we were rooting for the South Korean team, we quickly became the focus of verbal attacks such as "Go back home" and "traitor" throughout the game. While my citizenship and nationality defined me as a born-and-raised American, my ethnic and racial difference was all that mattered inside that space. We left physically unscathed but emotionally unsettled. I felt a sense of helplessness and anger that at a moment's notice, my friend and I could feel unsafe and vulnerable. It was ten years after the L.A. Riots/Uprising and I felt that there had been little progress in race relations and nativism and the idea of who could be a "real" American.

THE CHALLENGES OF GENDER AND ETHNICITY

While I didn't quite feel like a "real" American because of my racial and ethnic identity, I also felt out of place in a Korean world, often because of my resistance to the perceived gender imbalance in our family and community. My parents were always referenced in relation to my older brother. They were "Sang's mom" or "Sang's dad," and it was me who was chastised if I didn't call him "*oppa*" (big brother) even though he could boss me around by my given name. I protested against the unfair division of reproductive labor at home, of me doing the dishes and helping out with the cooking or cleaning on a daily basis, while my brother was left alone. Later on, the challenges of being a Korean-American teenager came down to separating the "good" Korean girls from the "bad" ones.

"Scary" or "bad" Korean girls were extremely skinny, always wore black clothing, wore heavy makeup, were materialistic, status-conscious and very exclusive/cliquey, and drove black Hondas with tinted windows. On the flip side, "good" girls were the "super-Christians": obedient, avid churchgoers who took care of their younger siblings, always helped out in the home without complaining, and could peel an apple in an unbroken spiral. I wasn't particularly religious and didn't attend church regularly. I also didn't wear makeup or have any interest in shopping or keeping up with the latest fashions. Between the binaries of FOB/twinkie and scary/crazy Christian, I didn't belong in either of these undesirable, problematic extremes. Instead, I tried to distance myself from being "Korean," opting to cling to a more "American" identity that I perceived as racially and ethnically unmarked and not as patriarchal.

The Korean-American Dream Marriage—Why Can't You Find a "Good Korean Boy"?

As an adult, the expectations of being a good Korean girl were about the pressures to marry "well." A corollary to the general "American Dream" story was the "Korean-American Dream," which featured a future Korean-American husband who was a doctor, lawyer, or businessman, preferably with an Ivy League pedigree, from an upper-middle-class background. When I graduated from college without a Korean Prince Charming in tow, my mom constantly nagged me with the stories of the sons and daughters of her friends at Young Nak church who accomplished the "Korean-American Dream marriage."

In a paradoxical way, the pressures of living up to the American Dream by pursuing a career that required a high level of education became a barrier to the Korean-American Dream marriage. Even my mom, the most fervent supporter of higher education, admits that she believes Korean-American men are threatened by a wife who has more education than him, and my Ph.D. was an impediment to attracting the perfect mate. When I talk with other Korean-American women who have "failed" to marry the "good, Korean boy," they also felt blamed for this undesirable situation. As second-generation Korean-American women, we're perceived as too educated, too aggressive, too career-driven, and (gasp) too feminist to make for "good" Korean wives.

I found myself dismissing Korean Americans as potential dating partners, especially eldest or only sons, because I imagined they came with the demanding mothers who would not approve of me as a "good Korean wife," given my career ambitions and my divorced parents. When the topic of dating would come up with my second-generation heterosexual Korean-American friends, many shared similar apprehensions about Korean-American men because it meant being trapped in the patriarchal, traditional roles for women as dutiful daughters, subservient wives, and sacrificing mothers that dictated our households growing up. I had rebelled against the expectations of being a good Korean girl as a kid, so why would I sign up for a lifetime of that responsibility as an adult?

The different expectations between my mother and myself reflect the ways ethnic pressures and gendered expectations create a divide between second-generation Korean-American women and their immigrant parents, especially in terms of dating and eventually marrying someone within the community with the proper socioeconomic class background, educational attainment, high status professional lifestyle and, of course, compatible blood type (traditionally, Koreans and Japanese place a lot of emphasis on blood types in dictating personality and temperament). Complicating the conversation for many families is the growing numbers of interethnic and interracial relationships for second-generation Korean Americans.

As someone in a long-term interracial relationship with a white partner, I am highly conscious of the phenomenon of Asian fetishes, the hyper-exotic image of Asian women in U.S. culture, and the phenomenon of "yellow fever." I am aware that rates of intermarriage are rising very quickly in the Asian-American community, especially for women, and that a majority of these relationships are between Asian women and white men. I question whether I am contributing to this problematic pairing and struggle with being seen as "that" Asian woman who hates her own racial/ethnic Otherness—the ultimate twinkie or racial traitor who has betrayed her own kind. These patterns reinforce a hegemonic masculinity rooted in whiteness at the expense of the emasculated Asian man in U.S. society while simultaneously encouraging the sexualization and exoticization of Asian women.

After six years together and counting, the racial differences between my partner and myself belie the notion that "love sees no color." Instead, I am often conscious of our racial difference and the reactions it can elicit from friends, family, and the general public, and I find myself at times trying to "manage" our differences to make them less visible. Family visits are fraught with both direct and indirect reminders of the cultural differences between my immigrant family and his. These constant negotiations have not faded over time but have become part of the daily fabric of our lives as an interracial couple.

While my friendships were largely with other second-generation Asian Americans from elementary school through college, since graduate school, I have been drawn to people with progressive politics. This is heavily influenced by my graduate training in sociology and the types of people drawn to that field of study. As a whole, my social network is filled with people who are committed to confronting sexism, racism, homophobia, and nativism, and understanding the ways these oppressions are intertwined in common roots of fear and ignorance. Beginning in graduate school, my Korean-American identity became the basis of my stronger identification as a person of color and as an Asian American more broadly. As a result, my social networks have shifted to include whites, people of color, other second-generation Americans, queer and LGBT-identified people, and international or recently immigrated individuals.

BEING ASIAN AMERICAN AT WORK

The White Lady with Chinese Eyes — the Louisiana Years

In my first job after college graduation, I joined Teach for America as a special education teacher in a predominantly black, poor community in rural Louisiana. For those two years, I found myself getting schooled in the ways class and race created deep inequalities in housing, educational attainment, and the distribution of resources. Along with a growing awareness of structural inequalities, I also found my Asian-American identity to be a constant reference point of difference for whites and blacks alike.

It was a constant joke among my predominantly Black students that my uncle was the famous Chinese martial artist Bruce Lee, in part because he was the only Asian person they "knew." While I tried to explain the impossibility of this relationship since my family was Korean in origin, my students would often refer to me as the "white lady with Chinese eyes." I would respond that I was as white as they were, which is to say, I wasn't white at all. But to them, I talked like white people, I dressed like white people, and I didn't live in their community—the only difference was my Chinese eyes.

But my white co-workers and the people in town didn't see me as one of them. I may not have been black, but I certainly wasn't white either. I received compliments from my co-workers about my great English skills and curious questions about "where I was (really) from." From my students, I was often asked how to say random words in Korean to which they would just laugh loudly and say that it sounded funny and not like a real language. A co-worker confided in me that "your people are such hard-workers and never cause any problems" (unspoken: unlike our black students) while another woman at Wal-Mart asked me enthusiastically where I got my "wonderful Orientalness from," as if it were a product on sale in one of the aisles where she could pick it up. While professionally as a teacher, race wasn't a hindrance, my Asian Americanness felt like a constant burden. I was marked by a heightened visibility in which I existed outside of the dominant racial identities and was accepted by neither.

But You Don't Look like a Professor

I still teach, but now I am a college professor in a small, liberal arts school in Pennsylvania. The demographics of the campus reflect a predominantly white student body, and the numbers concerning the diversity of faculty, staff, and administrators are even less diverse. I came to my job through a post-doctoral faculty diversity fellowship offered nationally to help attract people of color to liberal arts colleges, which tend to be less diverse than state institutions and larger research universities. Teaching in this environment for the last three years has made me more conscious of my identity as a person of color as well as an Asian American, given the very low presence of both on campus.

While my privileged position as a professor largely protects me from egregious acts of racism and discrimination, there are subtle ways in which race and gender have shaped my experiences here. The most common form is being mistaken for a student by other students, staff members, and faculty members. The most infuriating example of this occurred when I covered an introductory sociology class for an absent colleague, a class I had taught multiple times in previous years. As the students worked on the in-class assignment, one of the students spurned my offer to help, saying brusquely, "You're just a senior sociology major, what do you know about this?" When I quickly asserted my authority as a professor in the department, the student immediately apologized, visibly mortified. But his initial reaction had already revealed the ways he had perceived and immediately dismissed me.

While incidents like that are rare, I am often subjected to the surprised, "Oh, you're a faculty member? You look so young, just like a student!" when putting books on reserve at the library, checking out equipment, dealing with enrollment issues at the registrar, and many other everyday actions. Other socially awkward interactions have included being asked to vacate the copy machine by a fellow faculty member who assumed I was one of the student office workers, or being asked by a parent after the commencement ceremony what I planned to do now that I had graduated, seeing me as one of their child's friends rather than a professor. These moments of mistaken identity have led to a heightened awareness of regulating my behaviors, the tone of my voice, and even my appearance, to give off a more professional vibe. But being told that I don't *look* like a professor implies there is an implicit assumption of what a professor does look like that is highly influenced by race, gender, and age, and that often carries over into questions about whether I have the intellectual qualifications to be a professor. And while people tell me to take comments about my youthful appearance as compliments, I see it as part of the constant struggles of legitimacy that women of color in academia face day after day, year after year, during their professional careers.

But there are also positive aspects about my job that rest on my strong identities as Asian American and a person of color. Offering the only class in the curriculum focusing on Asian-American communities has allowed me to engage with students, many of whom have never learned about the histories of migration of this largely invisible and extremely diverse group in the U.S. For the few Asian Americans in the class, it was one of the first times they saw their own experiences legitimated as a field of study. Being a mentor for students, especially students of color, has been one of the most rewarding aspects of being a professor. In the past year, I have served as the faculty advisor for a newly-formed Asian-American student group that has gained some visibility and a sense of identity for many of the Asian-American students on campus who felt disconnected from the dominant campus community.

HOMELAND SECTION: LIVING IN LIMINALITY

I joke that I have become a "professional" Korean American, whose research and teaching focuses on the construction of transnational identities particularly within diasporic and homeland relations. The intersection of my personal and professional interests was a serendipitous outcome of the year-and-a-half I spent in Seoul conducting my dissertation research. At first, negotiating the city on my own terms as an adult was empowering and exciting. My eyes took in the skyscrapers, the neon signs, the PC *bang* (24-hour Korean Internet rooms), and the throngs of people crossing the street and hustling onto the subway who all looked like me! I heard Korean on the radio and on the streets, and I watched drama programs that featured Korean actors, an unusual sight for my U.S.-born-and-raised self who rarely caught a glimpse of an Asian-American actor, much less one whose accent and behaviors did not serve as a way to ridicule Asians. I felt reconnected to my Korean identity because I was finally creating a personal relationship with a country that I knew very little about but had defined my identity growing up. At home, I would often encounter people who had never heard of South Korea or only referenced it to the Korean War. But I saw that South Korea was an economic, political, and cultural contender in the global economy in its own right, emerging from the long shadow cast by the U.S.

But the honeymoon soon came to an end as I started experiencing the ways that Korean Americanness was not perceived and accepted as "really" Korean. My poor language skills made me regret my lackadaisical attitude towards Korean school as a child (something I would never admit to my mother). My numerous blunders in mundane, everyday interactions were a constant source of embarrassment because I "looked" Korean but did not behave as such. Usually after a surprised pause, I got the "Oh, you're an American" remark, dripping with condescension, from the checker at the grocery store, the teller at the bank, the taxi driver, or even the bus driver when I awkwardly tried to ask whether I was going the right way. As long as I kept my mouth shut, I felt I could "pass" as Korean in a complete reversal from my childhood, when I deliberately talked in unaccented English to prove that I was a "real" American. The overwhelming feeling that I felt more American in Seoul complicated the connection I felt with South Korea. This feeling was echoed by Korean-American friends who also felt that they were trapped in a permanent, liminal state—in the U.S., they were seen as Korean, in South Korea, they were seen as American.

In an ironic twist, I had become the "FOB" I dreaded from my childhood. "Fresh off the boat" from the U.S., I clung to familiar ways, my strong American accent in Korean betraying my foreignness. For the first time since my childhood, my social networks were almost exclusively Korean American and we would immediately switch to English when together. I became the anti-"twinkie," perceived as American on the outside and yellow on the inside, negatively judged for assimilating too much into white culture and losing touch with my Korean roots.

I also learned a lot about the gendered expectations of what it meant to embody "desirable" and legitimate Korean femininity. In fact, gender became the most frustrating aspect of my time in Seoul and a key factor in the distancing I felt from my Korean roots. Like many of the Korean-American second-generation women I interviewed, I constantly felt that I was alternately seen as "too fat," "too dark," and "too independent" by my South Korean family relatives, co-workers, and acquaintances. My decision to live on my own after a disastrous three-month stay with my grandmother created a tidal wave of disapproval that traveled across the Pacific to my mother in California. As an unmarried, single woman, I was expected to live with relatives as dictated by tradition, but I was too Americanized and not brought up properly to perform like other "good" Korean girls.

It wasn't just my family, but also my everyday observations of South Koreans that made me feel out of place. It was as if clones of the "scary" Korean girl from my teenage years populated the streets of Seoul. These women were distressingly thin, extremely pale, and impeccably dressed in the latest styles dripping with status markers of Louis Vuitton and Burberry. I lived near Sinchon-dong, an area near Ewha and Yonsei Universities, and watched in horror as young women demonstrated *aegyo* by childishly shaking their shoulders, stamping their feet, pouting and whining in a high voice, "*Oppaaaaaa.*"

As my initial dissertation project slowly dissolved and left me contemplating my life chances as a grad school dropout, a chance meeting with a key contact introduced me to a church and NGO in Seoul that offered legal, financial, travel, dining, temporary shelter, and religious services for ethnic Koreans from China, known as Joseonjok (Korenas living in China). It was the first time I had heard about Joseonjok and their plight. Over the next year, I gathered their stories of social discrimination and stigma while in Seoul, and realized there were commonalities as well as important differences with the Korean-American experience. Even though both Korean Americans and Joseonjok were Korean by blood and could trace their roots to the Korean peninsula and strongly identified with it as their ancestral homeland, they were often not seen as "real" Koreans by South Koreans. Particularly for Joseonjok, who came as labor migrants, their undocumented status in South Korea and the social and legal discrimination they endured made them feel less a part of the Korean family as *dongpo* and more Chinese.

I found myself identifying with some of the alienation Joseonjok felt and the complications of moving to a country where I was simultaneously familiar and foreign. I arrived in Seoul with romantic notions of instant belonging and acceptance—that after a lifetime of dealing with racism and discrimination as a racial outsider, I would be in a country where I was an insider. But my experiences in Seoul added more complicated layers to my earlier struggles around what it meant to be a "real" Korean and a "real" American. I realized that the hybrid condition of being simultaneously Korean and not Korean is what defines diasporic Korean communities around the world, whether they are Joseonjok or Korean American. Rather than limiting ourselves to the impossible goal of assimilating 100% to one nation or another, I think that "home" might be in the diasporic space "betwixt and between" nations where belonging and authenticity are more fluidly constructed.

CONCLUSION: *MIYEOK GUK* FOR OUR KOREAN-AMERICAN SOULS

While there is no official "Chicken Soup" for our souls, I think that we can tell our own stories and use them to empower and uplift our own community. Only our volume would feature *miyeok guk*, a popular Korean soup made from seaweed traditionally eaten on birthdays. As a community, we would be nourished and strengthened by our immigration stories, our common struggles with racism and discrimination, the ways gender and ethnicity impact our social networks and intimate relationships, and our negotiations between

American and Korean identities. The overarching theme across these stories is about the ongoing identity crisis of never fully belonging in either the U.S. or South Korea. They speak to the need for second-generation Korean Americans to pave our own future paths rather than getting stuck between unachievable extremes. We will never be (white) Americans, nor do we want to. We will never be "real" Koreans in a South Korean sense, nor do we want to. But we must think about how to create legitimacy and belonging as Korean Americans that encompass the broad spectrum of identities within it. Our demographics reflect our diversity: we are adoptees, biracial/multiracial, 1.5/second/third generation, some of us have the highest professional degrees possible while others have none. We come from intact families and broken ones, we are straight and queer. What is clear is that there isn't one "perfect" way to be Korean American. Rather than accepting the standard that we all must strive to be like the others, we, as second-generation Korean Americans, can break through the conventional narratives defined by dichotomies of American/Korean, men/women, and twinkie/FOB to create new spaces where all of us can belong as Korean Americans, despite our differences.

Chapter Eleven

Anyone Ever Tell You That You Look Like . . . ?

Dave Hahn

Ethnic identity is something I've struggled with my entire life. I was born in Piscataway, New Jersey, in 1977, to two Korean immigrants. I currently live in Atlanta, Georgia. For the past five years, I have worked as an Encoding Specialist at a large multi-national media company. My parents earned college degrees in Korea (which any Korean will tell you is an impressive feat) and moved to the United States separately in the late 1960s.

Growing up in New Jersey, which is largely a suburb of New York City and Philadelphia, exposed me to cultures from around the world. As much as I would like to picture the various cultures of New Jersey getting along like in a Coca-Cola commercial, this is not the case. Ethnic communities tend to be insular. They have their own shops, community centers, and places of worship. Most of my experience with Korean culture comes from what I observed at home while living with my parents. Unfortunately, most of what I've retained over the years is a weak grasp of the language and a fond connection to the food. My mother, like many Korean Americans, is a devout Christian and attends church multiple times throughout the week and every Sunday. Like many Korean-American children, the church was my first exposure to Korean-American communities.

KOREAN CHURCH

Some of my earliest memories consist of the time we spent with our first congregation in Morristown, New Jersey. Our congregation rented the church in the late afternoon, after the services of the primarily affluent Caucasian congregation's morning services had concluded. This was one of my first experiences feeling like Korean Americans were an underclass. It felt strange that we had to have our services late in the day, and it definitely felt like a borrowed experience worshipping in a large building with photos of unfamiliar people on the walls. Being so young, I was unaware of any of the circumstances surrounding the arrangement of the shared church space or the relationship between the two congregations, but I distinctly remember feeling like our group was different and lesser than the group that had services before ours.

This was my first experience with a larger Korean-American community, and it would frame my relationship with the community at large for the rest of my life. I attended that first Korean church in Morristown until I was eight years old. While there, I met Brian Chang, my first Korean friend. His family was distinctly different from my own. My father worked constantly, and my family dynamic was dysfunctional, but Brian's family seemed to be the opposite of mine in that regard. One key difference between his father and my own was that his father had an excellent command of the English language, whereas my father did not. His father was far more social, and therefore, learned the English language and customs far faster than mine had.

I believe that Korean-American communities are largely faith-based, so for my entire life, it has been difficult for me to participate in them. I am interested in non-religious Korean groups but they seem to be few and far between. When I went to college at Rutgers, there were plenty of Korean-American student groups, but they were predominantly faith-based, so I avoided them, partially because I had a negative experience with religious youth groups when I was a teenager. Against my wishes, my mom had sent me to a Korean-American youth group camp when I was thirteen. Prior to this camp, youth groups seemed more or less like play groups. We had spent most of our time playing in a sandbox and engaging in Bible studies. However, at this retreat, a more serious goal was sought: the concept of being a born-again Christian. Religious zealotry was on full display.

In the beginning, it seemed like a typical summer camp. We had Bible studies, ate Korean food, and had lots of recreation time. Towards the end of the retreat, things started to get strange. The evening services became more intense, as the congregation sought to have teens and pre-teens confess their sins in order to become born-again Christians. One night, I walked into the middle of an ongoing late-night service, and kids were writhing on the floor and supposedly speaking in tongues. It was like a scene from a bizarre Southern Baptist revival, and it left a bad taste in my mouth. After that retreat, I had no interest in maintaining a strong relationship with the church, because I saw it as an organization of emotional manipulations preying on the uncertain and insecure feelings of teenagers.

At some point, my family stopped attending our church in Morristown and we didn't go to any church for about a year. During that time, I began attending a weekly Korean school that was closer to Piscataway. This Korean school, an offshoot of the Korean church that it shared a building with, was supposed to be non-religious and more educational. I think this was the first time I really felt alienated by a Korean-American group. Everyone in the school already knew each other because they also attended the church, and I was just the kid who showed up on Saturday to attend Korean school. To be fair, I associated my alienation with being the "new kid." It obviously had nothing to do with my ethnicity since we were all Korean. However, I do think this experience laid the groundwork for my dislike of Asian-American groups at large, since this was my first experience being alienated from any group. At home, I had my neighborhood friends to play with. I felt very comfortable socially with my friends of different backgrounds and at that young age, we had no real understanding of ethnic differences.

Years later, my family began attending the same church that was associated with the Korean school. At this point, I had not attended the Korean school for several years, so my former Korean school classmates whom I had known as elementary school kids had grown to be teenagers like me. But there was a stark difference between myself and these kids, because they had defined and continued their social networks largely within the Korean-American church community, and were heavily involved in the church youth group when I was reunited with them. I had continued to develop social bonds with non-Koreans in my town, becoming completely Americanized by the time I was in middle school. I was very different from the kids in the youth group. By this point, I had lost most of my Korean-language skills, was not religious, and did not identify much with Korean culture. I was also in a somewhat rebellious teenage phase, so church did not seem especially attractive to me. My experiences at this particular church turned out to be my last encounter being a regular member of a large Korean-American group. After that, I went off to college at Rutgers University, and never regularly attended church again.

LOSS OF KOREAN LANGUAGE

Although my parents primarily spoke Korean at home, I spent an extensive amount of time socializing with non-Koreans. As a result, my grasp of the Korean language is virtually non-existent. I can only speak on a very basic level (mostly greetings and goodbyes), and I cannot read or write Korean at all. This is also partially the result of my oldest sister being raised to learn Korean. When she entered elementary school, her command of English was poor, so my parents were advised to raise me and my sisters to speak more English, so we would have an easier time in American schools. My parents did as they were advised, which led to the death of my grasp of the Korean language.

My father and I have always had a language barrier, because of his poor grasp of English and my minimal knowledge of Korean. We can communicate basic conversational thoughts to each other fairly easily, but we have trouble expressing more complex ideas or having in-depth conversations. As I get older, I regret this more and more, because I realize that it limits by ability to fully connect with Korean people and culture, including my father.

In middle school, a Korean student from South Korea transferred to my school. On his first day, I was called down to the principal's office because the kid couldn't speak English. The administration knew that I was Korean, and thought that I could translate for them. They were sadly disappointed to see that my grasp of the Korean language was absolutely pathetic. This student became the "weird foreign kid" at my school. I felt that I had to distance myself from him, so the other kids wouldn't associate me with him. I didn't feel too bad about this, simply because middle school is a socially brutal place, and it can get a bit like *Lord of the Flies* with boys at that age. However, looking back, it would have been nobler of me to embrace this kid and get him integrated into school instead of making him the pariah.

SUBURBAN KIDS, FRIENDS, AND DATING

Growing up in Piscataway, I had a very close and diverse group of friends. We joked that we were as ethnically diverse as the United Nations. The core group included me, a Jew, an Egyptian, a Hispanic, two African Americans, and a British kid, who was my childhood best friend. Being such close friends and coming from such diverse backgrounds, we enjoyed pointing out our cultural differences and ruthlessly mocking each other for them. I always felt much closer to these friends than I did to the Korean kids at church. Having such a diverse group of friends, I felt that homogeneous ethnic groups of friends were somewhat insular and dorky. At that point in my life, connecting with my ethnic identity was not high on my priority list, so when I went to college and saw the Korean or Asian kids walking in packs, they seemed like part of a culture that I didn't belong to. Throughout my college years, I maintained my friendships with my ethnically diverse group of friends.

Some of my feelings of not wanting to join Asian-American groups derived from my desire to blend into larger mainstream American society. I think that homogeneous gatherings of ethnic groups draw extra attention to themselves as an isolated group from mainstream American society. Any ethnic group that went out in public together in 1980s America can tell you that they often drew the ire of Caucasians when going out in public. I think this is still the case for many ethnic groups, but such instances are less frequent and overt.

I remember one particular church outing to a bowling alley when I was five years old. I was clumsy, and I slipped on the floor as I tried to roll the ball, so I fell down. My church group thought it was funny and cute. Being only five, I loved the attention, so I kept hamming it up and continued to slip on the boards. Apparently, our group's laughter and enjoyment drew the attention of the management, and we were reprimanded and ordered to not let me slip anymore because it would "damage the lane." This was ridiculous, because I was incapable of doing any actual damage to the lane. I was a small child throwing a ball that weighed five pounds, and I was wearing typical bowling shoes. I distinctly remember feeling that our group was singled out amongst the other bowlers simply because of our ethnicity. I have bowled a lot I my life, and I've seen white families bowl, and watched their kids slip and fall all day long. This is not an unusual occurrence at a bowling alley, so I don't think it is unfair to say that our church group encountered a subtle form of racism that day. I think these kinds of experiences happen less frequently in post-racial America, but in the back of my mind I still have this feeling of being watched, singled out, and defined as different when I'm out in public with a group of Koreans.

However, this does not mean that I did not seek to connect with other people who shared a similar experience to mine. Over the years, I've had numerous friends of Asian descent, including Chinese, Filipinos, Vietnamese, and Japanese. One experience we had in common was that everyone thought we were Chinese (I suppose the Chinese guy didn't mind this too much). Asian Americans generally all understand being perceived as "chinks." The racial divisions that exist in Asia largely disappear in America simply because we have a shared racist experience here. I work at a huge media company now, and there are a handful of Asian employees, and we are all specifically aware of the other Asians in the building. When we pass each other in the hallways, we acknowledge each other by exchanging head nods, even though a lot of us don't work together or know each other. These head nods are silent gestures of Asian solidarity, kind of like invisible fist bumps.

Ironically, my current best friend is Korean American. I met him at a summer camp in Korea when I was in tenth grade. We have been friends for nearly twenty years, and we celebrate our Korean identity in subtle, unspoken ways. We eat Korean food at restaurants frequently, and although we speak English to each other and are both culturally Americanized, we are proud of our heritage. However, most of the things we do have very little to do with being Korean, which is why I think we're such good friends. We silently enjoy the brotherhood of our shared ethnic identity without having to directly address it.

Not surprisingly, my parents have encouraged me to date Korean girls, in the hopes of marrying one. However, at this point in my life, my parents just want me to get married to anyone (except a black or Indian woman, because they're somewhat racist), but they would be ecstatic if I started dating a Korean girl. Thus far, I have only dated Caucasian girls. However, I don't have anything against dating Korean or Asian girls. In fact, I think Korean women are some of the most beautiful women in the world. Some of my earliest and most memorable crushes were on Korean females. However, I'm not around a lot of them, and when I am, it's in a religious context. Since I'm not religious, I don't end up meeting many dateable Korean girls. Sometimes when I go out to eat *bulgogi*, I see young attractive Korean women. I am attracted to these girls, and I would be happy to date them. However, I'm not within the social circle to really do so. This doesn't stop my mom from continuing to pester me about getting married and trying to set me up with girls in her church. She still does this even though I live in Atlanta and she lives in New Jersey.

Looking back, when I initially started dating girls, I did not have any interest in pursuing Korean girls for a number of reasons. The first reason was rebellion. I didn't want to do anything that would bring my parents that much joy. If I brought one Korean girl home, my parents would forever pressure me to marry that girl. Additionally, I think I wasn't interested in Korean girls because I was still coming to grips with my ethnic identity. "Would having a Korean girlfriend make me too Asian?" That's the kind of stupid self-hating thoughts that would swirl in the back of my mind.

Most of my post-college social life has been in hip American circles of slackers, artists, and musicians. Because of their assimilation into non-ethnic American culture, Asians in these groups tend to date non-Asians, and I'm no exception. In these social circles, people tend to be more open-minded, liberal, and progressive in their political and social thinking. Many seem to have a real interest in exploring cultural differences, and my ethnicity is not seen as a negative quality, so I feel very comfortable in these settings. However, as I grow older, I am feeling an urge to reconnect with Korean culture, and I am open to the idea of being in a serious relationship with a Korean woman, as long as she doesn't want me to go to church.

KARATE, MATH, AND OTHER STEREOTYPES

Although I don't like being generalized or categorized by mainstream America, I don't think Asian stereotypes are the worst. They are more positive than stereotypes associated with blacks or Latinos of being less intelligent, criminal minded, and lazy. Asian stereotypes reinforce the model minority myth. We are seen as hard-working, industrious, and quiet. We are also allegedly great at math and science, and our women are the sexual fantasy of Western men, whereas our men are viewed as asexual martial artists or computer programmers.

I am annoyed at the American media's portrayal of Asian men as not being sexually virile. I recently saw an online dating site commercial, where two white women were shopping in a frozen food aisle in a grocery store. However, instead of frozen food, there were men in the freezers, and the women were picking what kind of man they wanted. They eventually picked the "spicy" choice, and grabbed a Latino man from the freezer. I was offended but not surprised to see that every race except for Asians were portrayed in this commercial. While I'm not too torn up to be excluded from this terrible commercial, it is nonetheless an indicator of how mainstream American culture perceives Asian-American men.

Overall, Asian men aren't portrayed in the most positive light in American media. Sadly, portrayals of Asian men have not progressed much since the days of *Sixteen Candles*' Long Duk Dong, an offensive caricature of a nerdy, sex-crazed Asian exchange student with an exaggerated ambiguous Asian accent. Looking at the acting career of Ken Jeong (*The Hangover*) confirms this. Just the other day, I was in a gas station and the clerk asked me if anyone ever told me I looked like the guy from *The Hangover,* and insisted I say a line from the movie. I said the line to placate him. I did not find this to be humiliating so much as annoying and typical of random American ignorant behavior. But any Asian man can tell you they experience similar interactions on a regular basis. Really, I should have just told this guy to fuck off— he was Black and should have known better. Ironically, I usually encounter the most overt racist behavior from other minorities, mostly blacks and Hispanics.

I have been approached by people saying I look like a variety of Asian male entertainers, including William Hung, Bruce Lee, Jet Li, and the guy from the show *Heroes*. Apparently, I look just like any Asian on TV or in the movies. Once, when I was reporting a lost license plate to a police officer at the station, he asked if anyone ever told me I looked like William Hung. For the record, I look nothing like William Hung. Another time, while ordering a Guinness, a bartender told me I looked like the guy from *Heroes*. Again, I look nothing like this individual except for the fact that we're both Asian.

In the interest of not completely demonizing the media industry, I do believe there are actors in Hollywood busting stereotypes of Asian males. Daniel Dae Kim and John Cho have made strides as being sexually attractive leading men types. And I tip my hat to them for that. I appreciate these actors for being selective about their roles and not grabbing every stereotyped role where they're a computer programmer.

I have had a number of interactions with people that display a complete lack of tact and a total display of ignorance. On a hot summer day, a security guard at my work asked me, "Where's your hat? I thought your people always wore hats in this weather." I said, "I don't need one." As I was walking away I realized that he was referring to a rice farmer hat. Another time, a security guard looked at my driver's license and asked how I got the name David. I told her that it was from the Bible. She replied, "Oh! That's interesting! Your people don't typically have normal names."

These kinds of interactions with the public have shaped my understanding of my Asian-American ethnic identity. I am viewed and defined as an outsider to mainstream American culture. On a regular basis, I am asked, "Where are you from?" I understand that is a loaded question that inherently pigeonholes me as an outsider. When someone asks me this, I know that they are inquiring about my specific ethnic background. I do not like the nature of this question, so in my own subtle way of informing the questioner of his/her insensitivity, I'll answer, "New Jersey," and proceed with a boring five-minute discussion about New Jersey, thereby forcing them to rephrase the question. I have this exact interaction at least once a month.

I am occasionally reminded of my outsider status even at my job. We make lots of internal corporate videos (we are a multinational media corporation after all) and I frequently get asked to be in our videos as on-screen talent. Every time I'm requested to do this, I know it's probably going to be a video where they want a multicultural look. While I do find it humorous that I'm asked to participate in these videos solely because of my ethnicity, it is a reminder that I am distinctly a minority in the company, singled out to promote "diversity."

PARENTAL UNITS

This essay would not be complete without discussing my parents' influence on me, because they had a hand in every aspect of the formation of my ethnic identity. They have been married my entire life, but I was raised primarily by my mom since my dad worked at night. My mom worked in the Revlon factory and as a cleaning lady at Rutgers. She worked during the day and came home right after I did from school. My father, a pharmacist, worked from 2:30 PM and didn't return home until after midnight, seven days a week. My parents' work ethic is definitely something that has been imparted to me, and it is something I associate as a Korean-American quality. I recognize that an intense work ethic is largely a quality of immigrant groups regardless of ethnicity: just go to any top medical school and look at the student roster. As I've met more people over the course of my life, I've come to realize that I share a similar experience to anyone who is the child of first-generation immigrants. The clash of ancestral versus American culture, the desire to have their children retain a connection to their ancestral culture, and the instilled intense drive to succeed in traditional areas of success, such as law, business, and medicine, are commonalities among most immigrants.

In this regard, my parents were typical. My father pushed me to study hard, so I could become a doctor or lawyer when I grew up. I was strongly encouraged to perform well academically, but I did not receive a lot of positive reinforcement. Rather, I was made to feel a sense of disappointment for not living up to expectations if I didn't produce the desired results (straight A's). While this tactic of persistently pushing one's children to succeed academically worked for some, it did not really work for me. I had many non-Asian friends who were raised in more traditional American households that placed less emphasis on excelling academically. Upon seeing this, I was not pleased with how I was being raised and the expectations that were being projected onto me, so I rebelled by applying myself just enough to place into top classes in middle and high school, but not enough to actually achieve great grades.

By the time I went to college, it became obvious that I was not going to be fulfilling their lofty career aspirations for myself. As a result of my parents' influence, my two older sisters had both entered college as pharmacy majors. However, they both dropped out due to being incredibly unhappy entering a field solely to please my parents. By the time I went to college, my parents were terrified about what effect their influence might have on my success in college, so they let me pick what I wanted to do. My grades in high school were not great, and my parents had grudgingly accepted that I wasn't going to an Ivy League school. When I told them I was going to major in Communication Studies to work in TV or film, they were not pleased, but they didn't tell me what to do, which is not to say that they didn't express doubts about my chosen path.

After graduating from Rutgers, I had a series of underwhelming freelance jobs in the media industry, and my parents never failed to inform me of their disappointment, particularly my father. He didn't think that a job without 401K and health benefits was legitimate. Even when I got a job at my current company, one of the largest media companies in the world, they still didn't think it was good enough, because I initially worked as a freelancer. A few years ago, I finally got a staff position, and since then, my relationship with my parents has vastly improved, due solely to the fact that I have health benefits and a 401K. This seems completely unreasonable and insane to me, although, admittedly, I am happy that my parents are proud of me. My mother is happy now that she can brag to her friends at church that I work at a big media company that everyone knows about.

My parents also had many aspirations about who my friends would be and who they wanted me to date. Besides trying to influence what kinds of people I should associate with (all Koreans, basically), my parents spent a good deal of effort exposing me to Korean culture. In addition to sending me to the Korean school that I hated, they also sent me to Korea twice by myself for entire summers when I was in fourth and tenth grade. I studied Tae Kwon Do for several years, and eventually earned a first degree black belt. My mom also forced me to attend Korean Christian youth groups up until I went to college.

I am not unfamiliar with Korean culture. As I've gotten older, I've had the chance to become more comfortable with my Korean ethnicity, and at this point in my life, although I am very Americanized, I am completely proud to be Korean. But this was not always the case. Part of it was due to my feelings of shame of being Korean and having my differences shoved in my face and forcing me to embrace it. As an impressionable teenager, it's difficult to embrace being different. Teenagers want to fit in and will desperately do anything to achieve this. Being Korean and embracing my differences when I was one of the only Korean kids in school was a difficult teenage concept to grasp.

PERCEPTIONS OF MY HOMELAND

I've been to South Korea three times in my life. I have very little recollection of my first visit, since I was just a baby. The second and third time, I went to a summer program that I believe was sponsored by the Korean government to get Koreans kids living abroad acquainted with Korean culture. This program was like a summer camp where we took Korean language lessons and classes about Korean culture. Since I don't speak Korean well, there was a considerable language barrier. My perception of Korea at the time was that of a strange and other-worldly place where the American dollar stretched far to buy myself snacks and toys. As bad as my grasp of the language has always been, I have never felt rejected by Koreans anywhere, either in the United States or in Korea. There's always been encouragement from every Korean person I meet to immerse myself in more Korean culture and to tie myself more into the community at large.

In the past, I thought of Korea as a developing nation, living in the shadow of Japan and China. Lacking the manufacturing strength of China or the technological prestige of Japan, it was hard to be proud of Korean products in the 1980s and 1990s. Hyundai was known for cheap and crappy hatchbacks, and Korean consumer electronics were virtually non-existent. Things have changed dramatically in recent times, as Hyundai manufactures all kinds of cars as a respected brand, and companies like Samsung and LG have dominated the consumer electronics field to the point where Sony and Panasonic have both recently announced they'll be scaling back TV production. I am happy about this. For a long time, I've envied how enamored Americans are with Japanese and Chinese culture: sushi, samurai culture, anime, film, video games, art and design, and so much more. Admittedly, I enjoy all of these aforementioned aspects of Chinese and Japanese culture too. But I also felt like Korea got none of that love. Culturally, I think Korea is still catching up, but tremendous strides have been made. There are Korean movies that are regularly released that are regarded as "cool" by international audiences, which used to never happen, because Japanese and Hong Kong films were regarded as the cool ones. Americans love Korean food now, and it's not unusual for me to meet people who enjoy eating Korean food without being accompanied by a Korean person. The recent popularity of the Korean taco is testament to Korea's increasing popularity and influence. It makes me happy and proud that the general American public is finally enjoying and consuming real Korean culture.

CLOSING REMARKS

I admit that in some ways, I'm a living and breathing stereotype. I'm an Asian male who loves video games, knows martial arts, and works at a multinational media company in a technical capacity. Yes, I work with computers. Maybe I'm a self-hating Asian, and that's why I don't hang out with a lot of other Asian people. There will always be a little bit of that in the back of my mind. Every Asian American has experienced what it feels like to be treated like a "chink," and we're wary of being perceived as such. I am very comfortable with who I am now. When I was twenty-three, I got a tattoo on my right shoulder of a painting of eagles by the Korean artist Jang Seung-Op. People always ask me what the meaning behind it is, like I have some kind of secret Asian mystical metaphysical Buddhist meaning to it or something. I tell them it's just a painting that I liked. When I decided to get the tattoo, that's all it was. But it is also a symbol of the journey of the embracement of my heritage and a proud display of the beauty of Korean culture.

Chapter Twelve

Family Matters

Emerging Adulthood and the Evolution of My Ethno-Racial Identity

Sung S. Park

1984: I peered into the neonatal unit of the hospital, looking fearfully at my newborn brother. Five years my junior, at the time I thought, *he is zero years old*! To my relief and amazement, he looked just like me. I had been worried that since he was going to be born in the U.S., as opposed to being born like my parents or me in South Korea, he was therefore "American" and would look like an American. That is, he would look white. For the many months during my mother's pregnancy, I was excited about the possibility of having a playmate, but even as a child, I had a nagging feeling that something would not be quite right. How would people outside of our family know my sibling would be related to me since we wouldn't look the same? At age five, I equated citizenship with a specific racial or ethnic phenotype. I relayed this discovery to my parents, who laughed it off, saying we were all certainly Korean. Although their answer seemed straightforward and correct at the time, since then, I've challenged, changed, (re)defined, and (re)asserted my identity, knowing full well that there would be no single term that would encompass who I am today, and relatedly, who my family is.

Everyone is born into a family. On paper, my family's profile is similar to other Korean families. My parents owned a grocery store, we went to church, and I grew up mainly in various Queens neighborhoods where many Asian families resided. Over the course of my life, I have struggled to understand and clearly define my identity as American, Korean, Korean American, or even generically, "Asian" or "Asian American." However, even to this day, being a thirty-four-year-old woman, I do not have a consistent answer for the most sensitive questions: "What are you?," "Where are you from?," and "What is your background?" but pause for a moment before eventually responding with "I was raised in the United States and my parents are from South Korea."

This answer seems to satisfy inquirers just enough. It hints at the possibility of my personal struggles growing up as a second-generation daughter of immigrant parents, but precludes consideration of the fact that these struggles are never wholly resolved (nor, as I have learned, are they necessarily meant to be). In retrospect, my identity has been shaped by the consequences of my personal feelings of "otherness" that was neither American nor Korean, which then led to my isolation from most other Koreans except my parents. Consequently, until my late twenties, my desire to "be Korean" was synonymous with my desire to please my parents. It has only been through the development of personal relationships with other Koreans that I have begun to differentiate the relationship I have with my parents from my Korean identity.

ALL I REALLY NEED TO KNOW I LEARNED IN KINDERGARTEN

I immigrated to the U.S. with my parents at the age of one, and we lived in Queens. At that time, my grandmother took care of me while my parents worked sixteen hours a day, every day, at their grocery store. I spent most of the day with her, where she did various chores around the apartment. My grandmother explained how to make different Korean dishes as she was preparing them at the kitchen table. I helped with smaller tasks alongside her as she cleaned the apartment. She taught me how to sew. We conversed in Korean, all while I waited for my parents to come home from work. I wouldn't see them every day, as I was usually asleep by the time they got home, but I remember those rare occasions when I did see them.

By the time I was old enough to attend school, my parents were under the impression that the public school in our neighborhood was inferior to Catholic schools in terms of safety and the quality of instruction. Hence, despite our family not being Catholic, I started my education at a Catholic school in Astoria. I recall attending class my first day and realizing that there was only one other Korean as well as one African-American student in my class. I (and my non-white peers) experienced various types of tormenting from white classmates. In particular, students made comments about my looks and lack of English fluency. They told me I was Chinese, that I should marry my "cousin" (the other Korean student who happened to be male) and that I didn't belong there.

Given these unpleasant encounters, my immediate four-year-old's thinking was to stop attending school. I pretended to be sick, but my grandmother only believed this story the first time. She must have discussed this with my parents, and my mother eventually went to the teacher. She spoke with the nun who seemingly had no idea why I was having difficulties adjusting and had no friends. There was no particular resolution to the matter at hand. For the remainder of the year, I remember going to school every day with a heavy heart and a strong sense of trepidation.

Due to my difficulties in school, my parents invested in a tutor to teach me English after school. My father felt strongly that English proficiency was an integral part of my success in the U.S. I practiced speaking English to my parents every day and mimicking words with the proper intonation I heard from TV shows. My Korean was quickly replaced with my English sentences when speaking with anyone and everyone. The conversations with my grandmother slowly became one-way exchanges—I spoke less to my grandmother and just listened to whatever she had to say. Despite my improvements in English, I never really made any friends in Catholic school. To my relief, my family moved to Rego Park a year and a half later, and I ended up in a public school.

I was surprised on my first day at public school to see so many non-white faces in my class. I was initially placed in ESL, but quickly left after they decided I had exhibited English fluency. I felt comfortable in this school, where I was one of many non-white students, whose parents came from all over the world. These students were new to the U.S., struggling to learn English—exactly how I felt a couple of years earlier. Almost immediately, public school suited me well, as I made friends of varying backgrounds. My two best friends were Chinese and African American. Although there were some Korean students in my classes, they were mostly male students, who I did not develop close relationships with during those early years.

GOODBYES

Halfway through my elementary school experience, my grandmother left to move in with my father's brother who had just arrived to New York with his wife and two children. To me, this was a significant event for two reasons. First, given my parents' long working hours, she was the only connection I had to my Korean heritage, and secondly, because my role as my brother's sitter became even more important than before. Although my brother and I were taken care of for the next five years by live-in Korean babysitters while my parents worked, my perception was just that—they were just babysitters—and not family. Their responsibilities were limited to domestic chores and ensuring we were not in any immediate danger, while my responsibility was to make sure my brother was taken care of, in terms of helping with his schoolwork and overall well-being. Since my brother and I really only spoke English, our conversations with these babysitters were limited.

My brother had almost no understanding of Korean since he spent most of his time with me. He and I spoke to my parents in English, while they responded to us in a mixture of Korean and English. In conversing with them, I started to realize that I could still understand what they were saying to me, but had lost most of my fluency in speaking Korean. I remembered certain words but had difficulties putting grammatically correct sentences together. However, at the time, I did not see my language loss in a negative light, as my parents were both becoming increasingly fluent in English, particularly my mother. In fact, she had lost most of her Korean accent and could communicate in English much more easily than my father. Later on, I would find out that she had been particularly diligent about learning to speak English.

Every day, my mother would write down specific English responses and their Korean translations, in order to more readily communicate with her customers and vendors. I observed that customers would treat her differently than my father and other Korean workers, just based on her ability to answer their questions or to even recognize that they were making a joke and appropriately laugh. I saw time and time again that she could negotiate better with vendors to get the bulk discounts she needed. She argued, and most importantly, won, with companies that overcharged her on bills. Furthermore, a few years earlier, she had applied for and received her U.S. citizenship, while my father and I had retained our permanent residence status. I understood her command of the English language and American citizenship to mean that our family was just becoming more American. Hence, I did not see the need to relearn Korean.

This was seemingly not a big problem for me, except on the occasions when I was around other Korean adults who would lament to my parents (in Korean) that it was a shame that I could not speak Korean anymore. Although I never responded directly to these comments, inside I struggled to contain my disbelief and anger that they did not understand that I hadn't lost my language intentionally, but that it had gradually happened as I struggled to be accepted into an English-dominated society. This consistent stream of criticism by older Koreans made me less and less inclined to interact with Koreans, both young and old, for fear of being criticized.

BEING SCHOOLED—AS A RACIAL MINORITY

This fear loomed at the back of my mind as I went to Stuyvesant High School, which had a significant proportion of Korean students. They enjoyed each other's company, alternating between speaking Korean and English.

They discussed which churches they went to, and embraced their Koreanness together, even those who could not speak Korean fluently. Additionally, many of the Korean students were into high fashion, wearing designer clothes and carrying expensive handbags. They exuded a kind of confidence in materialism despite the fact that some of their parents also just barely scraped by. I couldn't relate to these types of image-conscious attitudes, and their evident understanding and unity in being Korean secretly made me re-evaluate who I was. I wondered why others had retained a strong affinity for their culture and Korean language skills while I could not. Were they right? Should I be ashamed? I'm not sure if I was alienated from this group voluntarily or involuntarily, but I know I enjoyed the company of a mish-mashed group of students that included Chinese, Indian, and Jewish friends who also did not join their respective ethnic groups during high school.

When it was time for me to go to college three hundred miles away, my parents did not understand that it was expected that parents were involved in the incoming freshmen's "move-in day," as my mother still operated a grocery store six days a week, while my father had made a career change by going to seminary and establishing his own storefront church. Therefore, there was little time for them to participate in a two-day-long university event. However, after some discussion, my father drove me to Baltimore, dropped me off at my dorm, wished me well, and rushed back to New York. I got settled in my room and explored the campus.

After living in New York City, I was surprised to see so few non-white faces. Evidently, I was not the only one who felt this way. In particular, one Korean student in my residential hall took it upon himself to identify other co-ethnic freshman. He asked them their names, asked if they were Korean, and then invited him or her to join him to hang out. This was the first time I saw an actual clique being formed over a period of an hour or so. By the end of the day, I was sitting en masse with a group of fifteen to twenty Korean students who were speaking to each other in both Korean and English. Most everyone else seemed at ease except for me. I realized at that moment that in this case, unlike high school, I had the opportunity to socialize with my Korean peers. However, I had some difficulty finding common ground with the other students based on anything else beyond our Korean heritage. I soon left the group and joined some other classmates I had met on campus.

In my efforts to make new friends, I met a variety of students through other avenues such as my work-study job and a non-denominational Christian fellowship. With respect to the former, I was surprised to see that I was the only Asian student in the office among mostly African-American and white students. I became friendly with these students, bonding through our shared experiences of funding our own education through a mix of loans, scholarships, and our jobs; how our families could not understand what it was like being here among generally privileged students; balancing our job with the demands of school; and our aspirations for lucrative professional jobs.

Although my own faith had lapsed, I joined a non-denominational Christian fellowship on a casual basis, ironically, to meet other students who were honest about their lapses of faith and difficulties reconciling what being Christian really meant for them. I opted to participate in this more liberal, non-denominational group rather than the more evangelical ones that were primarily comprised of East Asian students and had negative reputations on campus, both for their conservative views and lack of racial diversity.

Many of the most open students I met in fellowship happened to be African American, and they wound up being my closest friends (and still are). I believe we shared the same sentiments—feeling somewhat out of place at this private university, knowing we were economically disadvantaged, and accordingly, experiencing college differently than most of our white peers. My African-American friends also described their repeated experiences with racial discrimination in different settings, from the classroom to the workplace to retail stores. Through their stories, my eyes were opened to the injustices of racial minorities in the U.S.

Some of those themes regarding adjusting people's expectations resonated with me. Being a Korean American, people expected that I would be a studious student (I was), that I would be hard-working (I had to be), that my creative skills would be overshadowed by my quantitative skills (they weren't), and that I was a relatively docile person (I wasn't, but my silences were interpreted as such). I strove to understand if some of my characteristics and attitudes were rooted in who I "really" was, or stemmed from my living up to my parents' cultural expectations and the transference of their stigma, being foreigners in a racialized society. I became more aware that my actions and words could reinforce existing stereotypes about Asians and Asian women, and I questioned the underlying motivations for all my decisions. I actively held this sense of uneasy ethnic consciousness during my college years. Speaking with my African-American friends, I realized I was not alone. It was then that I felt a stronger sense of a minority identity based on cultural, economic, and racial dimensions.

Furthermore, in long discussions I had with my friends, it was clear that we strove to be upwardly mobile and to do better than our parents. In that sense, we were misfits, not only in school, but also in our own families. We discussed how our families had shaped who we were and our experiences, but ironically, we did not want to (nor did our families want us to) necessarily follow in their footsteps. The extreme pressure to be successful was always on our minds, and every small academic setback seemed like not only a personal disappointment but one that had a ripple-effect on our families, who had made great sacrifices to make sure we could accomplish whatever we set out to. As such, we narrowed our intellectual pursuits to fields that were seen as secure, profitable, and prestigious. I majored in economics and after completing school, soon joined the working world.

DOUBLE DUTIES

As I started working, it was clear to me that I was not well-versed in the normative behaviors of American office culture. Small talk at the water cooler about growing up highlighted how markedly different I was from my colleagues and supervisors, who discussed going to camp and vacationing overseas every summer. Given that my parents were small business owners who worked in an industry with very small profit margins, the word "vacation" was not in our household's vocabulary when I was growing up, unless you counted Sunday as "the day of rest."

My coworkers also all seemed to have expensive hobbies, like golfing, sailing, attending major concerts, or taking long weekend trips to the Hamptons. I wondered if everyone spent their money this way. With the burden of paying off my college loans, I didn't think about spending money I didn't have on these activities, and found it difficult to speak with coworkers about the standard Monday question: "What did you do this weekend?"

I spent my Saturdays helping my mom out at her grocery store so she could take a break. On Sundays, I helped out with youth ministry at my father's church. Fairly quickly, I began to feel like I spent all my free time after finishing my education helping my parents out with their jobs—something I had not expected to do while holding down a full-time job during the week. I started to feel a sense that I would never be able to enjoy my youth and have a normal life where I could enjoy my weekend like my coworkers. Instead, I was relegated to helping out my parents—something I had been doing for a long time growing up but wasn't sure I could do as an adult.

It was strange to be working in a grocery store after finishing my education, and particularly after working the week in an office where we routinely discussed "strategies" and "measurement plans." Customers were routinely surprised at my non-accented English. They were even more surprised when they learned that I could hold my own if they asked me about various items in the news. It infuriated me that they assumed I was an ignorant and uneducated person by virtue of working here and/or because they assumed my parents were also ignorant and uneducated. My infuriation had the two-pronged effect of making me both sympathetic and resentful towards my parents. On some particularly long Saturdays, I remembered that my father worked like this day in and day out for over fifteen years. An educated person back home, he was seen as nothing more than a blue-collar foreigner in the U.S. The times when I remembered this, I stifled my complaints and just tried to make it through the day.

As a working adult, it became clear that my parents also expected me to start helping them financially, something else I did not expect. I obediently provided a monthly allotment to them, but in conjunction with my spending weekends helping them out, I started to feel a mixture of both anger and confusion. I simultaneously felt burdened with responsibility and guilty that I could not do more for both of them. I was certainly perceived by American standards as "doing too much," but by Korean standards, I was "just being a good daughter." I spoke to my friends, who were either white or African American, but none of whom were children of immigrants, let alone Korean. No one could understand why I was feeling trapped. They simply said I should just say no and live my own life. The situation wasn't that simple for a variety of reasons incomprehensible to them.

My parents were economically less well-off compared to even my friends' parents who were from modest backgrounds. Their parents all had nine-to-five jobs that provided health care benefits and sometimes even a pension. My parents had no health insurance and definitely no retirement plans. Without these safety nets, I felt they were more financially vulnerable. My feelings were supported by evidence of mounting bills and summonses regarding their business, some of which I would have to read and explain the technical jargon to them. Additionally, my brother was in college, and I was the only one who had a viable, steady job. Wasn't it my place to step in and make sure things would be okay?

Secondly, my closest friends could not fully grasp (and maybe respect) the traditional Korean values and their influences on all aspects of my family life, even if, to the best of their knowledge, I happened not to exhibit any "Koreanness." I began to realize that my identity as a non-white minority did not fully encompass the complicated dimensions of immigrants' lives and more specifically, Korean immigrant lives, one of which was mine. It made me pause and reflect on the relationships I had and the possibility that I could have missed out on friendships with other Korean Americans who might have understood what I was going through.

I ended up finding a job in Washington, DC, that was both an intervention and an escape of sorts, allowing me to take a hiatus from the weekend grind I had in New York. However, I continued to send my family a check every month to help out with their expenses.

THE ART OF (AMERICAN) (OFFICE) POLITICS

When I began working, I realized my proper English grammar and academic credentials were not enough to start off on the right foot with my coworkers and managers. Initially, it started out with questions like, "How do you pronounce your name?" or "What do you want to be called?," both of which I found patronizing and insulting. But beyond these first encounters, I slowly realized that I wound up with more work than any other employee on my floor, despite the fact we were all essentially at the same level and making around the same amount of money. As I sat in the office in front of my computer at 10:00 pm one evening, I looked around and realized no one else was there. After spending hundreds of overtime hours completing projects that did not end up getting me anywhere in terms of a bonus, raise, or promotion, I addressed it with my manager. He said he expected me to "work hard" and in due time, I would get promoted. I outlined various reasons why I should be promoted, given my significant contributions leading a high-profile project. Comparatively, I saw my white, male peers get promoted in the same promotion cycle despite the fact that they held shorter tenures and less billable hours at the company. In other words, I found that some of the skills which I had developed as a student—a strong work ethic, attention to detail, and accuracy—were not as highly prized in the workplace as "fitting in." Furthermore, in some respects, I was at a disadvantage because I was not wholly "Americanized" in terms of various social norms that took place in the office around discussing leisure time, sports, and other topics which were not highly significant to me or my friends growing up.

After I had already been working there for over a year, a Vietnamese-American female joined the company. Our coworkers would confuse our names, calling us by the other, despite the fact we worked in different departments, had completely different physical builds, hairstyles, and voices. We both corrected people time and time again, but it continued to happen. I became upset that there was really no reason why this should be happening, and addressed it with my manager. Based on his body language, I could tell he immediately felt uncomfortable with the conversation. Even though I never used the words "race," "racial," or even "Asian," instead telling him that I thought it was unprofessional that she and I were confused for the other, he was dismissive, saying there was no bad will or harmful intent by calling us the wrong name.

Even in subsequent jobs where I held more advanced roles and responsibilities, I encountered the same issue, where coworkers would confuse me with another Asian woman. Even after correcting them, it happened over and over and made me realize that I—we—were seen as "all the same." Upon sharing this bit of information with my friends, my African-American friends could sympathize, but my Caucasian friends could not. They agreed it was wrong, but also thought I was taking it too seriously, since I was still otherwise treated with respect.

On the other hand, I noticed that I was immune to some forms of racism that other Asians experienced in the workplace. When I worked in the department of a large financial services company, where most of my colleagues were from China, Korea, or India on H1-B visas, they typically worked longer hours and with more intensity than the rest of the employees in the same department. Since most of them were hired for their technical aptitude, and not necessarily their fluency in English, many of my white colleagues would make disparaging comments about their inability to properly communicate in emails and during meetings. Although I agreed with them to the extent that command of the English language was not unimportant, I felt uncomfortable with their discussing "immigrants' inability to speak English" and their lack of office know-how. Since they perceived me as being "American" and not "one of these Asians on visas," they felt free to criticize and ridicule our coworkers in front of me.

To me, these professional experiences indicated that I was periodically classified as a racial minority and at other times as a nativist majority. I was confused with other Asian-American female employees, but my ethnicity was more or less "invisible" when comparing me to recent transplants. Moreover, I was oftentimes one of a handful of women in my department. I found my "Asianness" lent a sense of credibility when it came to the quality of my work, but my Asian *femaleness* could discount my ability to assume leadership roles, despite my contributions and assertiveness. Thus, my race and gender worked both for and against me in the workplace.

ETHNIC REVIVAL THROUGH COMMUNITY-BASED WORK

After consulting for two years in DC, I moved back to New York for a better professional opportunity. I assumed the same role in my father's church that I always had, which was as a Sunday school teacher, teaching Korean children in English while they usually responded to me in Korean. On the occasions when they could not explain what they meant in English, they would revert back to Korean, which I could usually understand.

Although I previously had a positive experience working with youth, when I came back a couple years later, I began to see things a bit differently. In particular, I saw them struggle with the same issues that I had experienced, such as conflict with their parents, assuming a tremendous level of responsibility for their siblings given their parents' demanding schedules, translating all sorts of bills and legal documents to their parents, experiencing racist comments from classmates and teachers, and feeling like their Korean background didn't really matter much or translate into anything valuable in the grand scheme of things in the U.S.

I also noticed that every person in the same family experienced their transition to this country in different ways, particularly when comparing siblings. Based on their birth order and the age at which they arrived to the U.S., children had different perceptions about their sense of identity, who their real friends were, and their futures in the U.S. In my conversations, I realized I was seeing a part of my own childhood in them. A new cohort of Korean-American children experienced the same growing pains I had. In this way, I started to feel a sense of belonging and responsibility to school; I started to teach the youth, not only about religion, but also about how to adjust to life in the U.S.

In a way, they taught me too, explaining different Korean customs and traditions that I had forgotten about. Among the families that attended church, it was clear that they were much more connected to South Korea than my family was, even among those who had been living in the U.S. for over fifteen years. We sometimes discussed Korean dramas and other types of shows that our families both watched on the Korean TV channels and read about in the Korean newspapers. They explained some of the pop culture that was prominent in Seoul. We mixed Korean, American, and other ethnic foods together, talking about what we did and didn't like. Their parents also often conversed during lunch with us about Korea and how Westernized Seoul in particular was these days compared to when my parents lived there. Some families who were legal immigrants would often travel to South Korea, as well as invite family members to visit them in New York, maintaining close ties to their family and the homeland. Each time someone visited the other, stories were exchanged about how rapidly South Korea was changing as an increasingly developed and modernized country, over a period of less than fifty years. I couldn't relate to these stories since I had never visited but found interest in knowing that South Korea had become increasingly liberalized in a way that began to mirror many social and cultural norms in the U.S. However, my parents often expressed how they had trouble catching up with the stories about the new infrastructure, neighborhoods, and even banking systems that didn't exist when they were there. They felt the Korea they knew had been transformed into something they could not quite understand. I became more aware that my parents were in the liminal state between foreigners of the U.S. and foreigners of South Korea, something I had not realized before.

As I continued to work at the church, I came to realize the importance of these relationships in terms of shaping my own ethnic identity. I became more comfortable and felt accepted among a handful of Koreans and their children. I realized my identity was based on the cumulative experiences of living as a Korean in the U.S., as an individual, as part of a family, and now, as part of a community through my work at the church.

As such, I mustered up the courage to temporarily suspend my financial obligations to my parents, not only for financial reasons, but because I associated much of my family obligation with a responsibility that was rooted in a cultural tradition that I had not chosen of my own accord. My parents' initial reaction was disbelief, then anger, but I communicated that I was firm in my decision, and that I would attempt to help them again once I was in a better financial position myself.

Although they expressed their unhappiness with my decision, there was nothing they could say or do to change my mind. I was initially fearful of being rejected by my parents, but they did nothing of the sort, beyond expressing their dismay with me. Over time, it became a relatively moot point, and I began to give back to my parents on my own terms. My decision to be in control of when and how to help my family was an important step in my becoming an adult, developing a different relationship with my parents than the one I had with them when I was a minor, and in the process, coming to terms with my Korean-American identity. I no longer equated loyalty to my parents with being authentically Korean. I could be Korean independently from my family.

THE EVOLUTION OF MY ETHNO-RACIAL IDENTITY

In continued search of my identity, and to validate my experience and the experiences of other Korean Americans like myself who had never really embraced our Korean identities, I started researching immigration. I was surprised to see a large amount of work that related specifically to Korean immigrants and their children. Reading about the lived experiences of Koreans in the U.S. in print—in journal articles, books, and blogs—was a wake-up call for me to continue giving back to the Korean community, as these authors had done. I continued to become immersed in the Korean community through academic involvement at the Research Center for Korean Community at Queens College. Through academic research, I began to understand the history of Koreans in the U.S., especially as it related to Korean Americans' ethnic identity formation and their trajectories in mainstream American society.

With this newfound ethnic consciousness, I began to seriously consider a research-oriented academic career as a meaningful way to continue studying and researching the lived experiences of immigrants and their families that were still untold. I chose to pursue the field of sociology, based on its breadth, both topically and methodologically, addressing multiple social mechanisms in studies of various aspects of social life. I subsequently committed to taking classes in the evenings after work for over two years in order to ascertain whether I was really ready for such a significant career shift, and to gain more training and guidance. With the encouragement and advisement of many professors and mentors, I applied to and was accepted to doctoral programs in Sociology, and am now being trained for my second career. My career change signals not only my interest and dedication to academic research and teaching, but my hope and commitment to make a broader impact to the immigrant community, particularly the Korean community, through my day-to-day academic work studying immigrant families. My career change is therefore positively associated with my emergent identity as a Korean-American woman.

Originally, my only connections to the Korean community were through my parents and their roles in the Korean community. Although my professional experience made me more aware of my minority status, it was through my engagement in the community as an adult that my ethnic identity was revived in a positive and meaningful way for me. Earlier during my college years, I questioned all my decisions and whether they were to a large extent actually predetermined based on socialization and my environment. After much reflection on the trajectory of my life and the various choices I've made, it is clear I cannot disentangle my identity and life choices from my family or the contexts and circumstances in which I was raised. As I mature, my identity continues to evolve based not only on my upbringing, but also on how I choose to engage with my family, and with the Korean community—two related, but distinct hemispheres of my world.

VI

Three Essays by Members of the Later Cohort

Chapter Thirteen

The Outlier

Katherine Yungmee Kim

I was in Berkeley on April 29, 1992; I was twenty years old, a visiting student living in a six-plex off Telegraph Avenue with a Korean-American roommate from San Francisco whom I met via a flyer on a telephone pole. Tony Lee was a strange Catholic lacrosse player who lined the walls of his bedroom with plastic bottles of his urine. He brought home girls to role-play nurse, and he would tell me the details in the morning, high-pitched mimicry and all. We had agreed to live together because we were both Korean American, and felt that the common ground ensured we would be more compatible than most others. In the end, though, we were barely cordial. I ran into him years later at a street-crossing signal, and it was hard for us even to manage to say hello.

Other than John Lee, a New Jersey-reared, M3-driving hallmate whom I met my freshman year at Vassar, I had no other real interaction with Korean-American men, save for one cousin and my brother. I moved to Berkeley on my own because my parents were in the middle of a divorce. I enrolled in two spring semester art history classes at Cal and got a job selling greeting cards and waitressing at a sushi joint. I stole cash from the card shop and ate leftover sushi from customer's plates after I bussed them. It was in the middle of this time that the riots occurred. I remember it wasn't quite yet dusk when the stores began to shutter. People were milling around in the middle of the streets. Curfew reminded me of the air raid drills in Seoul, with its ominous sense of urgency.

A friend came to the apartment a few hours later and told me he had seen a white kid pulled from his bike and indiscriminately beaten. That night, we watched a hot dog shop below my apartment get held up at gunpoint. It wasn't until the next day, when I went over to a friend's house that I found out that the Korean-American community in Los Angeles was being targeted. The news was on, and I saw one of the vigilante shopkeepers on his rooftop with his rifle defending his store. I was with a couple of white friends and when I saw the screenshot, I made this blasé comment: "Oh, that's my uncle."

I think I was trying to be funny. I was both casually deflecting my ethnic affiliation with the vigilante *and* acknowledging that he was "my people." A few years ago, I ran into one of the guys in that room. "Remember when you said, 'That's my uncle,'" he recalled, "that was so funny. I mean, that's crazy." After he went on about it, I started to realize that he actually thought that the man on the rooftop with the rifle *was* my uncle. And the fact that I didn't even bother to correct him pretty much encapsulates the heartbreaking and sometimes ludicrous moments I face as a Korean American. This futility of misinformation and misperceptions, and the weariness of having to explain something I see as so basic.

At a 4.29 (aka *Sah-ee-gu*, to commemorate the date of the Los Angeles riots) focus group for Korean Americans this past spring, I related my Berkeley anecdote as the example of where I was during the 1992 riots. I detailed how later studying the riots and photos and videos of the riots made me understand the significance of the event in Korean-American history, as our *baptê me du feu*, or our political awakening in the United States. One man in my focus group countered that although he also cerebrally felt the importance of the riots for our community, for him, 4.29 was a time of deep, personal devastation. His family's video store business in Koreatown was burned and looted, which subsequently broke his father's spirit and divided his family's memories into a before-the-riots and after-the-riots timeline. He made a short documentary film on his family's experiences and it includes several poignant interview clips with his parents.

I left the focus group that evening thinking about concepts of "ownership" in the Korean-American community, how there were people there whose first-hand experiences in the riots gave them the badge-of-honor authenticity of being on the front lines, of having personally endured. My grandmother was living on Wilshire and Normandie in a Koreatown nursing home—that was as close as I got—but she was kept entirely from harm's way and the most I did at the time was ask after her well-being in two or three phone conversations that year with my mother.

Old harbored feelings of alienation trickled in. I've long since reconciled them, but they can be persistent. My relationship to ethnicity has been an exercise in how to live with longing. I carry this inherited exile, and an incessant reckoning with perception, authenticity and acceptance. Starting with the emigration of my Second-Wave parents, my Korean-American experience has been atypical. It goes on to include my father's penchant for blondes and rural areas, my mother's startling business acumen, and our reverse migration. Being a Second-Wave child means to me that my parents came "earlier" than most Korean emigrés, and as a result, we lived completely isolated from a Korean community. Most of my parents' friends are non-Korean Americans. But I spent a great deal of time in Korea—visiting my grandparents at least every other year when I was growing up. The memories I have of their house on a one-way lane in Seoul are deeply embedded, and leave me with fond feelings about my homeland.

Even within my own family—my parents and my older brother—there is disparity in our relationship and reconciliation to that belonging. Recently, I was told that in the 1.5 generation, siblings' experiences within the family vary depending on the age at which they emigrated. It seems obvious and the same applies to my family. Each of us has a different relationship to being Korean American and to Korea, depending on our personalities and the narrative of our lives. Temperament shapes how we experience hope and sorrow.

KOREAN AND AMERICAN, NOT KOREAN AMERICAN

I was born on August 15, 1971, in Flemington, New Jersey—the last of four children born to my parents. Their first and third child died in infancy, but I didn't know of their existences until well into my childhood. As far as I knew, it was just me and my brother, who was three years my elder. My brother was born in Indianapolis, Indiana, where my father had found work as an electrical engineer.

I know that when I was in my mother's womb, my older sister, who was eighteen months old at the time, died after a sudden fever. I read this in medical paperwork that I later found in a pale pink album that also included a stack of both birth congratulations and sympathy cards. Both my siblings who passed were also born in Indiana, "Hoosiers," as my father liked to say. My father's command of English is excellent; though accented, his vocabulary and cadence come with ease. My father came to the United States in 1954, to Cambridge, Massachusetts, to study at an undergraduate level, and my mother also came to Massachusetts to study, though in 1966, and for her graduate degree. My parents were set up by mutual friends and they married in Massachusetts.

My parents spoke Korean to each other and to us, but we always responded in English. My listening skills in Korean are decent, but they are a far cry from comprehension. I tell people I understand about as much as a five-year-old child. I'm not sure how deliberate this not-learning was on my parents' agenda—it was partly circumstantial. We always lived in small, mostly white towns, some of them downright rural, where the sight of an Asian family was a complete anomaly.

The first town I lived in was Clinton, New Jersey, in a small middle-class development. I recall only white families around us. Our across-the-street neighbors were a family of devout Irish Catholics. I believe it was my mother's friendship with this family that led us to our Roman Catholic faith. We went to Mass frequently, though not regularly, without my father who was and remains cynical about organized religion. I took my Holy Communion and Confirmation in the Catholic Church—always in a white church; the concept of a Korean Christian church was completely unknown to me at the time and I've since distanced myself from religion.

At some point in the early 1970s, my mother's sister came with her family from Seoul to move into a small apartment a block away. They were the only other Koreans who I saw with regularity, this family of four. We often shared dinners at their house on the weekends. They had a happy, spare household. My cousins spoke perfect Korean to their parents, so my brother and I grew up fully aware and somewhat ashamed of our inabilities. When I turned seven, both of our families moved to different towns. We relocated to a more rural section of New Jersey, and they moved to a house near the Pennsylvania border, but we still saw each other about once every few months. Without them, I never would have had *any* interactions with other Korean Americans. Once or twice a year, my father would entertain visitors coming through JFK from Seoul, but they would simply visit for the afternoon and smoke cigarettes in the living room.

We rarely had visitors or phone calls. My father had a disparate group of white American friends, who came a few times a year to gamble, fix cars, or hunt. I remember going to their houses a handful of times in my life. I played with our neighborhood friends, but remember very little about their families or houses, just that they were very foreign and formal encounters. In the early years, kids would come over to our house from time to time, but I don't recall any feelings of shame or dislocation.

Throughout my childhood, we would visit Seoul for several weeks during the summers, so I was familiar with being in a Korean, albeit not Korean-American, environment. Because I don't speak Korean well and didn't grow up around other Korean Americans, I've been judged for not being "really" Korean, but I think my relationship with the actual homeland is deeper than a lot of the second-generation Korean Americans whom I've met. I grew up Korean and American, not Korean American. I attended third grade at *Kujong-gungmin-hakkyo* in Apkujong-dong, a neighborhood in southern Seoul, where we lived in the Hyundai Apartments, and I returned to Korea after college to live and work. I've been to Korea about twelve times, and each visit has lasted anywhere from two weeks to eighteen months.

Part of the reason we went back so often is that my father never reconciled leaving Korea for America. Because my father's family was quite affluent and well-established, our visits to Korea were gilded affairs. My grandfather was a Tokyo-educated physician, one uncle was a large steel magnate, while the other two were diplomats. My cousins were educated around the world at international schools, and there was always news of my uncles' latest postings: Riyadh, Quito, Kuala Lumpur, Hong Kong, Tokyo, DC. So within my family, even in Korea, the dinner conversation was an easy flow of Korean and English, with some Japanese and French thrown in for good measure. Several of the houses on my grandparents' street were ambassadors' or international CEOs' residences, so even in Seoul, we were around Caucasians. We were ferried around in black sedans with small fluttering Korean flags, by a chauffeur who doubled as a butler, and we would go to the Foreign Ministry or a Japanese restaurant or international markets. My grandfather would procure us Western goodies, like Frosted Flakes and Hershey's chocolates, at the black market in Namdaemun, so as to make us feel more at home. There were fine linens and foreign products and foodstuffs and fur coats and Ferragamo shoes in the vestibule.

Compared to our assiduously middle-class life in an old mill town in New Jersey, life in Seoul was aristocratic. We lived well for those weeks in the summer, which augmented my father's desire to return "for good"—this constant tumbling in his head of the exile's dilemma. The extreme wealth of my family in Seoul was always juxtaposed with the life of my mother's sister who sold shoes in an underground arcade near Chamshil. And then in turn, in America, with the dangers my aunt and uncle faced as they were frequently robbed at their dry cleaners in Flushing, New York. Growing up in a family of both the haves and have-nots made me very aware of class differences—my father's family looked down upon me visiting my mother's side, while my mother's side made constant remarks about my father's family's money and greed.

RACISM AND SCHISMS

Long shot: walking to my locker in the middle of fifth-grade class, a beefy white boy a grade above me at the end of the corridor. Centered in the doorframe, he sees me and makes the slanty eye gesture without a word from twenty-five feet away.

Fast forward two decades: a summer Saturday night on Fire Island, walking through the village looking for the market. Folks are drinking openly, fraternal gaiety abounds. I step into a doorway and bump into a man on his way out. He appears to be post-college-aged. I am thirty-two years old. He sees my face and makes the slanty eye gesture at me.

A fat middle schooler expressing hatred through discrimination in a textbook redirection is no small surprise. But I was completely floored by this grown man making racist gestures at a grown woman in the mid-aughts. The very first time a racist remark was directed at me was in the second grade and a biracial boy named Danny, whose skin was often referred to by classmates as "dirty," made me aware of how low he viewed my social status. I was surprised, then ashamed and afraid, and then angry, in that order. I began to brace myself—in middle school and high school—for racist remarks.

My father often felt discriminated against and was very vocal about it. His dignity was under constant assault in America. These confrontations never touched my mother; she would constantly tell me that it didn't matter what other people thought. To this day, she genuinely never cared.

Though popular in middle school and high school, I always knew that the reduction of an argument with a friend or a foe would come down to my race. That trump card could be easily tossed to demean me. Or more subtly, my Koreanness would be used to humor a situation—a parody of Chinese restaurant waiter lingo or sloppily choreographed martial arts. It succeeded in silencing me, though I was never ashamed of my looks or my race.

During my school years, my father's drinking increased steadily so much that my mother sent my brother away to boarding school to escape my father's abusive tirades. The atmosphere in my home was always deeply sad and volatile. So flowed the fear and shame from school to home. Because of this, I will never be able to differentiate "ethnicity" from the formation of my identity. I cannot sever shame from the secret of my father's addictions.

By ninth grade, I was drinking, and smoking cigarettes and pot. It was the small-town environment that I was in, but I was also one of the earlier and more enthusiastic users. I'd venture to say it was connected to my father's addictions. It was also these years that I started listening to hardcore, and I wore a black leather jacket, shaved part of my head, painted my room black, pierced my ears with safety pins and cut the Dead Kennedys symbol on the back of my hands. It was my way of putting my differences on display—being in control of being an outsider. My parents were oddly fine and slightly amused with my whole superficial transformation. I think because I was successful academically and socially, my parents never worried about me and let me do my own thing without too much supervision.

I lived this life of schism within schisms. By the time I was a junior, I was smoking pot almost every day, but I was still getting straight As and playing varsity sports. My dad was drunk when I came home, but I was Class President for three years in a row. When my parents split my senior year, I moved in with friends' families for weeks here and there and commuted from my mom's office in Cambridge, where we were living on a pull-out couch. I was increasingly on my own, finding independence and my own sense of happiness.

MY SOCIAL NETWORK: GENDER AND SEXUALITY

My first serious boyfriend was Canadian, a blond, blue-eyed soccer player whose mother and stepfather were alcoholics. He had left Toronto on his own to move in with his father and stepmother. We both had to strike out on our own early on. To be able to share those terrible experiences with someone who really understood, at that time in my life, was a kind gift.

My entire social network was mostly white—my friends, my parents' friends, my boyfriend, my neighbors. But it had been determined early on that I was to marry a wealthy Korean man. My Ewha alumna aunts—who were married to ambassadors—believed strongly in this fate. When I was a teenager, they set me up on dates with the sons of their friends, but I was quite tall—often taller than the boys—and my American demeanor was considered masculine and abrasive.

But it's not like I was a self-hating Korean who wasn't attracted to Korean men. My father introduced me to one of his friends' sons when I was in high school, and I remember really liking him and finding him handsome, but we only met a handful of times. And then within a few years, my parents divorced, and my mom began openly dating an Irish-American colleague. I was seventeen when my parents separated and twenty-two when my mom remarried her colleague. When this happened, every mantra about marrying a Korean man was erased.

As I came of age, I also became more and more aware of the pervasive Asian fetish—men of all races would leer at me and say hello in Mandarin and Japanese. It also coincided with when I moved to San Francisco, where I encountered for the first time a greater Asian-American population. When I was twenty, an African-American bus driver told me to "Get off the bus, Suzie." It was the first time I was addressed negatively for being an Asian woman. As a young woman, I wanted to be empowered sexually, but had to mitigate it with a certain type of negative racial attention.

After college, I worked in Asia as a journalist for almost three years when I was in my early twenties—first in Phnom Penh, Cambodia, and then in Seoul, Korea. I was working as an English-language journalist in both places, so I found myself in colonial enclaves, like the languid Foreign Correspondents' Clubs in both cities, and often squarely in the company of colonialists and their "native" girlfriends, some of them sex workers and many whom I befriended. Being at seedy nightclubs in this company augmented my awareness of the Asian fetish stereotype. Some of these men were johns, but they were also my journalistic and NGO colleagues; my beat in Korea was the U.S. Armed Forces, so I was often on base and socialized with GIs on Hooker Hill in Itaewon.

This experience certainly shaped me. As difficult and repellent as the scene was, I felt it was important to understand. Being in those arenas threw my undergrad thesis, a very American conversation of Otherness and the Male Gaze, out the window. In most of Asia, I was seen as a Westerner. Sometimes I was mistaken for a whore. But being a reporter forced me to stop judging—and I observed and listened and became very knowing in what people's perceptions of Korean women were. I had gone to Korea to reestablish my roots, find crony *kyopos* at Yonsei, extend my career, but in terms of gender and sexuality and engaging with the expat community, I was dealt a whole new set of cards.

    My experiences with racism don't even begin to address the subtlety of the "well-intentioned" folks, such as the men I've sat next to on planes with their stories of business trips in the 1980s and the Korean War. "Oh, I've been to Korea," they would relate, and I'd find myself nodding, thinking, "Here we go again." I've been asked multiple times if I am Sandra Oh or if I've read *The Joy Luck Club*. I once went to a book party in the Upper East Side, and an older socialite walked by me, and then turned to me and said, "I had a Chinese scarf once."

    I was twenty when I began befriending Korean-American women. I joined a group in Berkeley called KAWA—Korean American Women with Attitudes—comprised of Korean Californian women who went to Cal. Back in New York for my senior year at Vassar, I got to know a woman who was doing her history thesis on Korean-American women and their mothers—and she introduced me to another interviewee. It turned out that our fathers all went to the same high school in Seoul, and our mothers were all successful businesswomen. One had also lost a sibling and had dealt with grieving parents. The other to this day is my closest friend. Not only are we all Korean, but we share similar paths and experiences within Korean America and America as a whole. Not many Korean Americans I meet can or want to comfortably navigate the white world of America, and these women traverse race and class boundaries as well. My husband recently remarked how similar the three of our natures were, exclusive of us being Korean. My friendship with them has been very validating—we can find hilarity and cynicism in painful subjects—and they can be a real touchstone when I am feeling alienated.

    I've dated men from different races and countries, several who were half Korean. My college boyfriend was *hapa*—half Japanese American, half white—and we dated on and off for about nine years. We have a son, who is fifth-generation Japanese American and third-generation Korean American, not to mention a quarter white. Being in Berkeley during the Ethnic Studies heydey in the early 1990s, and dating this man who was very involved in his family's internment in the camps, made me identify very strongly with my pan-Asian-American identity. This only grew stronger raising my son, who is not entirely Korean.

When I returned to the States from Seoul, I started working at a progressive multiracial news service in San Francisco. My world shifted from pan-Asian American to identifying mostly with people of color. During this time, I was a single mom for four years; many Korean and Korean Americans couldn't even begin to comprehend my life, but for my progressive friends of color, it was just a matter of fact. As my family grows, it is also becoming more multiracial. My eldest son strongly identifies as being Korean American—he's already been to Korea four times—but he also has three sisters who are half Mexican, and another sister and brother who are half Jewish. His only cousin is half Jamaican. Because of the blending of our families, my ethnicity within my own family is but one and I've come to view the world through this lens.

My husband straddles separate worlds of his own. He is Jewish and secular, though his Bar Mitzvah was orthodox. He was raised by an Afro-Caribbean nanny and went to a Quaker school. Because he largely defines his nanny as his "mother" and his parents were active in the Civil Rights movement and the Black Panther Party, he majored in African-American Studies in college. Later, he became a chef, specializing in Vietnamese food. His grandfather was influential in Washington, DC, the way my grandfather was influential in Seoul, and our families have shockingly similar dynamics. His sister was born profoundly deaf and he had cancer at twenty-one, which made his early life a bit traumatic. We don't share race, but our personal experiences resonate with each other's, and when we came together, there was little question that we would eventually marry.

I have to confront being in the white man-Asian woman relationship, especially after being in a power-to-the-people Asian-American relationship for so long. Still sometimes it's not easy for me. Sometimes I get frustrated with his lack of interest about my community, or sometimes I feel judged, especially in my Korean-American or people-of-color professional circles, for being with "the white guy." I criticized him harshly for growing up with what I initially saw as "a black servant/master" relationship in this day and age. But we have the conversations—race is a constant topic. He scans situations and knows what my point of view will be. We have grown to live very separate public lives while keeping our home life as our sanctuary. I am proud and feel incredibly lucky that we've created such a great, loving, healthy, close-knit family.

A HEARTBREAKING EPIPHANY

Here's a quietly sad story. One cold night in 1995, when I was living and reporting in Seoul, I hailed a cab south of the Han River. There was already a man in the cab when I got in. We drove a few hundred feet before the cabbie stopped again to pick up two young women. It was bar time and the streets were packed with people looking for rides, and the girls were slightly drunk and they started chatting with the driver. They were being coquettish, one seated on the other's lap, and their cute conversation drew in the first passenger, and pretty soon, the four of them were bantering back-and-forth, flirting and laughing and having a grand old time. I remember sitting in my corner realizing that no matter how long I lived in Seoul, I would never have that facility. It was a heartbreaking epiphany that expedited my departure from Seoul, because I realized then that my romantic idea of permanently relocating to Seoul was illusory and faulted.

For a good half of my life, I expected to move to Korea and marry a Korean man. And then I moved to Korea, and realized I would never be a part of the society—that even there I was always to be the outsider. A friend of mine told me just the other day, "No matter where you go, no matter what community you're in, you'll always be an outlier."

About a year ago, I published a book on Los Angeles's Koreatown—comprised of about two-hundred photos from the late 1800s to the present day. In researching this publication, I got to know many community organizers, some of the oldest second-generation Korean Americans alive today, and many Korean-American scholars. I'm currently working at the Koreatown Youth and Community Center, which seems to tie together a lot of my interests—youth and community work, social justice, writing workshops, environmental activism, the Korean-American community, Koreatown. I am also a contributing editor at *KoreAm*, the only Korean-American monthly publication in print. Though my professional interests bring me to the community, I find myself in a constant state of liminality—this sense of dislocation. I often feel judged and there is a sometimes palpable mistrust or competition that I don't understand. In my work with ethnic communities, I can get frustrated with the lack of organizational structure and funding, which can underscore my anger at "the system." My decision to participate in the Korean-American community was very conscious, to advocate with my skills for my community.

As a fiction writer, I'm always aware of being pigeonholed into ethnic literature. Sometimes I feel like unless I write stories about my grandma and characters with names like "Snow Peony," no one will ever read my writing. When I moved to Los Angeles and met with a friend of a friend—they were old *Harvard Crimson* buddies—to get a job at the *Los Angeles Times*, he told me my best bet was to apply for the minority scholarship. I found his remark at the time to be condescending, given that he was a white third-generation *Times* staffer. Later, I found out that's how several of my Korean-American colleagues came to work there. As great an opportunity as it might be, I find it a sad indicator that for people of color to get work at the mainstream paper in Los Angeles, they have to enter in *as* minorities.

My family supports me in my endeavors, though my father doesn't quite understand why I am so interested in the Korean-American community, and often warns me of "bad" Koreans, who will embezzle or cheat me. He is filled with regret and recently told me he wished he had never come to America, because he and his friends agreed that given their family backgrounds, they'd have been better off in the end, "over there." But his position vacillates. He does often compare me and my experience in America to oil and water. One of his favorite admissions is "I didn't raise you… this fucking society did." My mother, who found tremendous financial success creating and selling her cartographic company, is a firm believer in hard work and optimism. She is board emeritus on several Asian-American organizations and just wants me to find personal happiness and success, and is thrilled that I'm doing community work, which she believes has always been my calling. She has no desire ever to go to Seoul again, as she finds the culture limiting and myopic. My brother could care less about his Korean ethnicity—it's a bit of a defensive posture as the relationship has been burdensome for him and riddled with land mines. Once when I pointed out a local business and mentioned it was Korean-owned, he shrugged his shoulders and said, "So?"

I haven't been to Korea in almost four years, and it's the longest I've gone my whole life. Part of it is because my grandmother passed away at the age of one-hundred in 2008—the incentive to visit is not there—and I have three young kids now to travel with and the expense is great. I've found so much solace in Los Angeles's Koreatown, which provides spiritual comfort and a Korean home in America, a perfect surrogate. But Seoul will always be another home for me and there in the hills remains the only childhood house where I can return and be enveloped in old memories. I smell the rosewood furniture and the smoke burning in the yards and I see the acacias and the mist in the air around *Bukgaksan* (a granite mountain located in the middle of Seoul) in the mornings. I hear the temple bells at dawn. I miss Korea viscerally, but I know I will go back soon. I won't be able to take the longing much longer.

Chapter Fourteen

할머니 안녕?
(*Halmuhnee Ahn-Nyung?*)

Alexandra Noh

To those who are familiar with the Korean language and the formalities that are a part of it, the title of this piece, which roughly translates as "Hello, grandma," may seem rude or impolite. As a 1.5-generation Korean American, I have been taught from a very early age to speak and act in certain ways that reflect the cultural traditions that our forefathers have developed and maintained. Under the influence of Confucian ideologies, I should be addressing my grandmother—an elder in the family—in a more respectful tone and manner. But if you knew the relationship between me and my grandmother, you would surely see that it is not a lack of etiquette that I have displayed. My grandmother, you see, is my best friend.

LEAVING ON A JETPLANE

As much as I wish I could, I cannot quite recall the events that took place when I was merely two years old; surely, this is a sentiment shared by most of us. So, *Halmuhnee* (Grandma), I'll start off my story with the ones that you and Mom have told me.

The room would fill with laughter when the three of us gathered to talk about the day I was born. Mom always said that she just wanted one daughter, nothing more. On one early morning in March in the late 1980s, in the delivery room of Baek Hospital in Seoul, South Korea, that is exactly what she got. As she went into labor, the doctor jokingly told Mom that her child wouldn't be able to breathe if she screamed too loudly. Mom believed him. Later, he admitted that she was the only woman that he had ever encountered in his entire career that gave birth without a peep. Naturally, you thought that something horrible had happened to your daughter and newborn grandchild, as you stood on the other side of the door. Thankfully though, we were both fine. A healthy baby girl was born, although the mother finally gave in and fainted at the sound of her child's cry. We should have known then that she was a force to be reckoned with.

My parents split up in the winter of 1990. Though you held your tongue for nearly twenty-five years, you made sure Mom knew how you felt about her naïve choice to marry the first man that she had dated. Knowing that the divorce courts in Korea were extremely partial to granting full custody to the father, my determined mother came up with a plan: to run. And so, we did. After quickly (and miraculously) gathering documents and registration forms, Mom packed one big suitcase full of basics and just a couple of hundred dollars in her pocket. Waddling alongside my mother, I boarded a plane and set foot on American soil for the first time.

SOAKING IT ALL IN

Growing up in Elmhurst, New York, a neighborhood that is considered to be the most ethnically diverse in the world, I learned to see past the skin colors and to hear past the accents early on in life. Our neighbors were not just Korean; they were Indian, Mexican, Russian, Chinese, Ukrainian, Black, Japanese, Puerto Rican, Greek, Polish, Vietnamese, and so much more. Because of the sheer diversity, I spent time with children and families from all over the world. Going to a public elementary school, there was no class, ethnicity, race, or religion that we shared. The only bonds that developed were due to true, sincere friendships built on companionship and love, no matter what languages we spoke at home or what types of spices lined our kitchen cupboards. On the playground, the Chinese boy was chosen first for basketball teams, the Jewish girl was chosen first for dodge ball, and I was always chosen as the goalie for our soccer games. Stereotypes and biases did not come to mind; not because we were unaware that they existed—we were fully conscious of society's dismal ignorance—but because we knew that judging a book by its cover was more detrimental to us than to anyone else. For instance, had we gone by the racial stereotype that "all black people are good at basketball," we would have had the shortest kid in the class who also couldn't dribble the ball more than a few feet at a time at the center of our games. Nearly two decades later, had the firm that I now work for hired accountants purely based on the idea that "all Asians are good at math," we may have found ourselves under the scrutiny of the Internal Revenue Service.

Like the majority of the population in the area, my family was not wealthy—quite the contrary, actually—but our hearts remained warm even

할머니 안녕? *(Halmuhnee Ahn-Nyung?)* 187

when the water was not. Splitting a one-bedroom, rent-controlled apartment between four adults and one child was less than ideal, creating rituals like full-blown wars in the morning for a semi-hot shower and checking the mirror in the elevator before stepping on to avoid the crooks that were sometimes known to rob and assault residents in the area. Although many may believe that the neighborhood and societal conditions that I lived in were not the best places for a small child to learn about life, I am thankful beyond words for having grown up in such an atmosphere. Much like being forced to climb the six flights of stairs in our ivy-covered apartment because of an elevator that was broken more often than not, maturing with a sense of hardship allowed me to broaden my sights and to overcome life's obstacles instead of avoiding or ignoring them. Sadly though, not everyone that I've encountered has been as open-minded and accepting of cultural diversity as the children that I grew up swapping lunches with. In a colorful world, it's unfortunate that there are so many people who still see in merely black and white.

One of the greatest problems regarding racism and racial stereotyping or biases, in my opinion, is rooted in the fact that the individuals who project such sentiments and opinions may be completely unaware of their ignorance and blatant disrespect. For example, while speaking with a former coworker at one of my previous jobs, we came across the topic of food. She turned to me and asked, "Do you have American food at home, too?" I was slightly confused, for two reasons: (1) In all of our interactions, I could not remember a single time that I had implied that I exclusively made—let alone ate— Korean food, and (2) I was pretty sure there was and still is no such thing as "American food." I responded, "Yes, I have American food at home. Do you?" It wasn't until then that she seemed to realize what a silly question she had asked, and her cheeks flushed as she quickly tried to change the subject. Another instance occurred on the street, as I passed by a stranger and he approached me, saying, "You look like a China doll! But since you're Chinese, I guess that just means you look like a doll!" As I blankly stared at his face and blinked my eyes rapidly to somehow help process what had just happened, his smile slowly faded, and I blurted out what seemed like the only logical response at the time, "I'm fucking Korean, now get out of my way." The stranger was taken aback, but quickly tried to patch things up with what he must have thought would be appropriate, "Chinese, Japanese, Korean, it's all the same thing!" At that point, I found myself laughing, as I finally looked at him dead in the eyes and said, "What are you? Dominican? Puerto Rican? Colombian? Mexican? Ah, never mind, it's all the same thing anyway, right?" Hammurabi would have been proud; my grandmother, perhaps not so much.

In a society that demands labels and dualities, I am frequently asked a vague question: "Where are you from?" Now, my answer to this question varies from time to time. When asked while at home, in New York, I reply with the county or neighborhood that I live in. If I am out of state or country, I respond with, "New York." The answer that I offer comes naturally, though I understand that it sometimes does not quite answer the true question that is being asked. When I am asked the question for a second time with a slight variation ("Where are you *really* from?"), I realize that what they wish to know is my ethnic background, and not where I reside. With a smile, I ask if they are inquiring about my ethnicity, then let them know that I am Korean. More often than not, they breathe a sigh of relief and smile back as they nod in what seems to be approval of my answer. I chuckle inside, wondering when such inane ignorance will end.

THE SANDWICH

Halmuhnee, do you remember? Even now, when I hug you and feel your head buried in my chest, I recall the days when I had to reach up to hold your hand and look up to have your warm eyes meet mine. It was on one of those days of carefree time on the school playground and math homework that did not require calculators that I suddenly became aware of my surroundings.

We only lived a few blocks away from the elementary school that I attended, but you accompanied me, both to and from, every single day. Occasionally, you scolded me for not "walking like a lady," and for coming home with scraped knees and bruises from playing sports with the boys. But no matter how hot or cold it got on those New York City mornings and afternoons, you held my hand and carried my schoolbag for me as you watched for cars that I incessantly seemed to ignore. Every afternoon, when the last bell would ring and the children would pour out of the large magenta doors, you stood by the foot of the stairs and waved your hand frantically for me to see.

"Areumah!" you would call out as you anxiously waved your arms. It was a gesture that I had become accustomed to, amongst the hustle and bustle of hundreds of children and their parents. But for some reason, at some point, I began to feel ashamed because of it. I wondered to myself, "Why couldn't my grandmother call me by my American name? Why did she always embarrass me in front of my friends by calling me by my Korean name?" My cheeks would flush as such silly questions permeated my mind, and I would scurry as quickly as I could to be outside of the school's gates and back at home. But you never so much as frowned at my actions. I would scamper across the street and you would be right behind me, reaching out to take the weight off of my back and to protect me from the dangers that I was so oblivious to.

할머니 안녕? *(Halmuhnee Ahn-Nyung?)*

When we got home, the door to our apartment would open and I would smell some sort of home-cooked meal. My stomach grumbled and I would quickly kick off my shoes at the door. Though it was not much of a distance, I would run into the bedroom to change and then to settle into a chair in the living room to eat. But that began to change, too. My friends at school would tell me about the sandwiches and burgers that they would eat when they got home. It was not until then that I became puzzled about the *jjigae* (stew) and *kimchi* (pickled cabbage) that my family and I always ate. Being the rebel without a cause that I had apparently become, I decided one day to refuse the food that you had so lovingly prepared for me. I pushed away the dishes and the warm bowl of rice as I asked you why you never made me sandwiches or burgers.

"Just eat it, we'll get you that stuff next time," you said.

"NO!" I so adamantly declared, as I stomped off into the bedroom, wishing I'd had a few bites before I had decided to become so mutinous.

I stayed angry at you until the next day. I huffed and I puffed, though I had no house to blow down, and I marched off to school, refusing to stick close by your side as you told me to. When school was over, I spotted you in the crowd but purposely walked past you, hoping to make sure you knew just how angry this little seven-year-old was. As the rusty elevator door slid open and we walked into our apartment, I grumpily took off my shoes and stormed into the bedroom.

"Areumah," you beckoned.

Admittedly hungry but determined to win the battle, I stuck my head out the door. I looked to the living room, where you stood with a sandwich in your hand. Nearly tumbling over, I threw open the door and ran over to you. The sandwich was from the small Chinese bakery that was a few blocks away. You went back into the kitchen and came back with some milk, as opposed to the barley tea that we always drank at home. I quickly ripped through the packaging and chomped away, until I looked up at you. The smile on your face at that moment is still embedded into my mind. You looked at me so lovingly, and the happiness that you felt from seeing me enjoy that snack was obvious in your voice as you asked, *"Ma shi ssuh?"* (Does it taste good?).

Not once were you late to take me back home. Not once did you chastise me for my foolishness. It was because of your unconditional love and amazing ability to understand me—even when I did not quite understand myself—that I was able to find and accept who I am. Because of your unabashed love, I learned that it is not what is on the dinner table that defines me; it is the knowledge in my mind and the love in my heart.

SEEING WITH EYES WIDE SHUT

In elementary and junior high school, students were grouped into classes according to their levels of academic performance. In high school, however, there were no specific classes that we belonged to. Aside from the "homeroom" in which we were assigned designated lockers to keep our belongings in, we travelled to and from the classrooms on our programs. Our daily schedules still provided a sense of structure, but there was one part of the day that always allowed a bit of freedom: lunch. Once we entered the cafeteria, we were free to roam around and choose where to sit, what to eat, who to talk to, and how to spend our free time. This is when I began to realize a change in my surroundings. Given the choice to hang out with whomever we wanted, the long lunch tables in the cafeteria were no longer a random mixture of colors and personalities. Instead, it was obvious that the majority of the students were gravitating towards others who belonged to the same ethno-racial groups. While the bright white tiles on the walls and the spaces between the tables created no clear division, we did. Whenever someone who did not belong to our "group" came along to have a seat, they were greeted with a smattering of unwelcoming looks and throats being cleared. The tables that we occupied were always the same, on the same side and location of the cafeteria, just like the faces that we surrounded ourselves with.

I do not believe it was racism that caused the divide. We, as individuals, had friends and classmates from all ethnic and racial backgrounds. We did not pass judgment on others because of the color of their skin, or where they had come from. Growing up in New York City, we were fully aware that the people that we encountered and interacted with should not be judged by their ancestries. However, the majority of my close friends were East Asian. These friendships formed from neighborhoods and ethnic enclaves to hallways and cafeterias, and, ultimately, wherever we went. We shared jokes about our strict parents and their traditional mentalities, such as their insistence that we focus on our studies and respect our teachers and elders at all times. We laughed about how vast the difference was between an A+ and an A– —at least to our parents—and how even the American dishes that we ate at home had Asian twists. Being around each other so much, we even began to understand short words and phrases of each others' languages, which were thoroughly incorporated in our jokes and everyday conversations. I firmly believe that it was neither hatred nor negative prejudices that separated us from the other ethnic and racial groups, but the comfort of familiarity and the ability to relate with one another without explanations that brought and kept us together.

The first high school that I attended was populated with Russian, African-American, Jewish, and Asian students. From classrooms to cafeterias, the sections of students that separated themselves from the others did not just create a sense of friendship, but solidarity among the group members as well. Some rather unfortunate consequences of such divisions, however, were the fights that occurred. Many times, there were altercations and quarrels that occurred between differing ethnic groups. In the earlier years of my high school experience, I wondered if it was a trend that was prevalent only in that particular school. However, when I transferred to a second high school after moving to a different neighborhood, I realized that the new school—and the many others that my friends and acquaintances attended—was not very different. Time and time again, crowds of students gathered near school grounds because someone had said or done something to get on someone else's nerves. One student's anger would quickly enrage members of the same ethnic group, and a small dispute would eventually escalate into high school "war."

Now, nearly a decade later, much has changed. Outside of school grounds and cafeteria walls, disagreements remain civil and between two individuals, rather than by groups. Living in Whitestone, New York, approximately twenty minutes away from Elmhurst, my life has changed in several ways. My neighbors are no longer from all over the world, but mainly Asian or Italian. Still, the majority of my close friends are East Asian—mainly first-, 1.5-, and second-generation Korean and Chinese Americans—many of whom I've known since high school. My friends and I frequently hang out in Flushing and Bayside, which are two areas in Queens with large Asian populations within close proximity of many of our homes.

With the notion of marriage looming above our heads, my friends' parents urge their children to date and commit to significant others from the same ethnic backgrounds, though the rate of intermarriages in the general population continues to increase. On the same note, most parents strongly "suggest" that we further our educations, though the reasoning behind such ambitions differs for sons and daughters. While men are urged to obtain degrees in the hopes of ultimately achieving higher occupational titles and the accompanying paychecks, women are encouraged to do the same, but in order to find mates who possess relatively positive attributes rather than for our own future careers. It is a double standard, to say the least—one that continues to affect Asian Americans while they further assimilate to the norms of an egalitarian society.

ME

When I was two years old, I waddled about in the neighborhood while clutching on to my mother's hand. Whenever we encountered an adult that I recognized, I bowed at a ninety-degree angle as I said, "*Ahn nyung ha sae yoh!*" (the formal way of saying "hello, how are you?") with a smile. Likewise, many of the traditions and customs of my heritage became second nature to me. I was taught how to read and write in Korean before I was enrolled in an English-speaking school. My mother and I ate Korean food and spoke to each other in Korean at home. In my squeaky, high-pitched voice, I bellowed out the Korean national anthem and other folk songs. To this day, these lessons remain embedded in my mind and I continually make an effort to keep it that way. Now, I cook Korean dishes and speak to my fellow Korean-American friends in "three languages": Korean, English, and "Konglish." "Konglish," a term commonly used among many Korean Americans, refers to a mixture of the two languages. For example, "친구들" (*chingudeul, meaning "friends"*) becomes "*chingus,*" which incorporates the grammatical rules of the English language to make a Korean word plural. Likewise, life as a 1.5-generation immigrant has been a great mixture of both worlds—the best, worst, and everything in between from both.

Over the years, I have not only become attached to and comfortable with Korean food, games, friends, conversations, and culture in general, but to companions, as well. I find myself more comfortable dating 1.5- and second-generation Korean men, not because I am not attracted to men from other ethnic groups, but because I find that a Korean-American mate maximizes both of our potentials as individuals to create a greater relationship. Communication is such a crucial factor in maintaining and improving a successful relationship, and I believe that the use of both Korean and English increases our chances of clearly delivering our thoughts and opinions to one another. Also, because the lifestyles and hobbies that many of the younger Korean Americans enjoy are similar in large cities like New York and Los Angeles—such as places to spend time and types of activities to do—there is a comfort in such similarities that allows us to almost immediately find common ground.

Traditionally, Korean heterosexual relationships were based purely on the Confucian and patriarchal ideologies. Complete with the "man of the house" and the housewife who diligently tends to her children and husband, the old-fashioned Korean couple may not appeal to modern egalitarian and feminist individuals. Personally, I believe in the traditional Korean balance of power and responsibility in a marriage. Though there are many people who argue that women deserve more respect and power, I understand and sympathize with the ideals that the elders of my heritage have followed. Much like the marvelous beauty and remarkable structure of the greatest tree in a forest, I find that a man deserves and needs to stand tall and proud in his environments. And much like the rich soil, sunlight, and rain that nourishes the tree, a woman is the foundation and source of successful growth. Although those elements of nature are oftentimes neglected, there is absolutely no doubt that the absence of such would lead to the inevitable demise of such marvelous beauty. Likewise, women in a traditional Korean marriage can frequently seem to be undermined and underappreciated to an outsider looking in. However, as long as her value is respected and treasured by her husband and children, I have confidence that the patriarchal structure that my ancestors have followed for numerous centuries can *and* will result in healthy and happy homes.

Regretfully, I have only visited Korea once since immigrating to the United States in 1990. That one trip, however, has left a lasting impression on me of a country that I had held so near and dear to my heart, yet was apparently rather foreign to the latter half of my Korean-American identity. Customs and rituals that I was so familiar with became challenging and confusing, such as the absence of tipping for services rendered (one cab driver was furious that I offered him a tip, while in New York, anything less than 15% evokes a cold, harsh stare), coming to terms with the fact that shopping meant going from an American size small to a Korean size medium or even large and—arguably the most disturbing and upsetting part of my trip—not being able to enter some establishments with my friends who were enlisted in the United States military. Granted, I gradually came to understand that the angry driver may have been offended because a young woman offered him more money than warranted, possibly implying that he needed the charity, that coming from one of the statistically most obese countries in the world to shop in one that is notably health and weight conscious meant perusing through a proportionately tailored marketplace, and that much of the night life in Korea—at the time, at least—was plagued with constant brawls and altercations between members of the American military that were stationed in Korea and the locals. I must admit, though, that the last tidbit still irks me to this day. Were the fights and exclusion from establishments due to a lack of communication because of the language barrier, or cruel ignorance on the part of the native Koreans in an act of ethnocentrism and xenophobia, or both? Overall, everything was more of an experience and I eagerly soaked it all in—both good and bad. I loved my heritage, although some aspects of it were inconsistent with my own ideals and principles as an individual, and I knew that a greater understanding of it would be the only way that I could expect personal growth.

Maintaining a happy medium between assimilating into American culture while preserving a level of cultural retention has not always been as easy as I would like, though. To this day, I try to sustain a steady relationship between myself and my Korean culture, by consciously engaging in conversations in Korean, asking my mother and grandmother for advice on spelling/grammar, learning to cook Korean dishes, observing the traditional holidays and customs, following Korean current events, and more. In the future, I intend to pass down such knowledge to my children, with hopes for them to lead and benefit from bi-cultural and ethnically rich lives as I have. Because of how much I value this aspect of my life, I would be devastated if I or any of my future generations were to lose that blessing.

FROM THE BOTTOM OF MY HEART

할머니 감사합니다. *Halmuhnee, gamsa hamnida* (Grandma, thank you).

Many 1.5- and second-generation individuals struggle with their identities. They wonder if they are immigrants or Americans, and how others perceive them. But, because of you, I feel fairly certain about who and what I am. After living in the United States for over twenty years, I realize that the color of my skin will always set me apart from the image of a "typical American." I also realize that this is nothing to be ashamed of, and that it is more of a blessing than anything else. I am fully bilingual and bi-cultural, and can relate with both ends of the spectrum. Because of such an advantage, I am now more successful in the labor market and in society as a whole.

It was on that fateful day that you instilled in me a sense of pride and confidence that I probably would have never been able to establish on my own. Because you set such a firm foundation for me which I have built on over the years, that one mundane sandwich opened my eyes to the world and my position in it. I smile, to this day, knowing just how lucky I am to have experienced such an unparalleled and powerful epiphany. Regardless of when and where we are, people are faced with difficult and uncomfortable questions such as "who, what, and why," about ourselves. Among such incessant curiosities and uncertainties, I find myself at an uncommon state of ease and comfort.

Who?

I am Alexandra Noh. I am the same little girl that you cradled in your arms even before my chubby little legs could carry my own weight.

What?

I am Korean. I am Korean American.
 I am a daughter, granddaughter, niece, cousin, friend, and lover.

Why?

I am who and what I am because of the strength and wisdom that you have molded me with. You have guided me to see that no label will make or break me, as long as I am sure and secure about myself. Even in a world that insists on boundaries between black and white, male and female, rich and poor, you have taught me that a love and fascination for life itself is what truly matters. I can cross boundaries and straddle the borderlines, because nothing can stop me from doing so but myself. And so, you see, I can enjoy my cheeseburgers and *kimchi*, too.

If there is one great thing that you have taught me, my loving, amazing grandmother, it is that the life I live is only as great as I let it be. For that, I will be forever grateful.

할머니, 사랑합니다. (*Halmuhnee, saranghamnida.* Grandma, I love you.)

Chapter Fifteen

What it Means to be Korean

Hyein Lee

What does it mean to be Korean? Is it a matter of citizenship, ethnicity, and cultural practice? Does it transcend material characteristics to include a shared mindset, values, and experiences? I only began wrapping my head around this question since moving to the United States in 2006, but it is one pertinent to understanding identity politics in a country where race permeates through informal and formal discussions.

I identify as "Korean," and define Korea as my homeland because it is where I was born, where I spent a significant part of my life, and where my family currently resides. I have lived nine years in the Republic of Korea, eight years in Hong Kong, and am entering my sixth year in New York City. In a couple of years, I will have spent equal amounts of time living in three different countries. People like to ask where I feel most at home, and I either say "nowhere" or "everywhere."

However, over the past couple of years, I have been actively grappling with understanding my own identity as a Korean living in the United States. Having attended international schools all my life, I sound like an American, however I do not identify as a Korean American. After all, I am still a foreigner transitioning to life in a foreign country. Legally, I am not a U.S. citizen or a permanent resident, and my status as a student on an F-1 visa is not only a pain every time I go through customs at the airport, but it also bars me from participating in day-to-day activities. Most importantly, I must pursue my studies and nothing else, in order to fulfill and not violate the intent of my stay in the U.S. On a more casual note, I often find conversation difficult when the subject matter turns to shared experiences of growing up in America.

These constraints, which ultimately draw lines between inclusion and exclusion, leave me ambivalent about my identity as a Korean living in the

U.S. This ambivalence is rooted in the fact that my life experiences have developed race awareness, but not much race consciousness. Growing up in a multicultural environment in Asia and moving to New York as an adult have resulted in a life mostly devoid of personal contact with racial conflict and identity politics. However, my interpersonal relationships and participation in organizational groups and larger communities (especially since moving to New York) indicate a quest to understand what it means to be labeled "Korean" or "Asian" in America. And while I cannot argue around academic discussions of citizenship or ethnic identity, I can attempt to analyze this quest by taking a closer look at particular decisions made in college and factors in my upbringing contributing to this personal confrontation of identity.

CONFRONTATION OF ETHNIC IDENTITY

On August 24, 2006, my father and I landed at JFK airport and made our way to a hotel in the Financial District in silence. New York City was the last place I wanted to be. Just a couple weeks prior, we were embroiled in a family feud over where I would go to college. My heart was set on Macalester, a small liberal arts school in St. Paul, Minnesota. Frustrated by the ethnic and socioeconomic homogeneity that defined my middle and high school experiences in Seoul, Korea, I was determined to attend Macalester—a college with one of the highest international student and faculty enrollment rates in the United States. Obsessed with the school's special emphasis on "internationalism, multiculturalism, and service to society," I was bubbling with aspirations of becoming the next Kofi Annan (a Macalester alumnus).

My parents, on the other hand, took one glance at the short list of schools I had been accepted to and bluntly refused to pay tuition for anything other than NYU because it was the only name they recognized and consequently the only name recognizable among friends, family, and Korean society at large. Education is central to social mobility and cultural capital in Korea. The informal categorization of American higher education fits into a larger framework of South Korean perceptions on foreign luxury commodities. To Koreans, Ivy League schools are the Chanels, Guccis, Porsches, and Ferraris of the education world. Non-Ivy League, yet well-known colleges such as NYU or UCLA, are equivalent to the Polo Ralph Laurens, Lexuses, and BMWs. Apparently, any school that falls beneath this bar is relegated to a list of seldom-referred-to family secrets.

Being a complacent teen, I considered my parents provincial for adhering to such superficial standards. I took parental coverage of college tuition for granted, and ungratefully sulked at being forced to go to a college against my will. In retrospect, my initial distaste for NYU meant I was void of the commonly romanticized expectations of living in New York City. It allowed me to absorb what the school and city had to offer tabula rasa style.

During my first semester, I took a Near Eastern Cultures course, where we read about Edward Said and the concept of orientalism, which he elaborates on in his book titled *Orientalism*. This was my introduction to the notion of race and ethnicity as a manmade institution. However, despite being intrigued by the notion of European imperialism forging a mythical, sexualized, oriental identity, I was personally apathetic towards discussions of race and ethnicity. Having spent all my life in Asia, I had no reason to define myself as a person of color or an ethnic minority. For me, it was simply an academic institution of thought that was not inherently rooted in my day-to-day life. I defined myself simply as "Korean."

Instead, I was invested in making the most of New York City and working towards a five-year plan culminating in a job at the *New York Times*. I immediately signed up to be a staff writer at NYU's daily newspaper. I was itching to live all the colors of New York City. Among many other new experiences, I observed a Ramadan fundraiser for Darfur, and I attended a flea market for plus-sized women at the LGBT Community Center. I also interviewed a local business man fighting Columbia University's expansion into Harlem, a student photographer capturing the lives of a homeless community in Jackson Heights, and an 81-year-old graduate student passionate about democratic politics.

It was fascinating how so many people had so many things to say. Working as a reporter brought me face to face with the politicization of voice, and ultimately, race. In the fall of 2007, I started writing a bi-weekly column on the international student experience. What started off as a wordy complaint on the school's neglect of international student parents turned into a foreigner's commentary on identity, gender, and social norms in America. However, I increasingly felt the need to take action as opposed to observing and writing from the sidelines, and it did not take long for the right opportunity to come along.

Towards the end of the fall semester, a Korean-American friend requested media coverage on a student club which strove to raise awareness on human rights violations in North Korea. Captivated by the notion of second-generation Asian Americans raising awareness on Korean peninsular issues, I started observing weekly meetings.

At the time, the club had a weekly turnout of about ten students, mostly Korean American, who were well versed in contemporary Korean history and culture. Considering there are over 4,000 Asian undergraduate students at NYU, this may seem like a dismal number. However, these students were personally committed to self-education and awareness. Several students expressed feeling a sense of responsibility as Korean Americans to bridge the gap between their ethnic heritage and American identity in a socially conscious way. Needless to say, this was completely inspiring. My take on bridging the gap was limited to taking friends to Korean restaurants, demonstrating how to haggle prices at *noraebang* (karaoke), and streaming K-pop videos on YouTube.

After getting to know Freedom 4 North Korea (F4NK) members on a personal level, I remember thinking, "These folks are more Korean than I am." This thought triggered the subsequent question, "What does being 'Korean' even mean?" Could I really say that I was Korean when I was completely detached from the history and sociopolitical issues of my alleged home country? Up until this point, I categorized Korean Americans under the pan-ethnic identity of Asian American. In doing so, I inherently believed them to be somehow "less Korean" than myself or other international students from Korea. However, I quickly discovered that many second-generation Asian Americans strongly identify with ethno-specific culture and subsequently possess high-octane ethnic attachment. There are over five student clubs with "Korea(n)" in its name at NYU – the most for any ethnic group. Ironically though, there is a hostile divide between the body of Korean-American and Korean international students, which is prevalent at many other college campuses. After writing the piece on the student group, I became a member not just to learn, but also because I felt it was my responsibility to bridge the polarization between Korean-American and Korean international students.

FINDING MY ETHNIC IDENTITY

As junior year started in the fall of 2008, I took classes on contemporary Asian and American history because I was intrigued by two things from my experience with F4NK: understanding my ethnic identity as a Korean living in America and social movements.

The 2008-2009 academic year was my learning curve on post-World War II U.S. foreign policy in East Asia: academic discussions of race, sexuality, and class, and theoretical discussions of capitalism and imperialism. I stopped writing for the school paper and ditched any journalistic aspirations for two reasons: (1) I was disillusioned by the not-so-invisible hand of the market dictating media production, and (2) employment sponsorship after graduation was a highly unlikely outcome in a dwindling industry like print journalism. Ironically, I abandoned journalism for utilitarian reasons, only to take up less practical opportunities at organizations focused on grassroots and community organizing.

Instead of going back to Korea the summer after my junior year, I decided to stay in New York to intern at a community organization mobilizing around peninsular issues. This organization consisted of an eclectic group of first-,

1.5-, and second-generation immigrants who were organizing predominantly on the Peace Treaty Campaign (PTC). The PTC is part of the greater National Campaign to End the Korean War. It aims to replace the outdated 1953 Armistice Agreement with a peace treaty, to promote demilitarization on the peninsula, and to normalize relations with North Korea. In doing so, the PTC hoped to indirectly address social issues by improving living conditions.

The internship program was best described as a class in Grassroots Organizing 101. I met amazing advisors who delved into alternative approaches to understanding history and translating theoretical frameworks of anti-imperialism into practice. We had weekly study sessions and conducted workshops for college students advocating the ratification of a peace treaty. We participated in solidarity pickets for other groups rooted in social justice. We shot a short film gauging public opinion on the Korean War and division.

As I threw myself into the program, I felt camaraderie and a sense of belonging with fellow community organizers who were mostly 1.5- and second-generation Korean Americans. The activities I was engaging in started becoming a part of my identity, and I began to view white males as symbolic of oppression, "the man," and a system of inequality.

However, unlike other community organizers, this was not because I personally experienced racial discrimination or injustice. The passion I felt was undoubtedly a byproduct of believing I could rectify injustice with the power of knowledge—a rather ubiquitous disease that seems to plague students mostly in the social sciences. I felt emotionally attached to the cause because I am Korean, and it concerned the future of all of my family who live in Korea. For the first time in my life, I felt something was worth fighting for. I idealized the student democratization movement of the 1980s in Korea and emulated "circles" by forging study groups with friends. I worked at a café in Koreatown, not out of financial necessity, but in a silly attempt to legitimize myself. Claiming to be a social justice advocate seemed hypocritical when I was a product of a lifelong private education and had no clue about "true suffering," as my father likes to say.

The flipside to finding a niche was the backlash from first-generation conservative groups. Frequently red-baited as a North Korean support group for promoting the establishment of diplomatic relations between the U.S. and North Korea, its members were constantly going into damage control mode even though the organization itself never instigated controversial debates in any formal or informal settings. It is interesting that the same tensions that exist between activists and conservatives in the Korean community in the United States also exist in South Korea.

After completing the internship, I began my senior year of college. By this time, my studies, extracurricular activities, and personal interests began revolving around East Asia-U.S. relations, and my social network drastically changed to predominantly Asian American. My closest friends in college consisted of international students from East Asia who, like myself, had spent a significant part of their lives in a third country or Asian Americans who exhibited strong ethnic attachment (i.e., bilingual, watched TV shows, or followed pop culture in the homeland), but at the same time distanced themselves from ethnically homogeneous social networks. We enjoyed spending time with each other because we all considered ourselves outsiders from our own ethnic groups because none of us had emotionally overpowering ties to a certain identity.

For example, I consider myself "Korean." However, having spent a significant amount of time living abroad in Hong Kong and the U.S., I still feel like an outsider when I visit my parents in Korea. It always takes a period of readjustment. I have to get used to reading and speaking in Korean to complete everyday chores, and I also have to update myself on the latest domestic issues and pop culture. Since most of my friends from Korea are Korean Americans who attended the same international school as me and have also since left to pursue college and a career in the U.S., I only have a couple of friends who permanently live in Korea.

Thus, I spent a lot of time in college with a diverse group of friends, including a friend from Hong Kong who also attended international school and spent several years living in Canada, a fourth-generation Japanese American who stressed the importance of cultural retention, a Filipino American who left an ethnic enclave in California in search of new life experiences, and a Korean who lived in Seoul and Seattle and actively resisted societal expectations of marriage or a white-collar job.

I had no problem befriending my white, black, and Hispanic classmates, but I found myself gravitating towards my Asian friends because it was easy to talk about our shared life experiences of being brought up bilingual under tiger moms and dads. We could vent without explanation about the frustrations of balancing filial piety and professional aspirations, especially as Asian women, in a modern-day setting. It was comforting to cook a big pot of *kimchi jjigae* and just talk in Konglish while hovering over a laptop and watching Korean TV shows online. There was one exception. One of my closest friends was a second-generation Venezuelan American from Miami. We talked about the similarities and differences growing up in our respective cultural environments, but mostly we talked about our immediate concerns with school, family, friends, the future, and society at large.

Although we were all different ethnicities, the common denominator turned out to be the fact that while we were proud of our ethno-specific heritages, it was not the dominant characteristic to how we defined ourselves. Culture and ethnic heritage were laid as foundations by our parents, but it was up to us to build character by using those foundations to navigate an increasingly transnational, capitalistic world. And although I was getting involved in seminars, fundraisers, exhibitions, and rallies for Peace on the

Korean Peninsula, these activities did not make me feel "more Korean." They actually made me feel more Asian American. Getting involved in social movements made me a proponent of ethnic solidarity as I began identifying as a person of color in the broader framework of race and ethnicity in America.

FAMILY INFLUENCES ON MULTICULTURALISM AND CULTURAL RETENTION

When I was two and my brother was barely a year old, our father's job indefinitely relocated us from Seoul to Hong Kong. Although my father worked in mainland Hong Kong, we lived on an island called Discovery Bay, located a 20-minute boat ride away. At the time, Discovery Bay was a small community, host to families from all over the world—most of whom had arrived in Hong Kong for the same reasons as us. My brother and I attended Discovery Bay International School (D.B.I.S), where over thirty-eight nationalities were represented despite the entire school population being only four hundred students. In a way, we received cultural diversity training throughout our childhood. D.B.I.S would host international food fairs, and the entire school would celebrate various holidays including Chinese New Year, Diwali, and St. Patrick's Day. Our teachers taught us to never hide from our ethnic heritage and to respect the traditions and values of our classmates.

However, as a child, I was oblivious to the obvious relationship of white Europeans as the colonizers and Asians as the colonized in day-to-day life in Hong Kong. I was definitely color-blind. I have fond memories of trading friendship bracelets with best friends from Australia and Taiwan, writing letters to a childhood crush from Ireland, and going on weekend trips with local friends.

Our household education reflected our school education. We were required to pick up an instrument, especially after a debauched attempt at ballet on my end. Our parents wanted us to have choices in life, choices they were never given. Our father wanted to show us the world, and made it a point to siphon off a part of his salary to travel abroad once a year. We spent summers backpacking through Europe, playing Uno for hours on trains that seemed to lead nowhere. We snorkeled through the beaches of Southeast Asia, pretending to be pioneers on deserted beaches. Of course these pseudo-Emersonian escapades were strictly regimented by our father, who adhered to self-created itineraries which always began with getting up at the crack of dawn in order to beat lines at any given tourist hotspot. Whether it was the Louvre in Paris, a national volcano park in Hawaii, or Harrods in London, we were the first ones there. "Early bird, catch worm, OK?" was his favorite saying whenever I whined at the unjustness of these so-called vacations.

Although our parents poured their efforts and funds into molding us into citizens of the world, they were simultaneously preparing us for our eventual return to Korea and planned incorporation into the Korean public education system. We spoke Korean at home and drilled academic exercises (especially in math and the Korean language) during summer break. I attended Saturday school for five years.

When it came to discipline, our parents were practitioners of physical punishment and fear tactics. If I wanted to be something other than a supermarket cashier, I was to work hard. If I wanted to be smart, I was to only listen to classical music. I was not to squander time or father's hard-earned money. I had to participate in mandatory family hikes every Saturday. These are just a few examples of family rules in line with our father's life philosophies of "A healthy body equals a healthy mind," and "Time is money."

In short, their parenting methods were dialectical and pushed us in two different directions simultaneously. The dichotomy of embracing cultural diversity while trying to retain our ethnicity defined our childhood. I emphasize that the latter was primarily enforced to prepare us for eventual assimilation back into Korea's ethnically homogeneous society with an education system valuing mathematical skill—not because they believed it was important to have a strong Korean identity.

However, what started out as a temporary relocation to Hong Kong prolonged itself into an eight-year, permanent stint. Towards the end of 1996, our family began planning for my secondary school education and possibly applying to boarding schools in England. However in the summer of 1997, the IMF crisis ravaged Asia, and the Lee family was unexpectedly shipped back to Korea.

SHIFT TO PRACTICALISM

Upon returning to Korea, our parents made the life-altering decision to enroll my brother and me in an international school. They had a change of heart after our sage headmistress at D.B.I.S advised them to "do what makes your children the happiest." Given the economic destitution of Korea at the time, I learned much later that our father went to great lengths to procure private school tuition for two children.

My middle and high school was the antithesis of D.B.I.S. The student population was 99.8 percent Korean, and about 80 percent of them were legally Korean American, having been born in the United States. Our graduating class was 100 percent Korean—there were no students of any other Asian heritage, let alone race. In addition, many students were from *"chae-*

bol" (multi-national business conglomerate) families. I had never seen such a high concentration of tweens decked out in designer labels. Friendships and cliques formed along class lines, and I became increasingly resentful of being on the lower end of the social stratum. I wondered what it was about the ways of the world that allowed some of my classmates to rent out rooms at bars and drop hundreds of dollars on alcohol in a night, while I had to get on the honor roll for a year to earn the rights to an outdated iPod. Consequently, my best friends in Korea were not from "*chaebol*" families, but were relatively middle class—children of pastors, professors, and office workers. Looking back, the indignation I felt during this time planted the seed for future dalliances in social justice.

In the meantime, our father was completely consumed with work and recovering from the IMF. Being the stalwart patriarch, he reassured us of financial stability, however the lines on his face and the grey in his hair were suddenly more pronounced. Our parents' focus in terms of household education shifted to self-sufficiency and financial independence after college. Bottom line, I needed to be financially independent the day I graduated. Thus it was imperative that we attend an Ivy League university. I began tutoring English in the seventh grade to save money and continued intermittently until sophomore year of college.

After moving to Korea, I began internalizing emotional problems stemming from adjustment issues, and my interaction with my parents gradually diminished. We still took family hikes as often as possible, and we started farming on the weekends, but this was no longer for recreational purposes, but rather for therapeutic, stress-relief purposes. However, there were perks to this newfound solitude and independence in pursuing activities. Sixth grade marked many firsts in my life: the first time I used a computer, the first time I went to a movie theater, the first time I bought a "pop" album (and no, there is no shame in admitting it was Britney Spears' ...*Baby One More Time*).

In retrospect, our parents were never helicopter parents. They pushed hard and had high expectations, but were indubitably more concerned with instilling proper work ethic, values, and frameworks for success as opposed to hovering over our daily activities. Consequently, my brother and I are financially independent after graduating from college, although I have recently committed to being a doctoral student with no income. Living in the multicultural, economically stable environment of Hong Kong, and the subsequent dramatic return to a homeland fraught with financial insecurity and political volatility pushed our parents to grapple with accruing cultural capital in their children, so that we may pursue success in America.

EXPLORATION OF THE IMMIGRANT IDENTITY

After graduating from college, I spent a year working at the Flushing YMCA as a Program Counselor at the New Americans Welcome Center (NAWC). The opportunity provided me with interpersonal interactions with a diverse population of immigrants. The NAWC aims to service low-income immigrants in New York City with the tools to achieve literacy, cultural competence, and self-sufficiency by providing a wide range of services (e.g., instructional, vocational, recreational, and family support). I helped adult immigrants, mostly from East Asia, as well as Latin America, South, and Southeast Asia, with referrals and enrollment in free literacy classes for ESL, computers, and citizenship. In addition to administrative work, I taught an ESL class of mostly women in their twenties to forties, who eagerly shared the tribulations and jubilations of living as an immigrant in one of the largest ethnic enclaves in New York City.

Through listening to stories of language, legal and cultural barriers, and the subsequent economic barriers they encountered, I began to understand the nature of racial discrimination as an institutional and systemic problem in the United States. Everything I read about in scholarly articles made a whole lot more sense once the issues were tangible and needed practical solutions, like finding Ms. Zhang a pro bono lawyer to fight a case of tax fraud, writing a letter on behalf of Mr. Kim to inform his employer of a family emergency so he wouldn't lose his job, or registering Ms. Lopez for an adult GED so she could qualify for better employment opportunities.

Just as I had identified with the Asian-American identity in college, I began connecting with an immigrant mentality while working in Flushing. I have no intentions of settling down in the United States for now, however, I would be lying if I said the thought never crossed my mind. I saw New York City as a new chapter of my adult life. The longer I spend time studying in New York and the less I visit Korea, the more I detach from sociopolitical issues affecting Korea. Now that determining a path in life is my main concern, notions of fighting for social justice have long since left my day-to-day activities. My focus has shifted to learning how to balance the search for finding "happiness" in life (a result of my education) and providing a means for sustainable living (a result of household teachings). Currently, I am figuring out my identity as a Korean adapting to life in America and finding a way to professionally explore my interest in sociopolitical issues, which is how I wound up in a Sociology program in graduate school.

SO, WHAT DOES IT MEAN TO BE KOREAN?

Living in New York City means Asians are culturally, politically, and economically relevant. My narrative is markedly different from those of older generations of immigrants who battled discriminatory practices in all-white environments. It is also markedly different from second-generation narratives involving identity politics. This goes to show that the identity of the foreign-born arriving in the U.S. has diversified in recent years. But thanks to the tireless efforts of immigrant predecessors, subsequent generations of Asian immigrants, as well as international students and temporary workers, now exercise the liberty of defining themselves within ethno-specific frameworks of identity. Expansion of ethnic enclaves means you can get off the train at Canal Street in Manhattan or Main Street in Queens and be transported to China. The immigrants I met at the YMCA consistently and proudly identified as "Chinese," regardless of whether they had been living here for twenty days as an undocumented worker or twenty years as a U.S. citizen.

I am just starting to understand my identity as a Korean in the U.S. Consequently, even though I speak English seamlessly, I am far from identifying as a Korean American, even symbolically. My parents have never lived in the United States, and I did not grow up in the United States. There is often a huge gap in relating to personal stories, which makes small talk quite challenging. On the other hand, in many ways I feel very Americanized. I am a fan of pop culture (namely reality TV) and I keep up with national affairs.

However, living in New York, the majority of people I have met have moved to the city from a different state or country. Thus everyone has a unique story involving migration, and diversity is the norm. Living in one of the most densely populated metropolitan cities in the world that also attracts millions of visitors every year means that race is simultaneously hyper visible and invisible.

I have only had two memorably racist encounters in the U.S. The first was when an inebriated white male joked, "Could your eyes be any smaller?" as he walked by me on the street. I was surprised and slightly amused that he did not use the word "chinky" or any other racial slur. The second was in a crowded subway train, when a black male repeatedly sneered, "Girl, you smell of fish." The moment was uncomfortable and awkward, and I was better able to empathize with why race is an emotionally charged, controversial, and timeless subject of discussion. These encounters demonstrate one bothersome expression of race: the sexual fixation on Asian women. It is not uncommon to be approached by non-Asian strangers with "Ni hao," or the question "Are you Japanese?" Those who do not like to waste time blatantly initiate conversation with, "I've always wanted to know what it would be like to sleep with an Asian girl"—this happened once in passing on the street and once at a bookstore. These incidents bring me back to Edward Said's *Orien-*

talism, which only furthers my curiosity on the various reasons why social phenomena like the Asian fetish exist.

Ultimately, the positive encounters living in a racially diverse city greatly outweigh the negatives. It is easy to meet people from all over the world and to gain firsthand insight into different life experiences. The multicultural nature of New York City makes interpersonal relationships traversing racial and class lines simple yet complicated. Graduate school has been a fresh start for me, and the days of grassroots organizing around social justice are now a chapter in the past. Now that I am up to my neck trying to comprehend the foundations of sociological theory and statistics, unlike the politically charged activities of my undergraduate years, I find myself befriending a racially diverse group of people.

I am still in the process of answering what it means to be "Korean"—specifically a Korean living in the United States. But the more I try to come up with a definitive answer, the more abstract the notion becomes. I think this is because the subjective nature of ethnic identity in America means its parameters constantly change according to the interactions between an individual, his/her activities, and how these activities are defined by greater social frameworks in a given environment. I consider myself a product of capitalism and globalization, and consequently, being Korean no longer boils down to living in a certain location, speaking a certain language, or practicing certain cultural traditions. It actually incorporates living in several locations, speaking several languages, and participating in several cultural traditions. Although I now spend significant amounts of time in New York and identify with elements of the Asian-American identity, I am still simply "Korean." Maybe all it boils down to is just that: believing it when you say "I am Korean."

VII

The Editors' Comments on the Essays

Chapter Sixteen

Major Findings about the Cohort Differences

Pyong Gap Min and Thomas Chung

The sixteen informants in Linda Park's study (2013) are all native-born Koreans who grew up in the 1960s and early 1970s. There were less than 70,000 Korean Americans in the United States in 1970. Almost all of the informants lived in middle- and upper-middle-class white neighborhoods. A predominant majority of their parents came to the United States as international students (W. Kim 1971: 26; Park 2013). At that time, younger-generation Koreans had great difficulties in retaining their language and culture, partly because of the small, limited Korean-American population and partly because of the U.S. government's strong assimilation policy. Park's chapter did not address the informants' Korean-language fluency or familiarity with Korean culture. However, she informed me that all of the informants, with the exception of one, could not speak Korean even moderately. The only one who could speak Korean moderately grew up in Koreatown in Los Angeles. Mostly professionals, most other participants lived in suburban neighborhoods in small cities with few Asian Americans.

Even if their parents tried to teach them the Korean language and Korean customs at home, it was very difficult for their children to learn and retain them because there were few Koreans or even Asians in their neighborhoods and schools. Moreover, her interviews with the informants revealed that the social and historical contexts in the 1960s and 1970s put so much emphasis on assimilation that teachers advised their parents to focus on teaching and speaking English at home (Park 2013). Thus, a few of her informants reported that while their parents usually spoke Korean among themselves, they would stop speaking Korean and would immediately switch to English when talking with their children. Like other Americans, they believed that their children should assimilate to America as quickly as possible to achieve social mobility, and that teaching their children the mother tongue (in this case, Korean) would prevent them from learning English.

Among the three authors of the identity essays included in Min and Kim's edited book (1999), Alex Jeong came to New York City at the age of nine, in 1976. Growing up in Korean enclaves (Elmhurst and Flushing) in Queens and, for all intents and purposes, forced to speak Korean at home, he seems to have been fluent in Korean. But Rose Kim, a U.S.-born Korean American who grew up in a suburban white neighborhood in Los Angeles, was thoroughly assimilated and knew only a little Korean from speaking with her grandmother, who lived in her household. The third informant, Ruth Chung, came to Los Angeles at the age of eight, but she, like Kim, spent her childhood and adolescence in a suburban white neighborhood, and consequently, she was not fluent in Korean. Moreover, these two younger-generation Korean women's pressure to fit in with white peers did not motivate them to learn Korean culture. We will come back to this issue in the next subsection when discussing younger-generation Korean Americans' social networks.

The three younger-generation essayists from the 1960s-1970s cohort embraced some Korean values as positive. Rose Kim said that she resented her parents' prohibition on her watching television on school nights, but indicated that she would impose the same restrictions on her own children. Jeong, an assistant district attorney at the time he wrote the essay in the 1990s, but now a Justice in Kings County Supreme Court, said that the strong work ethic he inherited from his father gave him an edge over his peers, most of whom were white Americans, at the Brooklyn District Attorney's office.

However, overall, they were more critical than proud of Korean culture. All three of these younger-generation Korean authors provided poignant critiques of some elements of Korean culture. Rose Kim was very critical of Korean patriarchal traditions that she witnessed at home. She commented:

> Some of my earliest memories are of suffering the degradation of being female, and for a long time I could not help but associate Korean culture with the oppression of women. I believe that my reaction was inevitable in a culture where women primarily held domestic, nonpublic roles as housekeepers, mothers, wives, and prostitutes. (See the first essay in part III.)

She said that when her parents invited guests to her home, she and her sister were "shuttled into the kitchen and forced to assist in preparing food for the guests" while her brothers "were allowed to sit with the adults in the living room." Ruth Chung also commented that during her adolescence, she was attracted more to white men than to Korean men, partly because of her resentment of what she considered to be "oppressive patriarchy within Korean culture."

Jeong became partially paralyzed in a car accident in his second year of law school. He presented a bitter critique of how Koreans viewed the disabled. He commented: "In all societies, the physically handicapped are subject to some prejudices and discrimination. Yet the bigoted attitudes I have encountered in the Korean community far exceed anything I have encountered in American society at large." The sixteen informants in Park's study criticized Korean immigrants and Koreans in Korea for not accepting them as "Korean" because of their inability to speak Korean. All of them had very uncomfortable experiences in Korea due to their language barriers. One male informant was even attacked by a man in Korea for not speaking Korean. They were very critical of the *danil minjok* ideology of Koreans that rejects U.S.-born Koreans based on their cultural differences. Their experiences of rejection by Koreans due to their language barrier hurt them greatly. As will be shown later, they were not accepted as American in the U.S., and to add insult to injury, due to their cultural differences, they were also not accepted as Korean in Korea.

The later cohort consists of ten essayists who grew up in the United States in the 1980s and early 1990s. The Korean-American population increased from about 69,000 in 1970 to nearly 800,000 in 1990 (Min and Kim 2013: 36). Only two metropolitan areas, Los Angeles and Honolulu, had sizeable Korean populations in 1970. By contrast, each of the following eight metropolitan areas—Los Angeles, New York-New Jersey, San Francisco, Baltimore-DC-Northern Virginia, Chicago, Philadelphia, Honolulu, and Seattle—had 25,000 or more Korean Americans in 1990 (Min and Kim 2013: 48). To provide a breakdown of the later cohort as a whole, six of the essayists grew up in the New York-New Jersey metropolitan area, two in Atlanta, GA, one in Los Angeles, CA, and one in Hong Kong.

Among the ten essayists from the 1980s-1990s cohort, two of them were fluent in Korean. Alexandra Noh, a 1.5-generation Korean who moved to the United States at the age of two, mastered both spoken and written Korean through her Korean-language education before she began attending an American public school in Queens, NY. Additionally, she honed her Korean-language skills by living with her grandmother and by attending a Korean church. Five essayists in the later cohort were able to speak Korean at the intermediate level, while the other three could speak Korean only at the most basic, beginner level.

A few women essayists from this cohort provided a similar critique of Korean patriarchal traditions. Helene Lee was vocal in exposing unfair treatment she received from her parents at home and from others in the Korean community, compared to her older brother. She wrote:

> My parents were always referenced in relation to my older brother. They were

"Sang's mom" or "Sang's dad," and it was me who was chastised if I didn't call him "*oppa*" (big brother) even though he could boss me around by my given name. I protested against the unfair division of reproductive labor at home, of my doing the dishes and helping out with the cooking or cleaning on a daily basis, while my brother was left alone. Later on, the challenges of being a Korean-American teenager came down to separating the "good" Korean girls from the "bad" ones. (See the first essay in part V.)

She said she dismissed Korean Americans as potential dating partners because of her fear that they "would come up with the demanding mothers who would not approve of me as a 'good Korean wife,' given my career ambitions and my divorced parents."

SOCIAL RELATIONS WITH KOREAN VS. NON-KOREAN FRIENDS

The earlier-cohort informants in Park's book chapter reported that, growing up, they knew they were Koreans, partly because that was what their parents emphasized at home and partly because they had physical differences from the white children and white students around them. Nevertheless, they grew up mostly interacting with white friends, with little contact with Korean or other Asian friends. The 1960s–1970s cohort had little opportunity to interact with other Koreans during their pre-college years because of the lack of Korean Americans in their neighborhoods or schools.

Upon entering high school and college in the late 1970s, the earlier-cohort informants had more opportunities to meet co-ethnic students, mostly Korean immigrants. However, many of them intentionally distanced themselves from Korean immigrants to "blend in" with white peers or to "act white." As one informant said, "We still hung out but you could tell that they were the weird ones and I guess there was that term called FOB, 'fresh off the boat.' I didn't want to look like that. I wanted to look like my blond-headed American friends and do what they do." Many of the Korean Americans from the earlier cohort also experienced some difficulties interacting with 1.5-generation Korean co-ethnic students, partly because they felt excluded by the latter due to their lack of Korean-language fluency. As one informant said, "So I didn't totally identify with them because they all had grown up in Korea, at least through some significant period of time. Korean was their first language and I didn't speak Korean and I didn't feel like I fit in with that group."

Only two younger-generation informants in the earlier cohort had significant numbers of Korean friends. Both of them were 1.5-generation Koreans who learned the Korean language prior to their migration to the United States and grew up in large Korean communities. One of them, Ruth Chung, came to the United States at the age of eight and spent her early years in Los

Angeles. During her college years, she lived in two segregated social worlds, one with Korean friends and the other with white friends. She tried to maintain a balance between the two worlds in her friendship patterns and tried to integrate them. The other informant was Alex Jeong, who arrived in Flushing, New York, in 1976, at the age of nine. Flushing, the major Korean enclave in New York City, had a substantial number of Korean immigrants and children, even in the latter half of the 1970s. In addition, Jeong said that his father made him always speak Korean at home.

Having grown up in the 1980s and early 1990s, the ten essayists comprising the later cohort had far more active interactions with co-ethnic friends than the informants in the earlier cohort. This is particularly true for six of the ten essayists who spent their childhood and adolescent years in Korean enclaves or multiethnic neighborhoods, mostly in the New York-New Jersey area. Three of the essayists grew up in predominantly white neighborhoods: Katherine Yungmee Kim, who grew up in New Jersey, and Thomas Chung and Brenda Chung , who are siblings and who spent their early and formative years in Atlanta, GA. Hyein Lee is the lone essayist from the later cohort who did not grow up in the United States. She spent most of her formative years in Hong Kong, and a few years in Korea, mostly attending English-language international schools.

More importantly, by the early 1980s, the number of Korean immigrant churches, which provided fellowship and co-ethnic social networks for Korean immigrants (Hurh and Kim 1990; Min 1992), had grown exponentially in major Korean communities. A predominant majority of young Korean children (about 75%) regularly participated in Korean immigrant churches in the 1980s and 1990s, accompanied by their parents (Hurh and Kim 1990; Min 1992). Among the nine essayists who grew up in the United States, eight participated in Korean churches during their childhood, at least for a few years, with seven of them attending Korean Protestant churches and only one attending a Catholic church.

Korean immigrant churches are known to provide ethnic education and strong co-ethnic friendship ties for second-generation Korean Americans (Min 1992, 2010). Yet, only three of the nine essayists who participated in Korean Protestant churches during their childhood seem to have enjoyed their participation and have continued as adults. Even the three essayists who have continued attending Korean churches as adults have not turned into ardent evangelical Christians like many other second-generation Korean Christians. None of them has talked much about their Korean church friends or the importance of their religious faith for their identity. The other six, including Sun K. Park, the son of a Korean pastor, experienced more alienation from other church members during their childhood. Four of them stopped going to church during their adolescence, while Sun K. Park still seems to reluctantly attend church, mainly to satisfy his father.

Sun K. Park was never particularly religious, but as the son of a devout pastor, he was forced to attend his father's church. Moreover, as the son of a pastor, other church participants expected him to be fluent in Korean, but he could not speak Korean. This language barrier, his lack of other Korean cultural elements, and Korean immigrants' exclusive focus on children's academic performances in the church made him extremely uncomfortable attending it. This uncomfortable experience in his father's Korean church seems to have led him to feel negatively about Korean ethnicity. His lack of Korean-language fluency and the corresponding expectations of Korean immigrant students continued to bother and marginalize him throughout his high school and college years, particularly because he grew up in areas of Queens, NY, with heavy concentrations of Koreans. Two essayists, Thomas Chung and Brenda Chung, are siblings who grew up in Atlanta in the 1980s and early 1990s. Both of them attended a Korean church as children, but they stopped going to church within a few years because they were harassed and marginalized by other Korean and Korean-American members of the Sunday school. Thomas Chung wrote: "My bad experiences with the church were some of the most significant factors that led to my subsequent (albeit subconscious) rejection of my Korean identity." We expected Korean children's participation in Korean immigrant churches to help them to maintain social ties with co-ethnic friends and Korean identity. But this unexpected finding, although never generalizable to younger-generation Koreans in general, suggests that participation in Korean churches can have a negative effect on some younger-generation Koreans' ethnic attachment.

We previously noted that the informants in the earlier cohort had social interactions primarily with white friends. By contrast, most essayists in the later cohort have close friendship and dating networks with members of different racial groups, including co-ethnic Korean Americans, other East Asians, other racial minorities, and whites. Sun K. Park and Helene Lee seem to feel more comfortable with white friends and dating partners. They worry about Korean immigrants' rejection of them due to their barrier in the Korean language and cultural differences when interacting with them. Dave Hahn, Hyein Lee, and Alexandra Noh seem to prefer East Asian friendship networks, including Korean friends. Bora Lee has many close friends who are East Asian and Latino. Sung S. Park's close friends consist mainly of whites and African Americans.

LINKAGES TO THE HOMELAND (SOUTH KOREA)

Five or six of the sixteen informants in Linda Park's book chapter have visited Korea, all during their college or post-college years, while only one of the three Korean-American essayists (Ruth Chung) in the earlier cohort has visited, at least at the time of the book's publication. A small proportion of the informants from the earlier cohort visited Korea during their college or post-college years, in the 1980s, when South Korea had started to achieve high economic development. Their parents were not prone to sending their children to their homeland during the informants' elementary or secondary school years, partially because Korea had a low global profile in the 1970s, which was not very appealing to the parents or to their children.

However, these selected informants who visited Korea as adults also had negative experiences during their homeland trips that may have weakened rather than strengthened their Korean identity. All of them experienced a strong sense of rejection as Koreans because they could not speak Korean and were culturally different in other ways. One informant commented on the language issue:

> I remember once when we went to Korea, it was post-college and I remember a taxi cab driver was lecturing me because I couldn't speak Korean and it was like, he has a point—I look Korean, why can't I speak? (See part II.)

Another male informant reported that he even encountered an incidence of physical violence for speaking English during his summer school trip to Korea:

> Actually in Korea, in summer school walking back one night, I was with one of the Korean-American girls speaking English down an alleyway when a drunken Korean man came out. And he was like "Why are you not speaking Korean?" and then he attacked me and we fought too. I tried not to fight but it ended up that he was very aggressive. It was a short battle pretty much. She dragged me away and he was throwing bottles around. Yea, it was crazy! (See part II.)

Younger-generation Koreans' experiences of being treated as foreigners in Korea for not speaking Korean and not following Korean customs have been documented in other studies (E. Kim 2010: 188-192; N. Kim 2009; Lee 2013). Because of their experiences of being treated as foreigners, their homeland trips only strengthened their American identity.

The vast majority (eight) of the ten later-cohort essayists visited South Korea at least once. Two of them spent many years in Korea. One of them, Hyein Lee, completed kindergarten and elementary school at an international school in Hong Kong and attended junior and senior high school at an international school in Korea. She completed her undergraduate college education at NYU and has been working on a Ph.D. at the CUNY-Graduate Center. Thus, she has a strong transnational Korean identity. The other informant, Katherine Yungmee Kim, was born and raised in a suburban neighborhood in New Jersey. However, in her essay, she reported that she had visited Korea twelve times, and that each visit lasted from two weeks to eighteen months. She completed third grade in Korea and returned to Korea after college to work for eighteen months. Therefore, she has strong attachments to both South Korea and the United States. She characterizes her identity as "Korean and American," not "Korean American." These two cases are representative of many people living in multiple national locations in this global age.

Among the other six essayists from the 1980s-1990s cohort who visited Korea at least once, Helene Lee spent a year and a half in Seoul conducting her dissertation research in 2004 and 2005. Her dissertation focused on the experiences of young 1.5- and second-generation Korean-Americans and multigenerational Korean Chinese during their homeland trips to Korea (Lee 2013). Her dissertation research and the accompanying prolonged stay in Korea were intertwined with some of her own personal identity issues as a second-generation Korean American. Upon seeing many people who looked like her, she initially felt re-connected with her Korean identity, which was vague and ambiguous prior to her extended visit. However, she said that this honeymoon period soon ended as she began to experience rejection as a Korean. Although she speaks and understands Korean at a basic to intermediate level, she felt rejected and alienated because of her lack of total Korean-language fluency and other "un-Korean" behaviors. The following paragraph captures this sense of rejection and marginalization:

> My numerous blunders in mundane, everyday interactions were a constant source of embarrassment because I "looked" Korean but did not behave as such. Usually after a surprised pause, I got the "Oh, you're an American" remark, dripping with condescension, from the checker at the grocery store, the teller at the bank, the taxi driver or even the bus driver when I awkwardly tried to ask whether I was going the right way. As long as I kept my mouth shut, I felt I could "pass" as Korean in a complete reversal from my childhood, when I deliberately talked in unaccented English to prove that I was a "real" American. The overwhelming feeling that I felt more American in Seoul complicated the connection I felt with South Korea. This feeling was echoed by Korean-American friends who also felt that they were trapped in a permanent, liminal state—in the U.S., they were seen as Korean, in South Korea, they were seen as American. (See the first essay in part V.)

We noted above that the earlier-cohort informants who visited Korea in the 1980s had similar experiences of being rejected as Korean due to their inability to speak fluent Korean in public with strangers. Many of the 1960s-1970s cohort experienced overt rejection from Korean taxi drivers and Korean college students in the 1980s because they were Koreans who were not speaking Korean. However, over the past two decades, there have been some positive changes in South Korea in terms of accepting foreigners and overseas Koreans. Helene Lee encountered a more subtle form of rejection in her everyday interactions with Koreans in South Korea in the mid-2000s. But, as we can see from her essay, their perception of her as an "American" based on her difficulties with the Korean language and her unnatural Korean behaviors has weakened the Korean side of her identity.

Two of the other four informants who had visited Korea at least once mentioned that their homeland tours helped to forge their Korean-American identity. Thomas Chung participated in an educational overseas Korean summer camp held at Seoul National University between his sophomore and junior year in high school in the early 1990s. It was his second trip to Korea; he had made his first trip during his childhood. Although he felt somewhat alienated from other participating overseas Korean students, he reported, he improved his Korean-language skills drastically during the tour by spending time with his extended family members and wandering around various parts of South Korea. He said, "I also felt closer to my Korean roots, and it strengthened my desire to explore and cultivate that part of me." He made his third visit to Korea at the age of twenty-five to watch the 2002 World Cup soccer tournament, which was co-hosted by South Korea and Japan. He said that watching the World Cup soccer games played in various cities in Korea and joining other Koreans in cheering for the South Korean national team really kindled his Korean identity. We cite here the last several sentences from a paragraph in which he discussed his participation in the World Cup soccer games:

> I was surprised at how readily I adopted South Korea as my team. Although I had lived my entire life in the States, I even rooted for Korea when they played the U.S. On my last night in Korea, we attended the South Korea vs. Portugal match. The Reds upset the powerhouse Portuguese, which advanced the team to the next round. Pandemonium swept the entire nation that night. People paraded, chanted, and wept with joy. I felt like I was walking in a dream world. As I marched and chanted alongside the countrymen of my parents and ancestors, I truly felt proud to be Korean. (See the third essay in part IV.)

The other informant, Dave Hahn, made his second and third tours to Korea as a teenager. He participated in a summer roots education program for overseas Koreans, which was sponsored by the Korean government. He made this noteworthy comment regarding his ethnic education tours and his acceptance by Koreans: "I have never felt rejected by Koreans anywhere, either in the United States or in Korea. There's always been encouragement from every Korean person I meet to immerse myself in more Korean culture and to tie myself more into the community at large." As noted in the previous two subsections, many earlier-cohort informants complained about having been rejected by both Korean immigrants in the United States and by Koreans in Korea for not being culturally Korean. In his personal essay, Dave Hahn also mentions that he feels prouder of his Korean background because of the increasing popularity of Korean culture, the rise of Korean economic development, and the increase in quality and use of Korean-made cars and electronic products in the United States in the 2000s. No doubt, the popularity of Korean-brand cars and electronics and Korean culture in the United States must have boosted the Korean identity of most other later-cohort informants.

More later-cohort essayists visited Korea and did it at earlier ages than the earlier-cohort essayists. Both groups encountered rejection as Koreans in Korea due to their language barrier and cultural differences, which strengthened their American identity. Nevertheless, a few essayists in the later cohort discussed how much their visits to Korea strengthened their Korean identity. Studies of ethnic identity have neglected to examine the role the home country of younger-generation ethnic Americans and their experiences during their visits home play in the formation of their ethnic identity.

EXPERIENCES WITH RACIAL PREJUDICE AND DISCRIMINATION

There were not many Asians in the United States in the 1960s and early 1970s. Moreover, Asian countries were seen either as enemy countries to the United States in terms of political ideology or poor countries with little to no global visibility during the Cold-War era. Thus, there were high levels of racial prejudice and discrimination against Asian Americans during the period.

Linda Park's book chapter based on her personal interviews with sixteen younger-generation Korean Americans from the 1960s-1970s cohort includes plenty of comments that illustrate their experiences with racial prejudice and discrimination. For example, a second-generation woman bitterly recounted her experiences with dating due to racial discrimination:

> It was very blatant. First of all, I can't date the white people. This is a small city in Texas. I was always considered "Oriental," so it wasn't considered that I could date the white people. It's hard to explain. It's just, that's just the way it was. (See part II.)

A female informant recalled a particular incident that occurred to her younger sister:

> I remember when my sister ran for student council in Ohio and she was like class president and all that, but someone scrawled on her campaign posters "Remember Pearl Harbor." I don't think the community viewed itself as racist even though I think it probably was extremely so. (See part II.)

At that time, native-born Asian Americans were perceived as foreigners and frequently asked "where they are from," "what they are," and "when they plan to go back home." Another informant who spent her childhood in the East Coast and the Midwest commented:

> Oh clearly there were a lot of questions like "what are you?" I'm not sure if that was being discriminating against [. . .] I've been told I speak English very well and asked "when are you going to go back?" [. . .] More people were just ignorant and I came to appreciate that later. Obviously it was becoming burden-some to have to continuously explain who you were. (See part II.)

The later cohort of younger-generation Korean Americans did not experience the overt, blatant forms of racism that the earlier cohort encountered. However, all of the essayists from the later cohort discussed their experiences with subtle forms of racism or racial stereotypes, which they encountered in schools, residential neighborhoods, and at their workplaces. Dave Hahn, who works for a communication company in Atlanta, Georgia, devoted three or four pages of his essay to discussing how often he heard people making stereotypical statements about him. For example, a security guard at his work asked him on a hot summer day, "Where's your hat? I thought your people always wore hats in this weather?" He told the security guard that he did not need one. Walking away, he realized that the man was referring to a rice farmer's hat, the kind that was visible in old Asian villages, and an image that was a pejorative Western stereotype of Third World Asians. However, he was most "annoyed at the American media's portrayal of Asian men as being not sexually virile." Many essayists were annoyed and sometimes hurt because they were often called "Chinese," "chink," "Chinaman," etc. Alexandra Noh wrote that when she was passing a stranger he approached her, saying, "You look like a China doll! But since you're Chinese, I guess that just means you look like a doll." These two essayists from the later cohort also expressed their concerns about "positive" stereotypes of Korean Americans as hard-working and successful.

Three essayists from the later cohort encountered more serious forms of prejudice and/or discrimination. Two Korean-American siblings, Thomas Chung and Brenda Chung, grew up in the suburbs of Atlanta, GA, in the 1980s and 1990s. They were among the only Asian kids in their largely middle-class white elementary school. Brenda complained that the students in her class would ask her why she closed her "slanted eyes" when she laughed. She recollected that she would come home crying over her being singled out in school due to something she could not change. When she got older, she encountered other types of racist remarks by white students, such as "My daddy killed a bunch of you guys in the war." The white student meant to indicate the Vietnam War, which shows his ignorance of Asian peoples (inability to separate Koreans from Vietnamese). However, Brenda was more hurt by his malicious intent than by his ignorance. Her brother, Thomas, also encountered similar prejudice during his elementary, high school, and college years. Both Brenda and Thomas also discussed their parents' experiences with racial rejection and racial taunts by black customers in their retail store. Thomas said he often heard black customers calling his parents "Chinese and ching chong" and screaming "Go back to your country" when arguing with his parents about their refund/return policy and other aspects of business transactions.

Sung Shim Park gave specific examples of how she was unfairly treated at her workplace in Baltimore. She felt that she was assigned more work than her white co-workers, yet did not receive raises, bonuses, or promotions while she watched her white peers get promoted. She also complained that her co-workers confused her name with a Vietnamese-American woman's name. She and her Vietnamese-American colleague corrected people time and time again, but she said they continued to make the same mistake. She told the manager about the problem, without ever actually mentioning race or racism. She said that the manager dismissed it, saying "there was no bad will or harmful intent" by calling them the wrong names.

INNER STRUGGLE FOR ETHNIC IDENTITY

Growing up, the informants in the earlier cohort were very conscious of their Korean backgrounds, not only because of their parents' emphasis on it, but also because the dominant white society emphasized this ascribed racial characteristic to identify them (Park 2013: 179). However, they often felt ashamed of their Korean background and thus tried to hide it as much as possible. As noted in some of the informants' previously cited comments, they "acted white" publicly and tried to keep their Korean sides private. Ruth Chung, a 1.5-generation Korean woman, grew up in a suburban white middle-class neighborhood in Los Angeles in the 1970s. She commented on her effort to hide her Korean side in her early high school years:

> I was ashamed of my Koreanness and anything that hinted at my difference. I believed that I had to reject my culture and deny who I was if I wanted to be accepted by my friends and American society . . . By virtue of being nonwhite, I was excluded from society's perceptions of beauty and value. And yet I tried desperately to be white and actually came to believe that I was successful . . . (See the third essay in part III.)

When minorities absorb the racist messages in a white-dominant society, they come to replicate the negative messages in their own minds, believing that members of their ethnic or racial groups are actually inferior to white

Americans in intelligence, beauty, and other characteristics. This symptom or tendency is referred to as "internalized racism." Rose Kim reports that when she transferred to a high school in a predominantly Hispanic and Asian neighborhood, she tried to minimize her interactions with minority students. She recognized that her thinking that minorities were inferior to whites in her high-school years was a kind of internalized racism:

> Somehow I had developed the notion that white students were superior, and felt disdainful toward my classmates. I never participated in school events, spent lunches in the school library . . . Many years later, I recognized these feelings as being the possible result of living in a society where Asian Americans are not recognized as members of the mainstream. When I read about the concept of internalized racism, the replication of racist prototypes within one's own mind, I finally was able to come to terms with my past, conflicted feelings. (See the first essay in part III.)

"Acting white" out in public and acting as a Korean inside the home were possible during childhood, particularly for the essayists from the earlier cohort. However, it became increasingly difficult as they reached adolescence and adulthood. They realized that, culturally, they could act like perfect Americans; however, they could never hide their non-white physical differences. This realization led them to undergo many psychological struggles. To resolve these inner struggles, younger-generation Korean Americans, like many other younger-generation American children of immigrants, tried to accept their ethnic sides later in their lives, in late adolescence or young adulthood. They usually began their ethnic journeys when a particular incident at a particular moment led them to visually recognize their physical differences from whites. Ruth Chung recognized her physical difference from other white students at a specific moment in her high school senior year. The following paragraph from her essay vividly captures how she felt when she recognized this difference:

> I was walking down the mirror-paneled hallway of my high school, talking and laughing with a group of friends. For a brief moment as we walked past the mirrors, I caught my reflection in the midst of my friends. What struck me at that moment was how visibly different I was from them. Because most of the faces that I saw around me were white, I had come to believe that mine was too. In that devastating moment of truth, I was confronted with the reality that no matter how much I tried to deny it, I was inevitably who I was and that it was useless and foolish to ignore that fact. I recognized that in my desire to belong and fit in, I had been deluding myself to the point of thinking that I was actually white. (See the third essay in part III.)

Once they accepted the ethnic components of their identity, younger-generation Korean Americans began to resolve their inner struggles and began to recover and cultivate some self-confidence. They came to realize that their holding of both Korean and American cultures and identities was not a conflict, but a blessing. The following paragraph from Ruth Chung's essay, along with the quotation in the previous paragraph, again delivers the main point:

> This incident served as a catalyst for painful soul-searching and marked the beginning of an inner journey toward greater self-acceptance. Until that point, my struggle with ethnic identity and the denial of my Koreanness had been largely unconscious, but I began to see that the cost of my denial was too high a price to pay. I accepted the reality of my biculturality, that I was inevitably both Korean and American, and that I had a unique opportunity to learn from both cultures, rather than rejecting one for the other. For the first time since that moment in the second grade when I wished I was a blond-haired girl with the last name Smith, I began to see my bicultural experience as a blessing and an opportunity rather than a curse. (See the third essay in part III.)

However, many other younger-generation Koreans did not start searching for their ethnic roots until they were in college.

We expect the experiences of the essayists composing the later cohort to be more conducive to the formation of their Korean ethnic identity than the earlier cohort. As already noted, only three of the nine essayists (remember that Hyein Lee lived in Hong Kong in her early years) grew up in suburban white neighborhoods. The others grew up in Korean enclaves or multiracial neighborhoods with active or moderate interactions with Korean immigrants. Moreover, all of them had access to Korean Protestant or Catholic churches, which helped Korean immigrants and their children with ethnic fellowship and cultural retention. We already noted that the later cohort experienced subtle forms of prejudice and racial stereotypes in comparison to the more blatant forms of racial discrimination encountered by the earlier cohort. Accordingly, the later cohort are unlikely to have tried to hide their ethnic background due to being scared by the dominance of white society, and thus they are also unlikely to have lived with much racism-induced inner struggle.

We have found that only two of the ten essays indicate that the authors tried to not publicly display their ethnic side to avoid racial rejection. Read the following paragraph from Helene Lee's essay:

> From an early age, I learned that being too ethnic came at a social cost, because popular kids were never FOBs [Fresh Off the Boat]. Public displays of Koreanness were to be avoided at all costs. During my teenage years, when image meant everything, I started to feel like expressions of ethnicity were safe only within the private realm of the home and the family. (See the first essay in part V.)

Helene Lee's attitude reflected in the above paragraph is similar to the phenomenon of "acting white," which is associated with the earlier cohort. The following paragraph in Brenda Chung's essay also suggests the author's reluctance to identify herself as Korean to other people:

> There were many more instances of discrimination, both at school and at the store. Sadly, there are too many to list or even to remember. What I do recall is that I grew up with a reluctance to bring any undue attention to my ethnicity. It's not that I was ashamed to be Korean, but rather that calling myself Korean seemed to invite negative interactions. It is said that people determine their self-worth based on the reactions of others. (See the first essay in part IV.)

Most of the other essayists from the later cohort did not mention hiding or even having the desire to hide their ethnic background in their early years. However, they may have still experienced inner struggles over how to maintain a balance between their Korean and American identities, or how to integrate them, especially as they grew older and more aware. However, unlike the earlier-cohort informants, none of them seem to have felt scared by the absence of Korean/Asian culture and/or the limited size of the Korean/Asian population. Most later-cohort essayists took issue with Koreans' rejection of second-generation Korean Americans for their loss of the Korean language and culture; they also resented the Korean communities in South Korea and the United States for treating women as second-class citizens. Interestingly, none of the later-cohort essayists seem to have felt ashamed of their Korean background in their earlier years or at the time of writing their essays.

SUMMARY AND CONCLUSION

As expected, the study participants from the later cohort learned the Korean language and Korean culture much better than those from the earlier cohort. The larger Korean population in the United States and a more multicultural policy in schools helped them to learn their ethnic language and culture. Moreover, the later-cohort essayists were also more involved in co-ethnic friendship and dating networks. In addition, more of them visited their mother country, with some of them having positive experiences for their ethnic identity. The advantages in these three contributing factors helped them to maintain stronger and more positive ethnic identity than the study participants in the earlier cohort.

As expected, the essayists from the later cohort largely experienced subtle and less serious forms of racial prejudice and discrimination than the earlier cohort. As a result, they were able to accept their Korean ethnic identity more as a choice, compared to the participants from the earlier cohort, who were forced to accept the Korean or Asian racial assignment and had no choice in the matter. The participants from the earlier cohort, ashamed of accepting Korean identity because of negative images associated with Korea, tried to "act white" (behave like white people). However, they realized they could not hide their non-white physical characteristics. This dilemma put a great deal of psychological pressure on them until they began their ethnic journeys. By contrast, much stronger internal factors helped the essayists from the later cohort generally embrace their ethnic identity from their early years. Additionally, Americans accepted Korean culture and Koreans much better in the 1980s and early 1990s than in the earlier period. Accordingly, the essayists from the later cohort experienced much less inner psychological conflict over identity issues.

However, the two groups of study participants show some interesting similarities, albeit with moderate differences in degree. The majority of the study participants from both cohorts are women. Some of the female participants from both cohorts are very critical of patriarchal customs they experienced in their parents' homes, Korean communities, and Korea. Moreover, because of their language barrier and unfamiliarity with Korean customs, most informants from the earlier cohort encountered rejection as Korean by people in Korea during their homeland tours, which weakened their Korean identity. One female essayist from the later cohort (Helene Lee) also reported that she had similarly uncomfortable experiences of being recognized as "American" due to her inadequate Korean-language skills and lack of intimate familiarity with some of the more subtle aspects of Korean culture. A few informants from both cohorts also reported that their sense of rejection due to their language barrier led them to minimize interactions with Korean immigrants or church members, which subsequently contributed to weakening their Korean ethnic identity.

This study contributes to understanding the formation of ethnic identity among Korean and other Asian Americans by showing the significant differences in younger-generation Korean Americans' ethnic identity formation between the two cohorts, influenced by the four contributing factors. It also theoretically contributes to studies of ethnic identity in general by creating a typology of four different forms of ethnic identity in the four different contexts made by the cross-classification of three internal factors and one external factor and by connecting two Korean cohorts' different identity formations with two of the four contexts.

Younger-generation Korean-American children who are growing up in major American metropolitan areas today (in 2013) have even more advantages in forming their ethnic identity smoothly over the later cohort who grew up in the 1980s and early 1990s in terms of both internal and external factors. The Korean-American population grew from about 800,000 in 1990 to over 1.7 million in 2010. About two-thirds of Korean Americans live in the fifteen largest Korean population centers, where they have access to Korean TV and radio programs, as well as many Korean restaurants and supermarkets. Each of these Korean population centers has over a hundred Korean religious organizations, anywhere from dozens to over a hundred Korean weekend schools, and numerous other Korean ethnic organizations. Additionally, Korean-American children growing up in the 2010s have the advantage of new technological products and the Internet, which make it far easier to access Korean dramas, music, and other media, which can contribute to ethnic identity formation. There are even smart phone applications that are designed to aid in Korean-language education, in addition to Korean dictionary applications. Some of the 1980s-1990s cohort essayists were young enough to have access to the Internet when they were still in school. But none of the older members of that cohort had had Internet access until they were in college or later. Additionally, the Internet was not what it is today in the 1990s. It is much easier to visit Korea now than it was twenty years ago. Results of a survey study conducted in the late 2000s show that the vast majority of Korean-American adolescents have visited Korea at least once, with two-thirds having visited it twice or more.

Finally, the Korean economic, diplomatic, athletic, and cultural influence in the globalized world is now much stronger than it was in the early 1990s. While these internal sources of Korean ethnic identity have grown tremendously over the last two decades, the level of white racism has decreased in the same period. By virtue of these changes in the three internal factors and the external factor contributing to the formation of ethnic identity, younger-generation Korean-American children and adolescents are likely to accept their Korean ethnic identity at early ages, without much inner struggle. Most of them are likely to accept strong or moderate Korean ethnic identity, but not because they are not accepted as American by others. They will do so mainly because they are equipped with Korean cultural content and social networks and they feel proud of being Korean. They may be accepted as American in most situations. However, they will choose Korean identity in addition to American identity, because they know that being Korean is really a part of them and that, even publicly, accepting their Korean side will not hurt them (as it may have hurt the essayists from the 1960s-1970s cohort).

A small proportion of younger-generation Korean-American children and adolescents are likely to be highly acculturated to American society, thus, they are likely to lose the Korean language and customs over time, if they haven't already. Unlike those younger-generation Koreans who grew up in the 1960s-1970s, these highly assimilated younger-generation Koreans will not have a psychological problem because they are well accepted as Americans by others. However, they may not enjoy the same levels of flexibility in behavior and creativity in thinking that younger-generation Korean Americans with strong Korean-American identity enjoy. To reiterate, today's younger-generation Korean Americans are not forced to accept the Korean or Asian label, but have the luxury of choosing whether or not to add Korean ethnic identity to their American identity. This combination of identities is likely to enrich their lives, because they can pick and choose the best aspects of both cultures.

Although we emphasize the differences in ethnic identity between the two cohorts of younger-generation Korean Americans in this book, we are also aware that there are substantial individual differences among members of each cohort. Moreover, we also know that younger-generation Korean-American individuals often hold multiple identities, as Korean, Korean American, Asian American, American, or transnational. Depending on particular situations, one form of identity is likely to be more salient than the others (Nagel 1994; Okamura 1981). For example, second-generation Korean Americans who participate in an Asian-American softball league are likely to have stronger pan-Asian identity when playing softball games with other Asian-American members than when attending a Korean ethnic church. When second-generation Koreans encounter repeated rejection and discriminatory treatment in Korea due to their sub-par Korean-language skills and cultural differences, they are likely to hold fairly strong American identity, at least during their stay in Korea.

Finally, other axes of identity, such as gender and disabled status, can be stronger than their ethnic or racial identity for some Korean Americans. For example, younger-generation Korean women who have witnessed women's subordination in their families, in the Korean community and/or in Korea with great frequency may hold stronger gender identity than ethnic or racial identity. Disabled and homosexual Koreans are likely to identify more strongly with their disabled status or sexual orientation because prejudice and discrimination against these groups are more salient in the United States than racial prejudice. As we can see in this book, Alex Jeong, a Korean disabled man, devotes most of his essay to criticizing Korean immigrants' prejudiced attitudes towards and discrimination against disabled persons.

References Cited and Additional References on Ethnic Identity

Alba, Richard. 1990. *Ethnic Identity: The Transformation of White America*. John Wiley.
Alba, Richard, and Reid Golden. 1986. "Patterns of Ethnic Marriage in the United States." *Social Forces* 65: 202–223.
Alba, Richard, and Victor Nee. 1997. "Rethinking Assimilation for the New Era of Immigration." *International Migration Review* 31: 826–74.
Alba, Richard, and Victor Nee. 2003. *Remaking American Mainstream: Assimilation and Contemporary Immigration*. Cambridge: Harvard University Press.
Alumkal, Anthony. 1999. "Preserving Patriarchy: Assimilation, Gender Norms, and Second Generation Korean American Evangelicals." *Qualitative Sociology* 22: 129–140.
———. 2001. "Being Korean, Being Christian: Particularism and Universalism in a Second-Generation Congregation" In *Korean Americans and Their Religions: Pilgrims and Missionaries from a Different Shore*, edited by Ho-Youn Kwon, Kwang Chung Kim, and Stephen Warner. University Park, PA: Pennsylvania State University Press.
Anderson, Benedict.1983. *Imagined Communities*. London: Verso.
Bailey, Benjamin. 2000. "Language and Negotiation of Ethnic/Racial Identity among Dominican Americans." *Language in Society* 29: 555–582.
Bakalian, Anny. 2003. *Armenian-Americans: From Being to Feeling Armenian*. New Brunswick, NJ: Transaction.
Bakalian, Anny, and Mehdi Bozorgmehr. 2010. *Backlash 9/11: Impact and Reaction of Middle Eastern and Muslim Americans*. Berkeley: University of California Press.
Bankston, Carl III, and Min Zhou. 1996. "Religious Participation, Ethnic Identification, and Adaptation of Vietnamese Adolescents in an Immigrant Community." *Sociological Quarterly* 36: 523–534.
Banton, Michael. 1997. *Ethnic and Racial Consciousness*. Harlow: Addison Wesley Logham.
Barkan, Elliot. 1995. "Race, Religion, and Nationality in American Society: A Model of Ethnicity—From Contact to Assimilation." *Journal of American Ethnic History* 14: 38–101.
Barth, Fredrik (ed.). 1969. *Ethnic Groups and Boundaries: The Social Organization of Culture Differences*. London: Allen & Unwin.
Berry, John. 2003. "Conceptual Approaches to Acculturation." In *Acculturation: Advances in Theory, Measurement, and Applied Research*, edited by Kevin M. Chun, Pamela Balls Organista, and Gerado Marin, pp.17–37. Washington, DC: American Psychological Association.

Benson, Susan. 1981. *Ambiguous Ethnicity*. Cambridge: Cambridge University Press.
Bentley, Carter G. 1987. "Ethnicity and Practice." *Comparative Studies in Society and History* 29: 24–55.
Beyer, Peter, and Rubina Ramji (eds.). 2013. *Growing Up Canadian: Muslims, Hindus, and Buddhists*. Montreal, Canada: McGill-Queens University Press.
Bonacich, Edna, and John Modell. 1980. *The Economic Basis of Ethnic Solidarity: Small Business in the Japanese American Community*. Berkeley: University of California Press.
Bozorgmehr, Mehdi. 1997. "Internal Ethnicity: Iranians in Los Angeles." *Sociological Perspectives* 40: 387–408.
Brubaker, Rogers. 2009. "Ethnicity, Race, and Nationalism." *Annual Review of Sociology* 35: 21–42.
Calhoun, Craig. 1993. "Nationalism and Ethnicity." *Annual Review of Sociology* 19: 21–39.
Chan, Sucheng. 1991. *Asian Americans: An Interpretive History*. Boston: Twayne Publishers.
Chen, Carolyn. 2002. "The Religious Varieties of Ethnic Presence: A Comparison between a Taiwanese Immigrant Buddhist Temple and an Evangelical Christian Church." *Sociology of Religion* 63: 215–238.
Chong, Kelly H. 1998. "What it Means to be Christian: The Role of Religion in the Construction of Ethnic Identity and Boundary among Second-Generation Korean Americans." *Sociology of Religion* 59 (3), 259–267.
Chung, Ruth. 1999. "Reflection on a Korean American Journey." Pp. 59–68 in *Struggle for Ethnic Identity: Narratives by Asian American Professionals*, edited by Pyong Gap Min and Rose Kim. Walnut Creek, CA: Altamira Press.
Cohen, Steven. 1985. *American Modernity and Jewish Identity*. New York: Tavistock Publications.
Cornell, Stephen. 1996. "Variable Ties that Bind: Content and Circumstances in Ethnic Processes." *Ethnic and Racial Studies* 19: 265–289.
Cornell, Stephen, and Douglass Hartman. 1998. *Making Identities in a Changing World*. Thousand Oaks, CA: Sage Publications.
Cummings, Bruce. 1997. *Korea's Place in the Sun: A Modern History*. New York: W.W. Norton and Company.
Danico, Mary Yu. 2004. *The 1.5 Generation: Becoming Korean American in Hawaii*. Honolulu, HI: University of Hawaii Press.
Das Gupta, Monisha, 1995. "What Is Indian About You? A Gendered Transnational Approach to Ethnicity." *Gender and Society* 71: 572–596.
Despres, Leo. 1975. *Ethnicity and Resource Competition in Plural Societies*. The Hague, Netherlands: Mouton Publishers.
Dhingra, Lavina, and Rajimi Srikanth (eds.). 1997. *A Part, Yet Apart: South Asians in Asian America*. Philadelphia: Temple University Press.
Dormon, James. 1984. "Louisiana's Cajuns: A Case Study of Ethnic Group Revitalization." *Social Science Quarterly* 65: 1043–1057.
Dublin, Thomas (ed.). 1977. *Becoming American, Becoming Ethnic: College Students Explore Their Roots*. Philadelphia: Temple University Press.
Eckstein, Susan, and Lorena Barberia. 2002. "Grounding Immigrant Generations in History: Cuban Americans and their Transnational Ties." *The International Migration Review* 36 (3), 799–838.
Enroe, Cynthia. 1981. "The Growth of the State and Ethnic Mobilization." *Ethnic and Racial Studies* 4: 123–136.
Erikson, Thomas. 1993. *Ethnicity and Nationalism. Anthropological Perspectives*. London: Pluto Press.
Espiritu, Yen Le. 1989. "Beyond the Boat People: Ethnicization of American Life." *Amerasia Journal* 15 (2): 49–67.
———. 1992. *Asian American Panethnicity: Bridging Institutions and Identities*. Philadelphia: Temple University Press.
———. 1994. "The Intersection of Race, Ethnicity, and Class: The Multiple Identities of Second-Generation Filipinos." *Identities* 1: 234–273.

Fisher, Maxine. 1978. "Creating Ethnic Identity: Asian Indians in the New York City Area." *Urban Anthropology* 7: 271–285.
Fong, Eric, and Emi Ooka. 2002. "The Social Consequences of Participating in the Ethnic Economy." *International Migration Review* 36: 125–136.
Fugita, Stephen, and David O'Brien. 1991. *Japanese American Ethnicity: The Perspective of Community*. Seattle, WA: University of Washington Press.
Gans, Herbert. 1979. "Symbolic Ethnicity: The Future of Ethnic Groups and Cultures in America." *Ethnic and Racial Studies* 2: 1–20.
Garcia, Alma M. 2004. *Narratives of Mexican American Women: Emergent Identities of the Second Generation*. Walnut Creek, CA: Altamira Press.
Glazer, Nathan, and Daniel Moynihan (eds.). 1975. *Ethnicity: Theory and Experience*. Cambridge, MA: Harvard University Press.
Glenn, E. Nakano. 1983. "Split Household, Small Produce, and Dual Wage Earner: An Analysis of Chinese American Family Strategies." *Journal of Marriage and the Family* 45: 35–46.
Glick Schiller, Nina, Linda Basch, and Cristina Szanton Blanc (eds.). 1992. *Towards a Transnational Perspective on Migration: Race, Ethnicity, Class and Nationalism Reconsidered*. New York: New York Academy of Science.
Glick Schiller, Nina, Ayse Caglar, and Thaddeus Guldbrandsen. 2006. "Beyond the Ethnic Lens: Locality, Globality, and Born-Again Incorporation."*American Ethnologist* 33: 612–633.
Gold, Steven. 2002. "From the Jazz Singer to What a Country! A Comparison of Jewish Migration to the United States, 1880 to 1930 and 1965 to 1998." In *Mass Migration to the United States: Classical and Contemporary Periods*, edited by Pyong Gap Min, pp. 253–284. Walnut Creek, CA: Altamira Press.
Goldscheider, Calvin, and Alan Zuckerman. 1984. *The Transformation of the Jews*. Chicago: University of Chicago Press.
Gordon, Milton. 1964. *Assimilation in American Life: The Role of Race, Religion, and National Origin*. New York: Oxford University Press.
Greeley, Andrew. 1976. *Ethnicity in the United States: A Preliminary Reconnaissance*. New York: John Wiley.
Grenier, Guillermo, and Lisandra Perez. 2003. *The Legacy of Exile: Cubans in the United States*. Boston: Allyn and Bacon.
Halter, Marilyn. 2000. *Shopping for Identity: The Marketing of Ethnicity*. New York: Shocken Books.
Hammond, Philip E. 1988. " Religion and the Persistence of Identity." *Journal for the Scientific Study of Religion*: 27: 1–11.
Hammond, Philip E., and Kee Warner. 1993. "Religion and Ethnicity in Late-Twentieth Century America." *Annals of the American Academy of Political and Social Science* 527: 55–66.
Hannan, Michael. 1979. "The Dynamics of Ethnic Boundaries in Modern States." In *National Development and the World System*, edited by John Meyer and Michael Hannan. Chicago: University of California Press.
Heckter, Michael. 1974. "Political Economy of Ethnic Change." *American Journal of Sociology* 79: 1151–1178.
———. 1975. *Internal Colonialism: The Celtic Fringe in British National Development*. Berkeley: University of California Press.
———. 1978. "Group Formation and the Cultural Division of Labor." *American Journal of Sociology* 84: 293–318.
———. 1987. *Principles of Group Solidarity*. Berkeley, CA: University of California Press.
Heckter, Michael, Debra Friedman, and Malka Appelbaum. 1982. "A Theory of Ethnic Collective Action." *International Migration Reivew* 16: 212–234.
Hing, Bill Ong. 1993. *Making and Remaking Asian America through Immigration Policy, 1850–1990*. Stanford, CA: Stanford University Press.
Hong, Joanne, and Pyong Gap Min. 1999. "Ethnic Attachment among Second-Generation Korean Adolescents." *Amerasia Journal* 25: 165–189.
Hsu, Ruth Y. 1996. "Will the Model Minority Please Identify Itself: American Ethnic Identity and Its Dilemma." *Diaspora* 5: 37–64.

Huntington, Gertrude Enders. 1998. "The Amish Family." Pp. 450–479 in *Ethnic Families in America: Patterns and Variations*, edited by Charles H. Mindel, Robert W. Habenstein, and Roosevelt Wright Jr. Prentice Hall: Upper Saddle River, NJ.

Hurh, W. M. 1980. "Towards a Korean American Ethnicity: Some Theoretical Models. *Ethnic and Racial Studies* 3 (4).

Hurh, Won Moo, and Kwang Chung Kim. 1989. "The 'Success Image' of Asian Americans: Its Validity and Its Practical and Theoretical Implications." *Ethnic and Racial Studies* 12: 512–537.

Hurh, Won Moo, and Kwang Chung Kim. 1990. "Religious Participation of Korean Immigrants in the United States." *Journal for the Scientific Study of Religion* 29: 19–34.

Itzigsohn, Jose, Carlos Dore Cabral, Esther Hernandez Medline, and Obed Vasquez. 1999. "Mapping Dominican Transnationalism: Narrow and Broad Transnational Practices." *Ethnic and Racial Studies* 22: 316–339.

Jacobson, Jessica. 1997. "Religion and Ethnicity: Dual and Alternative Sources of Identity among Young British Pakistanis." *Ethnic and Racial Studies* 20: 238–256.

Jacoby, T. 2004. "What it Means to be American in the 21st Century." In *Reinventing the Melting Pot: The New Immigrants and What It Means To Be American*, edited by Tamar Jacoby. New York: Basic Books.

Jenkins, Richard. 1997. *Rethinking Ethnicity: Arguments and Explorations*. London: Sage Publications.

Jeong, Alex. 1999. "A Handicapped Korean in America." In *Struggle for Ethnic Identity: Narratives by Asian American Professionals*, 69–74, edited by Pyong Gap Min and Rose Kim. Walnut Creek, CA: Altamira Press.

Jimenez, Thomas. 2004. "Negotiating Ethnic Boundaries: Multiethnic Americans and Ethnic Identity in the United States." *Ethnicities* 4: 75–97.

Jo, Moon H. 1999. *Korean Immigrants and the Challenge of Adjustment*. Westport, CT: Greenwood Press.

Kalmijn, Mathijs. 1998. "Intermarriage and Homogamy: Causes, Patterns and Trends." *Annual Review of Sociology* 24: 395–421.

Kao, Grace. 2000. "Group Images and Possible Selves among Adolescents." *Sociological Forum* 15: 407–30.

Kao, Grace, and Kara Joyner. 2006. "Do Hispanic and Asian Adolescents Practice Panethnicity in Friendship Choices?" *Social Science Quarterly* 972–992.

Kasfir, Nelson. 1979. "Explaining Ethnic Political Participation." *World Politics* 31; 365–388.

Keyes, Charles (ed.). 1981. *Ethnic Change*. Seattle: University of Washington Press.

Kibria, Nazli. 2000. "Race, Ethnic Options and Ethnic Binds: Identity Negotiations of Second Generation Chinese and Korean Americans." *Sociological Perspectives* 43: 77–95.

———. 2002. *Becoming Asian American: Second-Generation Chinese and Korean Identities*. Baltimore: The Johns Hopkins University Press.

Kim, Chigon, and Pyong Gap Min. 2010. "Marital Patterns and Use of Mother Tongue at Home among Native-Born Asian Americans." *Social Forces* 88: 233–256.

Kim, Eleana. 2010. *Adoptee Territories: Transnational Korean Adoptees Remapping Kinship and Rewriting Citizenship*. Durham, NC: Duke University Press.

Kim, Nadia. 2008. *Imperial Citizens. Koreans and Race from Seoul to LA*. Stanford, CA: Stanford University Press.

———. 2009. "Finding Our Way Home: Korean Americans, 'Homeland' Trips, and Cultural Foreignness." In *Diasporic Homecomings: Ethnic Return Migration in Comparative Perspective*, edited by Takeyuki Tsusada, pp. 409–430. Stanford, CA: Stanford University Press.

Kim, Warren. 1971. *Koreans in America*. Seoul: Po Chin Chai.

Kitano, Harry, and Roger Daniels. 1995. *Asian Americans: Emerging Minorities*. Englewood Cliffs, NJ: Prentice Hall.

Kuran, Timur. 1998. "Ethnic Norms and Their Transformation through Reputational Cascades." *Journal of Legal Studies* 27: 623–659.

Lan, Shanshan. 2012. *Diaspora and Class Consciousness: Chinese Immigrant Workers in Multiracial Chicago*. New York: Routledge.

Lapidus, Ira. 2001. "Between Universalism and Particularism: The Historical Bases of Muslim Communal, National, and Global Identities." *Global Networks* 1: 37–55.
Lee, Helene. 2013. "Transnationalism and 'Third Culture Kids': A Comparative Analysis of Korean American and Korean Chinese Identity Construction." *In Koreans in North America: Their Twenty-First Century Experiences*, edited by Pyong Gap Min, pp. 157–172.
Lee, J. S. 2002. "The Korean Language in America: The Role of Cultural Identity in Heritage Language Learning." *Language, Culture and Curriculum* 15 (2), 117–133.
Levitt, Peggy. 2001. *The Transnational Villagers*. Berkeley and Los Angeles: University of California Press.
Levitt, Peggy, and Mary Waters. 2002. *The Changing Face of Home: The Transnational Lives of the Second Generation*. New York: Russell Sage Foundation.
Lieberson, Stanley. 1985. "Unhyphenated Whites in the United States." *Ethnic and Racial Studies* 8: 159–80.
Light, Ivan. 1986. "Ethnicity and Business Enterprise." In *Making It in America*, edited by Mark Stolarik and Murray Friedman. Lewisburg, PA: Bucknell University Press.
Light, Ivan, George Sabagh, Mehdi Bozorgmehr, and Claudia Der-Martirosian. 1993. "Internal Ethnicity in the Ethnic Economy." *Ethnic and Racial Studies* 16: 581–591.
Lopez, David, and Yen Espiritu. 1990. "Panethnicity in the United States: A Theoretical Framework." *Ethnic and Racial Studies* 13: 198–224.
Manning, Nash. 1989. *The Cauldron of Ethnicity in the Modern World*. Chicago: University of California Press.
Mckay, James, and Frank Lewis. 1978. "Ethnicity and Ethnic Group: A Conceptual Analysis and Reformulation." *Ethnic and Racial Studies* 4: 412–427.
Mckay, Jay. 1982. "An Explanatory Synthesis of Primordial and Mobilizationist Approaches to Ethnic Phenomena." *Ethnic and Racial Studies* 5: 395–420.
Massey, Douglas. "The New Immigration and Ethnicity in the United States." *Population and Development Review* 21: 631–652.
Min, Pyong Gap. 1991. "Cultural and Economic Boundaries of Korean Ethnicity: A Comparative Analysis." *Ethnic and Racial Studies* 14: 225–241.
———. "The Structure and Social Functions of Korean Immigrant Churches in the United States." *International Migration Review* 26: 1370–94.
———. 1996. *Caught in the Middle: Korean Communities in New York and Los Angeles*. Berkeley: University of California Press.
———. 1998. *Changes and Conflicts: Korean Immigrant Families in New York*. Boston: Allyn and Bacon.
———(ed.). 2002. *The New Second Generation: Ethnic Identity among Second-Generation Asian American Professionals*. Lanham, MD: Rowman and Littlefield.
———. 2005. "Religion and the Maintenance of Ethnicity among Immigrants: A Comparison of Indian Hindus and Korean Protestants." In *Immigrant Faiths: Transforming Religious Life in America*, edited by Karen Leonard, Alex Stepick, Manuel Vasquez, and Jennifer Holdaway, pp. 99–122. Walnut Creek, CA: Altamira Press.
———. 2008. *Ethnic Solidarity for Economic Survival: Korean Greengrocers in New York City*. New York: Russell Sage Foundation.
———. 2010. *Preserving Ethnicity through Religion in America: Korean Protestants and Indian Hindus across Generations*. New York: New York University Press.
———. 2013a. "Korean-American Residents in Korea: Transnational Lives between the United States and Their Homeland." In Younghee Cho (ed.), *Emigration Trends and Policies of Major Sending Countries from Korea*, pp.121–151. Gyeonggi-do, Republic of Korea: IOM (International Organization for Immigration) Migration Research and Training Center.
———. 2013b. "The Socioeconomic Attainments of Korean Americans, Compared to Native-Born Whites and Other Asian Groups, in the NY-NJ-CT Consolidated Metropolitan Statistical Area." Research Report 5, the Research Center for Korean Community at Queens College.
Min, Pyong Gap, and Mehdi Bozorgmehr. 2002. "Immigrant Entrepreneurship and Business Patterns: A Comparison of Koreans and Iranians in Los Angeles." *International Migration Review* 34: 707–738.

Min, Pyong Gap, and Youna Choi. 1993. "Ethnic Attachment among Korean American High School Students." *Korea Journal of Population and Development* 22: 167–179.

Min, Pyong Gap, and Chigon Kim. 2009. "Patterns of Intermarriages and Cross-Generational In-marriages among Native-Born Asian Americans." *International Migration Review* 43: 447–470.

———. 2013. "Growth and Settlement Patterns of Korean Americans." In *Koreans in North America: Their Twenty-First Century Experiences*, edited by Pyong Gap Min, pp. 35–56. Lanham, MD: Lexington Books.

Min, Pyong Gap, and Rose Kim (eds.). 1999. *Struggle for Ethnic Identity: Personal Narratives By Asian American Professionals*. Walnut Creek, CA: Altamira Press.

———. 2000. "Formation of Ethnic and Racial Identities: Narratives by Young Asian American Professionals." *Ethnic and Racial Studies* 23: 735–760.

Min, Pyong Gap, and Young Oak Kim. 2009. "Ethnic and Sub-ethnic Attachments among Chinese, Korean, and Indian Immigrants in New York City." *Ethnic and Racial Studies* 32: 758–780.

Nagel, Joane. 1985. "The Political Mobilization of Native Americans." In *Majority and Minority: The Dynamics of Race and Ethnicity in America*, Fourth Edition, edited by Norman Yetman. Boston: Allyn and Bacon.

———. 1986. "The Political Construction of Ethnicity." In *Competitive Ethnic Relations*, edited by Susan Olzak and Joanne Nagel. New York: Academic Press.

———. 1994. "Constructing Ethnicity: Creating and Recreating Identity and Culture." *Social Problems* 41: 152–178.

Nelson, Candace, and Marta Tienda. 1985. "The Structuring of Hispanic Ethnicity: Historical and Contemporary Trends." *Ethnic and Racial Studies* 8: 49–74.

Nielsen, Francois. 1980. "The Flemish Movement in Belgium after World War II: A Dynamic Analysis." *American Sociological Review* 50: 133–149.

Novak, Michael. 1973. *The Rise of Unmelting Ethnics: Politics and Culture in the Seventies*. New York: Macmillan.

Oboler, Suzanne. 1995. *Ethnic Labels, Latino Lives*. Minneapolis: University of Minnesota Press.

Okamoto, Dina G. 2003. "Toward a Theory of Panethnicity: Explaining Asian American Collective Action." *American Sociological Review* 68: 811–842.

———. 2006. "Institutional Panethnicity: Boundary Formation in Asian American Organizing." *Social Forces* 85: 1–25.

Okamura, Jonathan. 1981. "Situational Ethnicity." *Ethnic and Racial Studies* 4: 425–465.

Okihiro, G. Y. 2001. *The Columbia Guide to Asian American History*. New York: Columbia University Press.

Olzak, Susan, and Joane Nagel (eds.). 1986. *Competitive Ethnic Relations*. New York: Academic Press.

Omi, M., and H. Winant. 1994. *Racial Formation in the United States*, 2nd Edition. New York: Routledge.

Padilla, Felix. 1986. "Latino Ethnicity in the City of Chicago." In *Competitive Ethnic Relations*, edited by Susan Olzak and Joane Nagel. New York: Academic Press.

Park, Linda. 2013. "Authenticity Dilemma among Pre-1965 Native-Born Koreans." In *Koreans in North America: Their Twenty-First Century Experiences*, edited by Pyong Gap Min, pp. 173–194. Lanham, MD: Lexington Books.

Patterson, W. 2000. *The Ilse: 1st Generation Korean Immigrants in Hawaii, 1903–1973* (Hawaiian Studies on Korea). Honolulu, HI: University of Hawaii Press.

Phinney, J. 2003. "Ethnic Identity and Acculturation." In *Acculturation Advances in Theory, Measurement, and Applied Research*, edited by Kevin M. Chun, Pamela Balls Organista, and Gerado Marin, 63–81. Washington, DC: American Psychological Association.

Portelli, A. 1991. *Death of Luigi Trastulli, and Other Stories: Form and Meaning in Oral History*. Albany, NY: State University of New York Press.

Portes, Alejandro. 1984. "The Rise of Ethnicity: Determinants of Ethnic Perceptions among Cuban Exiles in Miami." *American Sociological Review* 49: 383–397.

Portes, A., and L. Hao. 2002. "The Price of Uniformity: Language, Family, and Personality Adjustment in the Immigrant Second Generation." *Ethnic and Racial Studies* 25 (6): 889–912.
Portes, Alejandro, and Dag McLeod. 1996. "What Shall I Call Myself? Hispanic Identity Formation in the Second Generation." *Ethnic and Racial Studies* 19: 523–546.
Portes, A., and R. G. Rumbaut. 1996. *Immigrant America: A Portrait*. Berkeley, CA: University of California Press.
Portes, A., and R. G. Rumbaut. 2001. *Legacies: The Story of the Immigrant Second Generation*. Berkeley, CA: University of California Press.
Portes, A., and R. Schauffler. 1994. "Language and the Second Generation: Bilingualism Yesterday and Today." *International Migration Review* 28: 640–658.
Rayaprol, Apana. 1997. *Negotiating Identities: Women in the Indian Diaspora*. New Delhi: Oxford University Press.
Reitz, Jeffrey. 1980. *The Survival of Ethnic Groups*. Toronto: McGraw Hill.
Romanucci-Ross, Lola, and George De Vos (eds.). *Ethnic Identity: Creation, Conflict, and Accommodation*. Walnut Creek, CA: Altamira Press.
Roosens, Eugene. 1989. *Creating Ethnicity: The Process of Ethnogensis*. Newbury Park, CA: Sage Publications.
Rosenberg, S. 1985. *The New Jewish Identity in America*. New York: Hipocrene Books.
Rosenfeld, Michael. 2001. "The Salience of Pan-National Hispanic and Asian Identities in U.S. Marriage Markets." *Demography* 38: 161–175.
Rubin-Dorsky, Jeffrey, and Shelley Fisher Fishkin (eds.). 1996. *People of the Book: Thirty Scholars Reflect on Their Jewish Identity*. Madison: University of Wisconsin Press.
Rumbaut, Ruben. 1994. "The Crucible Within: Ethnic Identity, Self-Esteem, and Segmented Assimilation among Children of Immigrants." *International Migration Review* 28: 748–794.
———. 1995. "The New Californians: Comparative Research Findings on the Educational Progress of Immigrant Children." In *California's Immigrant Children*, edited by Ruben Rumbaut and Wayne Cornelius. San Diego: Center for U.S.-Mexican Studies, University of California, San Diego.
Scott, J., and D. Alwin. 1998. "Retrospective vs. Prospective Measurement of Life Histories in Longitudinal Research." In *Crafting Life Studies: Intersection of Personal and Social History*, edited by J. Z. Geile and G. H. Elder, Jr. Thousand Oaks, CA: Sage Publications.
Segal, U. A. 2002. *Framework for Immigration: Asians in the United States*. New York: Columbia University Press.
Shim, T. Y., M. S. Kim, and J. N. Martin. 2008. *Changing Korea: Understanding Culture and Communication*. New York: Peter Lang Publishing, Inc.
Shin, Gi Wook. 2006a. "Ethnic Pride Source of Prejudice, Discrimination." *Korea Herald*. August 2, 2006.
———. 2006b. *Ethnic Nationalism in Korea: Genealogy, Politics, and Legacy*. California: Stanford University Press.
Sidel, Ruth. 1994. *Battling Biases: The Struggle for Identity and Community on College Campuses*. New York: Penguin.
Smith, Timothy. 1978. "Religion and Ethnicity in America." *American Historical Review* 83: 1155–85.
Song, Miri. 2003. *Choosing Ethnic Identities*. Oxford, UK: Polity Press.
Steinberg, Stephen. 1989. *The Ethnic Myth: Race, Ethnicity, and Class in America*, Second Edition. Boston: Beacon.
Suárez-Orozco, C., and M.M. Suárez-Orozco. 2001. *Children of Immigration*. Cambridge, MA: Harvard University Press.
Suh, Sharon. 2004. *Being Buddhist in a Christian World: Gender and Community in a Korean American Temple*. Seattle: University of Washington Press.
Takaki, Ronald. 1989. *Strangers from a Different Shore: A History of Asian Americans*. Boston: Little, Brown.
Takenaka, Ayumi. 1989. "Transnational Community and Its Ethnic Consequences." *American Behavioral Scientist* 42: 1459–74.

Taylor, Ronald. 1979. "The Black Ethnicity and Persistence of Ethnogenesis," *American Journal of Sociology* 84: 1401–23.
Tuan, Mia. 1999a. *Forever Foreigners or Honorary White? The Asian Ethnic Experience Today.* New Brunswick, NJ: Rutgers University Press.
———. 1999b. "Neither Real Americans nor Real Asians?: Multigenerational Asian Ethnics Navigating the Terrain of Authenticity." *Qualitative Sociology* 22 (2): 105–125.
Tweed, Thomas. 1997. *Our Lady of Exile: Diasporic Religion at a Cuban Catholic Shrine in Miami.* Cambridge: Oxford University Press.
van den Berge, Pierre L. 1981. *The Ethnic Phenomenon.* New York: Elsevier.
Vo, Linda. 1996, "Asian Immigrants, Asian-Americans, and the Politics of Ethnic Mobilization in San Diego." *Amerasia Journal* 22 (2): 89–108,
Wallman, Sandra. 1978. "Boundaries of 'Race': Processes of Ethnicity in England." *Man* 13: 200–17.
Waters, Mary. 1990. *Ethnic Options: Choosing Identities in America.* Berkeley: University of California Press.
———. 1994. "Ethnic and Racial Identities of Second-Generation Black Immigrants in New York." *International Migration Review* 28: 795–820.
———. 1999. *Black Identities: West Indian Immigrant Dreams and American Realities.* New York: Russell Sage Foundation.
van den Berge, Pierre L. 1981. *The Ethnic Phenomenon.* New York: Elsevier.
vo, Linda. 1996, "Asian Immigrants, Asian-Americans, and the Politics of Ethnic Mobilization in San Diego. *Amerasia Journal* 22 (2): 89–108,
Wei, Williams. 1993. *The Asian American Movement.* Philadelphia: Temple University Press.
Werner Sollors (ed.). 1989. *The Invention of Ethnicity.* Oxford: Oxford University Press.
Williams, Raymond Brady. 1988. *Religions of Immigrants from India and Pakistan.* New York: Cambridge University Press.
Woldemikael, T. M. 1989. *Becoming Black American: Haitians and American Institutions in Evanston, IL.* New York: AMS Press.
Yancy, William, Eugene Ericksen, and Richard Juliani, 1976, "Emergent Ethnicity: A Review and Reformulation," *American Sociological Review* 76 (1976): 391–403.
Yang, Philip. 2011. *Asian Immigration to the United States.* Cambridge, UK: Polity Press.
Yanow, D. 2003. *Constructing "Race" and "Ethnicity" in America: Category-Making in Public Policy and Administration.* New York: M.E. Sharpe, Inc.
Yinger, J. Milton. 1980. "Toward a Theory of Assimilation and Dissimilation." *Ethnic and Racial Studies* 4: 249–64.
———. 1994. *Ethnicity: Sources of Strength? Sources of Conflict?* Albany, NY: State University of New York Press.
Yu, E. Y., and P. Choe. 2003–2004. "Korean Population in the United States as Reflected in the Year 2000 U.S. Census." *Amerasia Journal* 29 (3): 2–21

Index

assimilation policy, 22, 23, 36, 211
authenticity dilemma, 21, 23–24

criticisms of, Korean culture, 59–60, 81, 98, 137; patriarchal customs, 44, 67, 83, 136–137, 137, 138, 142, 212, 213–214, 225, 226, 228; prejudice against the disabled, 55, 60, 213, 228
cultural foreigner (rejection of overseas Koreans based on cultural differences), 24, 27, 31, 31–33, 37, 142, 143, 217, 218; Kim, Nadia. See authenticity dilemma

danilminjok. See cultural foreigner
data sources, 15–17

ethnic culture, 7–8, 35–37, 52, 58, 84, 95–96, 103, 104, 115, 119, 120, 145–148, 167, 191, 192, 211, 213; See also criticisms of Korean culture
ethnic identity : ethnic consciousness, 65, 97, 98, 126, 149, 167, 168–169; ethnic pride, 85–86, 154, 194, 224; for Black Nationalists, 15; for Jewish Americans, 14; four major contributing factors to, 5, 7; global identity, 208; hypernated American identity, 13–14; multiple identities, 4, 121, 228; rejection of, 103, 104; struggle for, 66, 68–69, 84, 85, 90–91, 143, 145, 157–158; symbolic

ethnicity, 12; transnational identity, 141; typology of, 12–15
ethnic social networks, 8–9, 81–82, 90–97, 95, 96, 111, 128, 182, 192, 214, 215, 226

FOBs, 134–135, 135

Garvey, Marchus. See Black Nationalists

heritage tours. See linkages to the homeland

Joseonjok, 143

Korean churches, 90, 120, 133, 145–147, 166–167, 176, 215–216
Korean immigrants, three waves of, 22–23
Korean Students Association, 90

Lee, K. W., 50
liminality, 141, 142
linkages to the homeland, 10–11, 67, 79–80, 104, 111, 113–114, 119, 141–143, 154, 174, 176–177, 179, 183, 193, 216, 219–220, 226, 227
Los Angeles Times ' Minority Editorial Training Program, 50

the model minority myth. See stereotypes of Korean and other Asian Americans

237

organization, of the book, 17–18

pan-Asian ethnic ties and identity, 47, 51, 127, 139, 140, 141, 206
pressure to be high-status professionals, 70–71, 153, 162, 205

racial prejudice and discrimination: acting white, 64–65, 68, 214, 222, 223, 224–225; against blacks, 11, 105, 110, 162; against Korean and other Asian Americans, 11–12, 25–30, 46, 78, 94, 101, 106, 107–108, 117, 136, 139, 140, 149, 152, 157, 158, 164–166, 178, 187, 207, 220–222; blacks' racial prejudice against Koreans, 78, 106, 107; blending in, 25, 26, 27, 48, 154, 214; internalized racism, 46, 222, 223

the Smithsonian National Portrait Gallery, 39
stereotypes of Korean and Asian Americans, 64, 68–69, 72, 124, 140–141, 150–152, 162

research methods of the book, 4

Sah-ee-gu, 173–174
The Shin Han Il-Bo, 45

Takaki, Ronald, 72
Twinkies, 134

X, Malcolm. See Black Nationalists

About the Contributors

THE EDITORS

Pyong Gap Min is Distinguished Professor of sociology at Queens College and the Graduate Center of the City University of New York. He also serves as director of the Research Center for Korean Community at Queens College. The areas of his specializations are immigration, ethnicity, immigrant businesses, immigrants' religious practices, and family/gender, with a special focus on Korean and Asian Americans. He is the author of five books, including *Caught in the Middle: Korean Communities in New York and Los Angeles* (1996) and *Preserving Ethnicity through Religion in America: Korean Protestants and Indian Hindus across Generations* (2010). *Caught in the Middle* (1996) received two national book awards while *Preserving Ethnicity through Religion in America* (2010) received three national book awards. He is the editor or co-editor of nine books, including *Koreans in North America: Their Twenty-First Century Experiences* (2013). He received the Distinguished Career Award from the International Migration Section of the American Sociological Association in 2012. He also received the "Proud Koreans Award" from the Association of Overseas Korean Journalists in 2013. He was the only recipient of the award from the Korean community in the United States.

Thomas Chung is a writer and editor for the Research Center for Korean Community at Queens College. He studied English literature, creative writing, African-American studies, film studies, and French at Oberlin College and Georgia State University, and received his BA in English from Georgia State University. He is co-editor (with Pyong Gap Min) of *Koreans Who Have Empowered the Korean-American Community*, which will be published in 2014. In addition to writing essays and sociological articles, he writes fiction and non-fiction, and will begin a PhD program in sociology at the Graduate Center of the City University of New York in fall 2014. Thomas lives in Brooklyn, New York.

THE CONTRIBUTORS

Brenda Chung is a freelance web designer residing in the Portland, Oregon area. Her focus has been collaborating with independent artists to enable them to gain a wider audience for their photography, painting, and other types of art. She writes poetry and short stories as a hobby. She is also A+ certified as an IT Technician and has a PC Hardware Specialist Certificate.

Ruth H. Chung, PhD, is professor in the Graduate School of Education at the University of Southern California, where she teaches in the marriage and family therapy program as well as global executive doctorate in Education. As a Counseling Psychologist, her areas of expertise are in acculturation and cultural identity of Asian-American immigrants and immigrant family adjustment issues. She taught for a year in Korea as a Fulbright scholar, and served as the project director of the Korean American National Survey with funding from the Overseas Korea Foundation.

Dave Hahn is an Encoding Specialist and has worked in the media industry in the post-production field for the last ten years. He was born and raised in the suburbs of New Jersey and received a BA in Communications from Rutgers University in 1999. In his spare time, he enjoys jogging, filmmaking, studying various martial arts, and hanging out with Goliath, his beloved dog. Dave currently resides in Atlanta, Georgia.

Alex Jeong is a judge for the New York City Criminal Courts of Kings County (Brooklyn). He was appointed to this position by Mayor Michael Bloomberg in October of 2005 and was reappointed in January of 2010. He received his undergraduate degree from Colgate University and his JD from the George Washington University School of Law. Jeong worked for the King's County District Attorney's Office prior to becoming a Criminal Court judge.

Katherine Yungmee Kim is the author of *Los Angeles's Koreatown* (Arcadia Publishing, 2010) and the communications editor for KYCC (Koreatown Youth and Community Center). She is also a contributing editor at *KoreAm Journal*. She received her BA in English literature from Vassar College, and an MFA in creative writing from Columbia University, where she was a Fiction Fellow. Kim has worked as an editor and reporter at the *Cambodia Daily*, Yonhap News Agency, *The Far Eastern Economic Review*, and Pacific News Service. She is currently working on a documentary graphic novel on the history of the Demilitarized Zone in Korea. Katherine lives in Los Angeles, California.

Rose M. Kim, PhD, has been an assistant professor of sociology at the Borough of Manhattan Community College/City University of New York since 2007. She received a BA in art & design from the University of Chicago in 1990 and a PhD in sociology from the Graduate Center of the City University of New York in 2007. Prior to graduate school, she worked as a reporter at *New York Newsday* and the *Los Angeles Times*, as well as freelancing for other publications. She was part of a team of journalists and photographers that won a Pulitzer Prize for its coverage of the 1992 L.A. *riots/insurrection/saigu*, an event she re-examined in her dissertation thesis. Her research areas include racialization, mass media discourse, and public higher education.

Bora Lee is the development coordinator at Korean Community Services of Metropolitan New York (KCS) and is responsible for KCS' fundraising and communications efforts. As a fundraiser, Bora connects donors with an opportunity to invest in a better community. Prior to KCS, Bora oversaw fundraising efforts at the Coalition for Asian American Children and Families (CACF). Additionally, she dedicated two years to national service as an AmeriCorps VISTA, increasing capacity for organizations serving the immigrant community of New York City. Bora serves as Co-Chair of Immigration Advancement Matters' Emerging Leaders Council and as part of the Advisory Board of MinKwon Center's Young Adult Movement Builders. She graduated from CUNY Queens College with a bachelors of arts in sociology and urban studies.

Helene K. Lee received her PhD in sociology from the University of California, Santa Barbara in 2009. She is assistant professor at Dickinson College in the department of sociology. She is currently at work on a book manuscript, *Bittersweet Homecomings: A Comparative Analysis of Ethnic Identity Construction in the Korean Diaspora*, which explores the impact of return migration to the ancestral homeland, South Korea, on two diasporic Korean communities—Korean Americans and Korean Chinese (*Joseonjok*). Her continued research interests focus on how diasporic individuals negotiate the intersections of ethnicity, gender, and nationality within multiple national contexts.

Hyein Lee is currently pursuing a PhD in Sociology at the Graduate Center of the City University of New York. Her research and teaching interests are rooted in issues surrounding immigration, stratification, class, and family behavior. She is currently working on a dissertation on upwardly mobile Asian Americans and cosmopolitan elites. Hyein was born in South Korea and currently lives in Brooklyn, New York.

Alexandra Noh is director of Public Relations of an entertainment and business marketing company, and the chief operating officer of a consulting firm—working with new technologies and market deregulation. She studied English, business, psychology, and sociology at Queens College, receiving her BA in 2011. While enjoying life in New York City with her friends and family, she has worked with a number of organizations, such as the American Red Cross, Milal Mission, New York Blood Center, and more. She hopes, through her entrepreneurial pursuits, that she will soon be able to give back and to help the Korean-American community thrive.

Linda Sujin Park holds a PhD from the School of Human Ecology, Department of Human Development and Family Studies at the University of Wisconsin-Madison. Her doctoral studies include two minors: research methods in cultural studies and social welfare with a focus on policy, along with two master's degrees in social work and business management. As a cultural gerontologist, Linda's research focuses on the contextual influences over the life course on ethnic identity formation of second-generation Korean-American Baby Boomers. Linda's passion for working with students has earned her four mentoring awards and she is committed to various diversity initiatives working towards improving campus climate and promoting inclusiveness. She is the Communication Chair-elect for the Emerging Scholars and Professional Organization of the Gerontological Society of America. Linda is a second-generation Korean American and an active member of both Korean- and Asian-American communities in Madison, Wisconsin, where she also practices as an independent cultural broker within the Korean immigrant and international student community.

Sun K. Park holds a BA in English (SUNY Buffalo, 2006) and graduated from Stuyvesant High School. He enjoys writing and reading when he's not honing his culinary skills. He is also working on a collection of short stories that can be described as a Millennial's cultural examination of ordinary life. Sun is currently managing a store in Howard Beach and lives in Bayside, New York.

Sung S. Park is currently a doctoral student in the sociology department at the University of California, Los Angeles, studying issues at the intersection of family demography, immigration, and aging across the life course. Using quantitative methods, Sung has investigated the nature and quality of intergenerational relationships between aging parents and adult children within both immigrant and non-immigrant families. Her dissertation focuses on understanding the relative importance of familial networks for migrants' and non-migrants' economic and social well-being. In her former career, she held numerous leadership roles in quantitative research groups at Fortune 100 corporations.